YUMMY

A History of Desserts

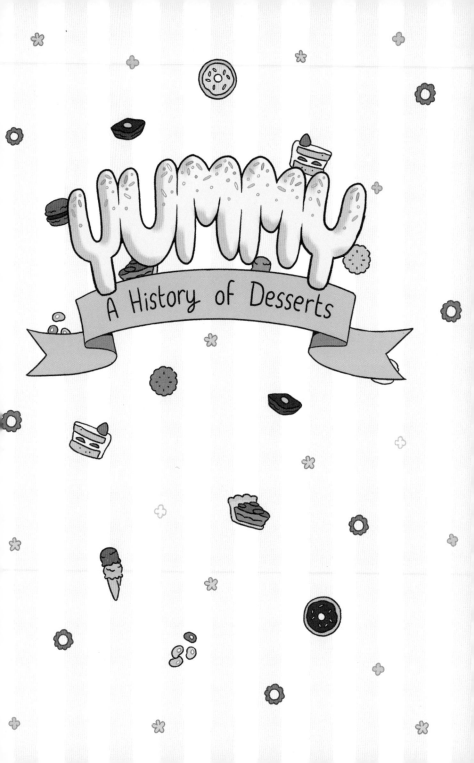

Yummy was illustrated, colored, and lettered digitally.
All recipes were made and enjoyed by the author.

All rights reserved. Published in the United States by RH Graphic, an imprint of
Random House Children's Books, a division of Penguin Random House LLC, New York.

RH Graphic with the book design is a trademark of Penguin Random House LLC.

Visit us on the web! RHKidsGraphic.com • @RHKidsGraphic

Educators and librarians, for a variety of teaching tools, visit us at RHTeachersLibrarians.com

Library of Congress Cataloging-in-Publication Data is available upon request.
ISBN 978-0-593-12437-6 (hc) — ISBN 978-0-593-12438-3 (pb)
ISBN 978-0-593-12542-7 (lib. bdg.) — ISBN 978-0-593-12439-0 (ebk)

Designed by Patrick Crotty

MANUFACTURED IN CHINA
10 9 8 7 6 5 4 3 2 1
First Edition

RH
GRAPHIC
A comic on every bookshelf.

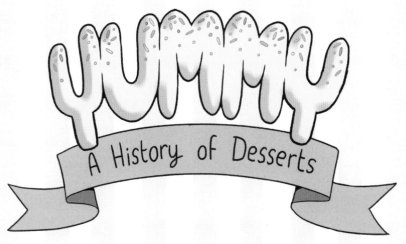

A History of Desserts

Victoria Grace Elliott

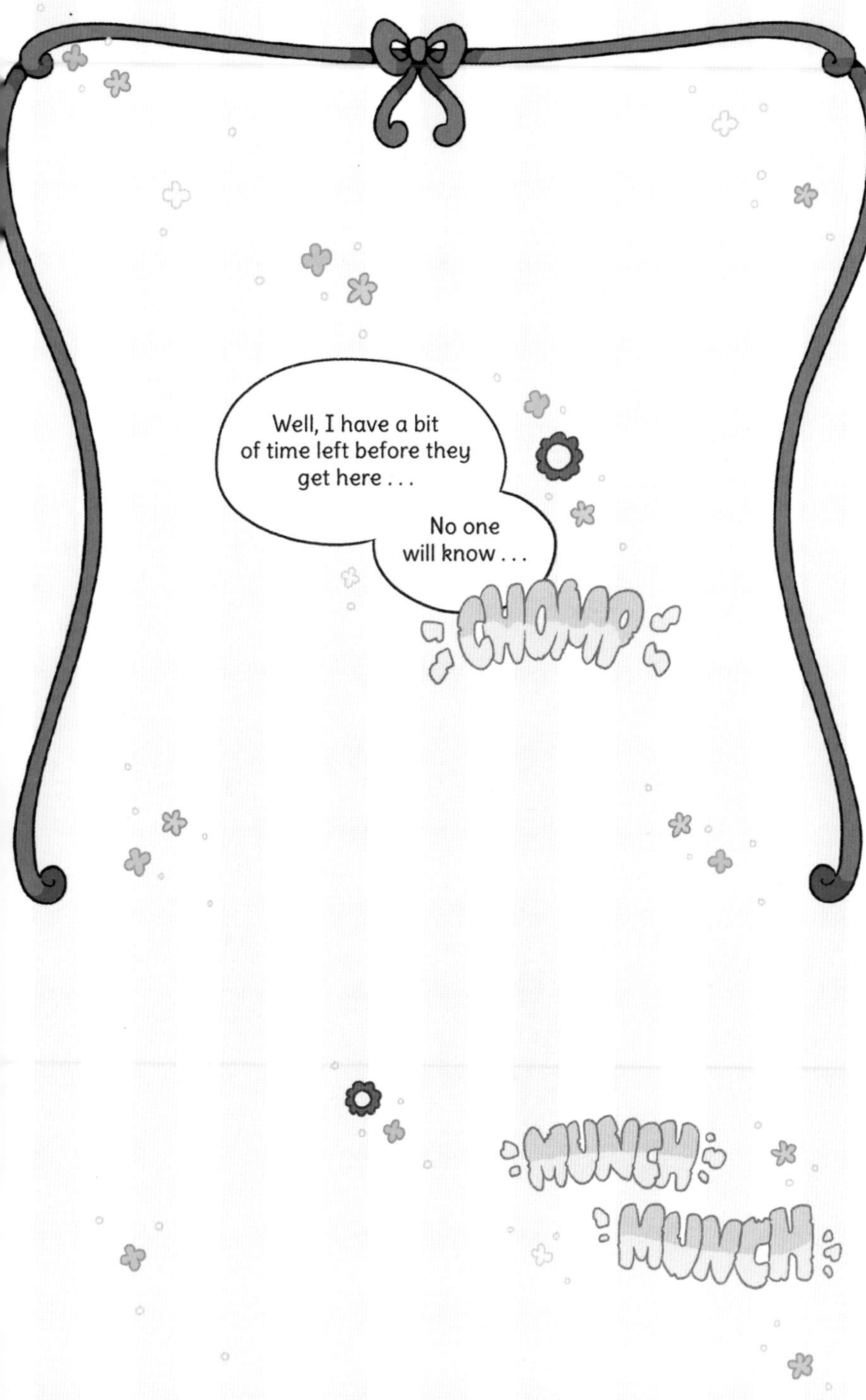
Well, I have a bit of time left before they get here . . .
No one will know . . .
CHOMP
MUNCH
MUNCH

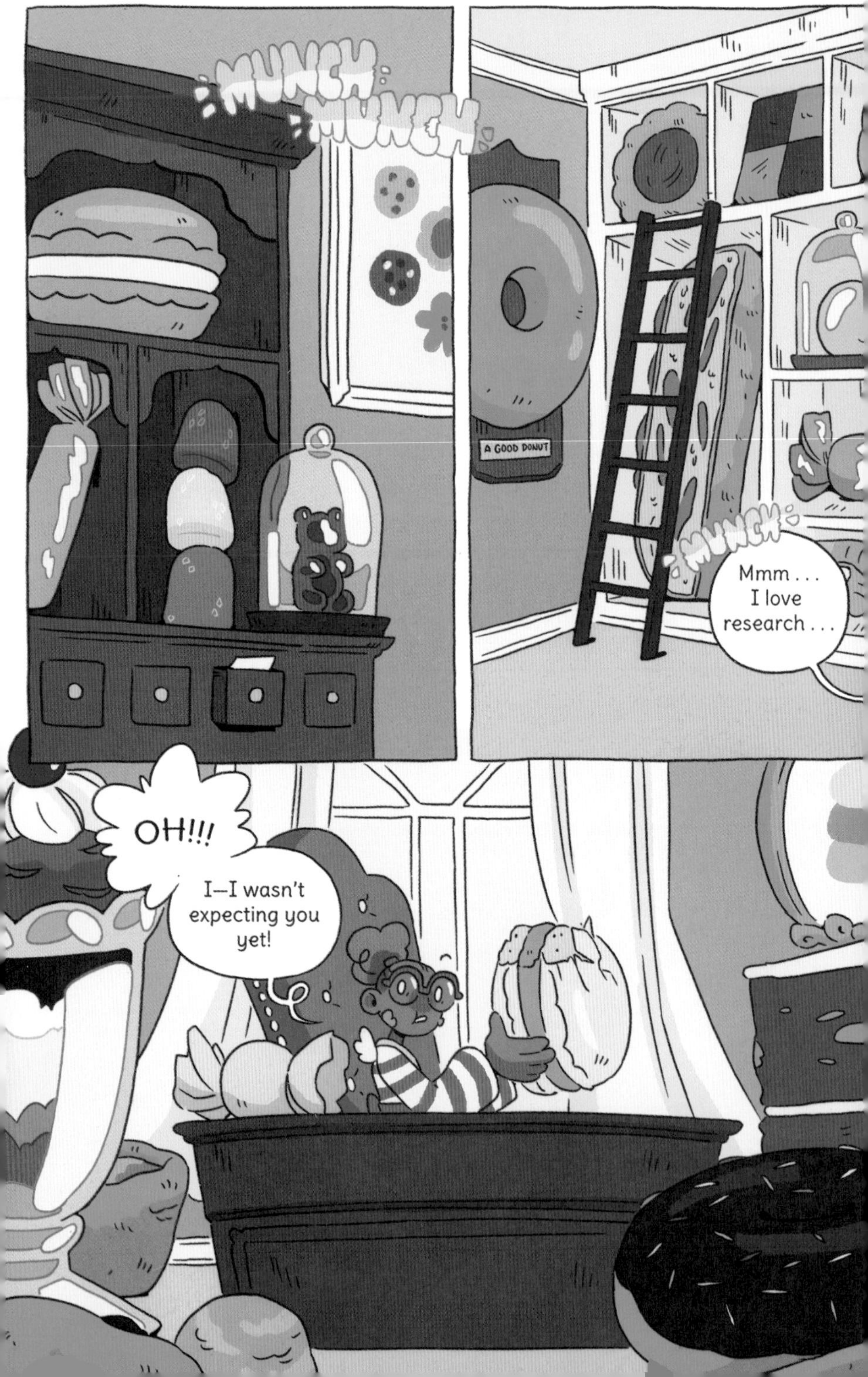
MUNCH
MUNCH
A GOOD DONUT
MUNCH
Mmm . . . I love research . . .
OH!!!
I—I wasn't expecting you yet!

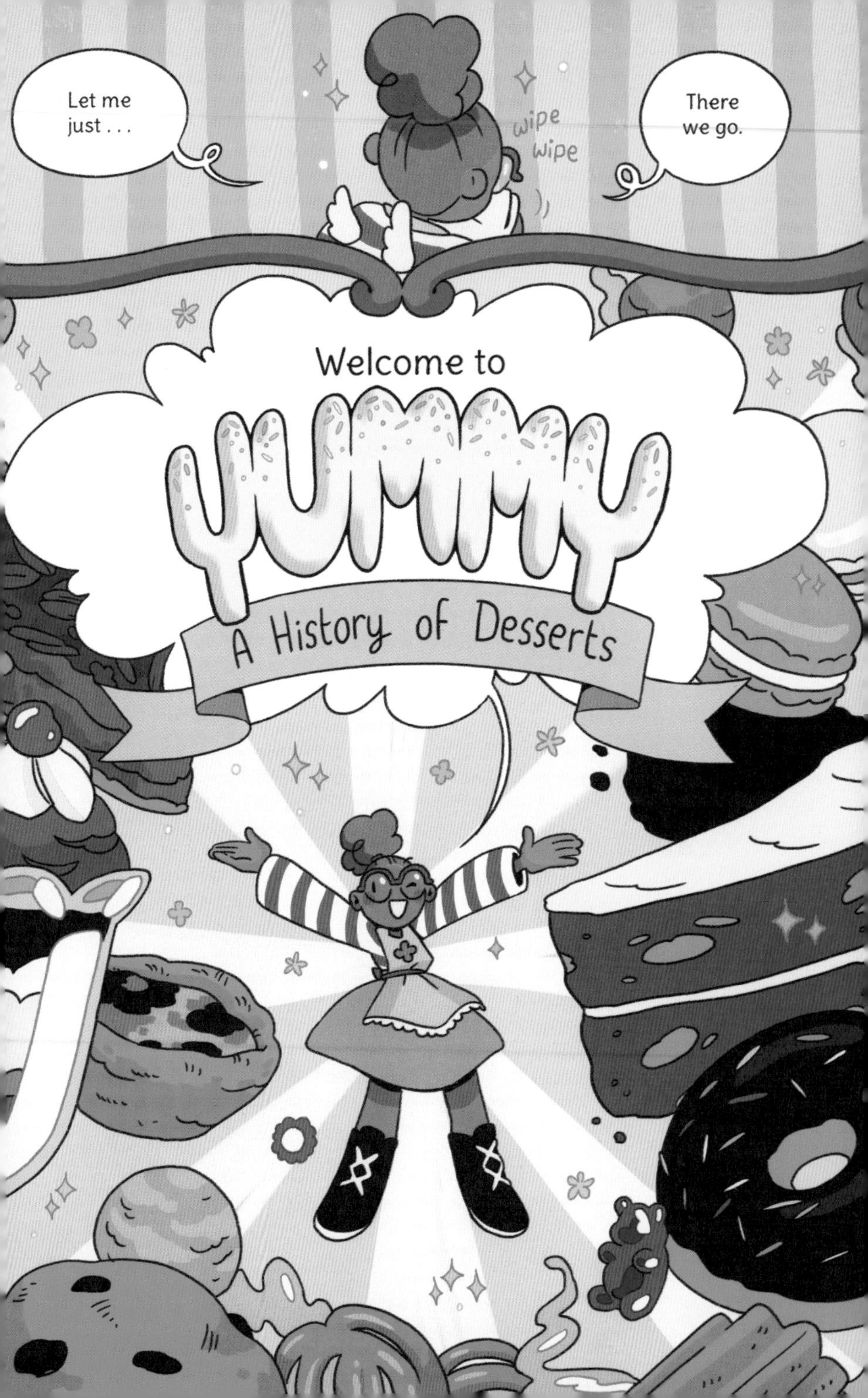
Let me just . . .
wipe wipe
There we go.
Welcome to
YUMMY
A History of Desserts

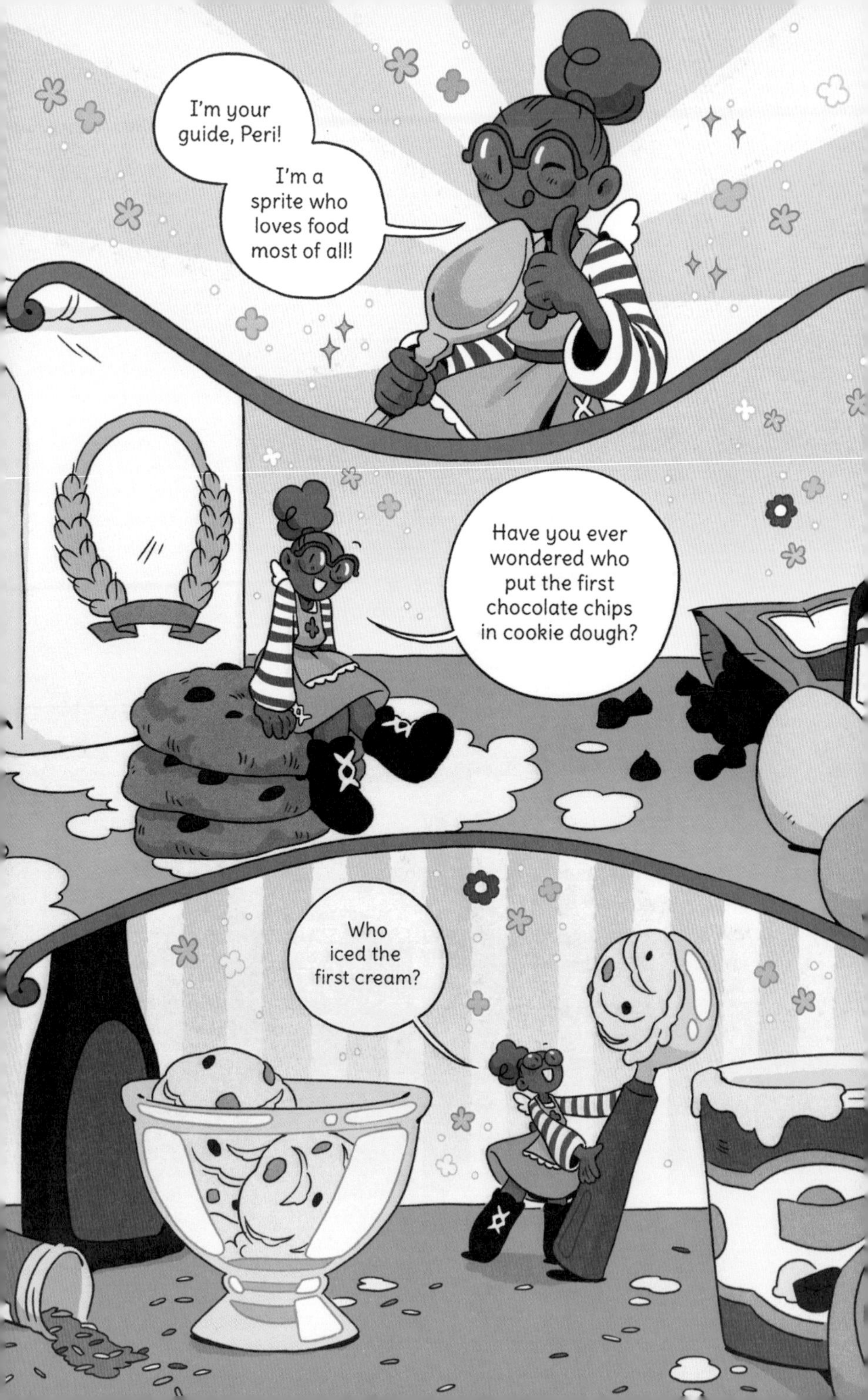
I'm your guide, Peri!
I'm a sprite who loves food most of all!
Have you ever wondered who put the first chocolate chips in cookie dough?
Who iced the first cream?

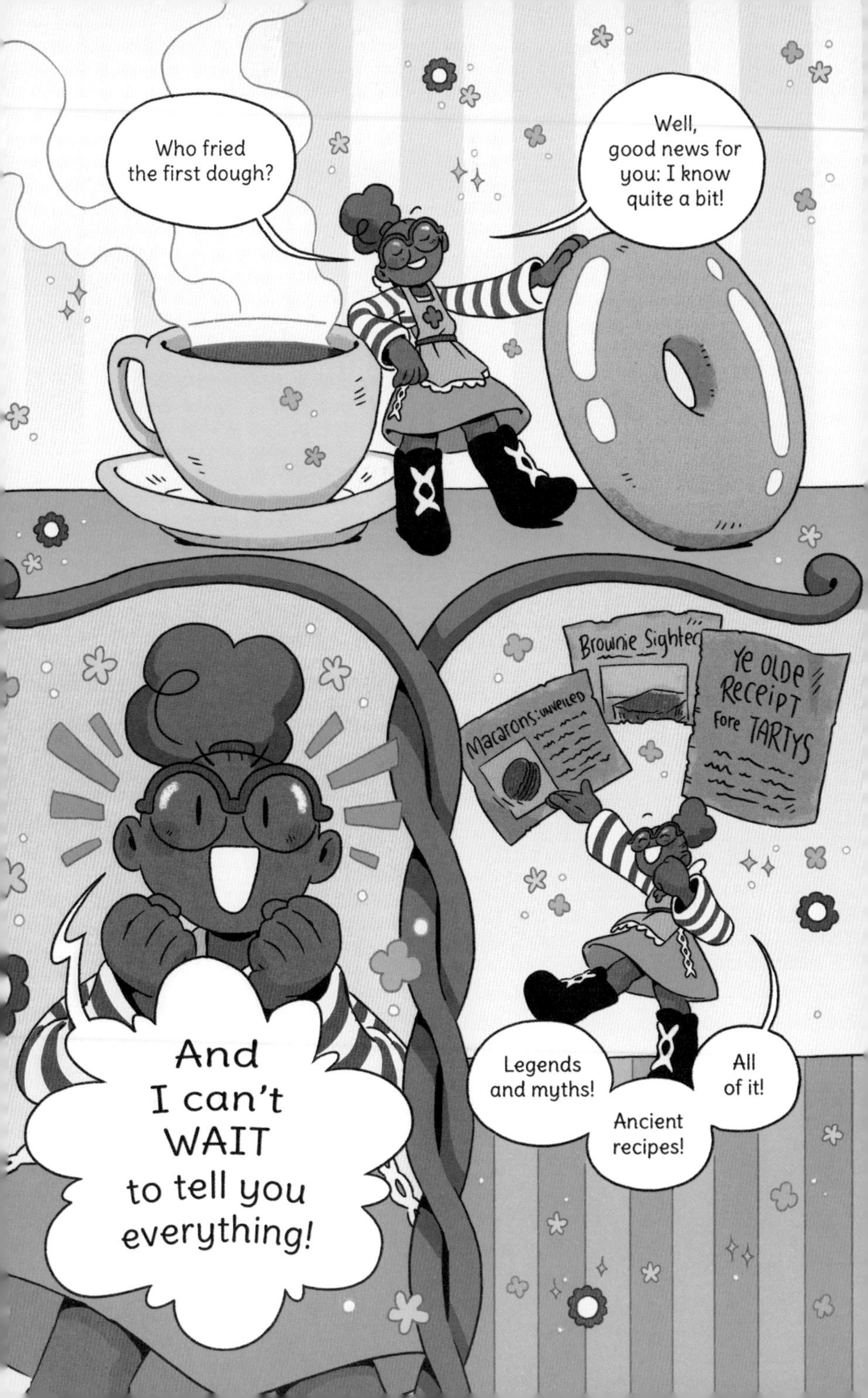
Who fried the first dough?
Well, good news for you: I know quite a bit!
Brownie Sighted
Macarons: UNVEILED
Ye OLDE RECEIPT Fore TARTYS
Legends and myths!
Ancient recipes!
All of it!
And I can't WAIT to tell you everything!

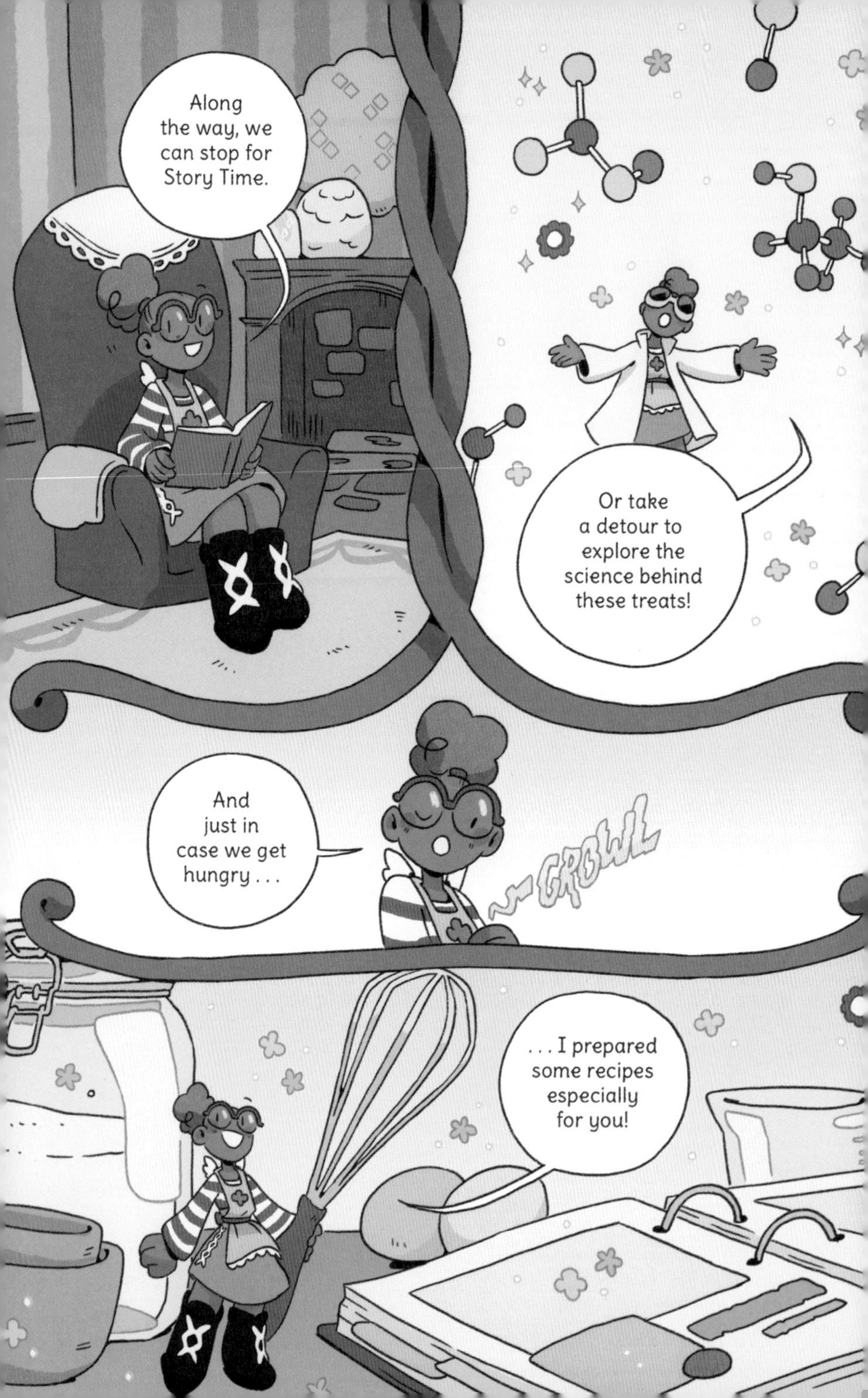
Along the way, we can stop for Story Time.
Or take a detour to explore the science behind these treats!
And just in case we get hungry . . .
GROWL
. . . I prepared some recipes especially for you!

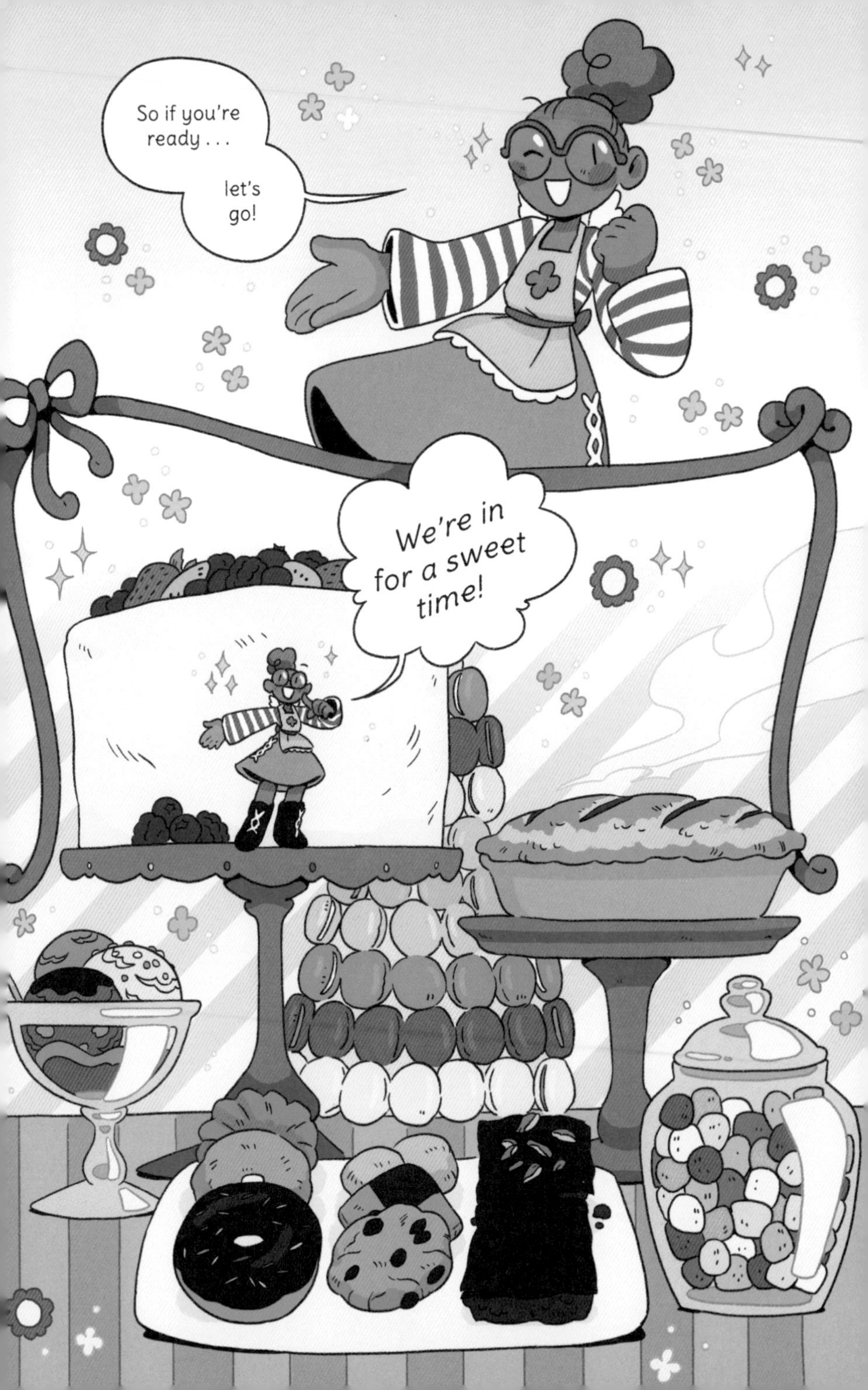
So if you're ready . . .
let's go!
We're in for a sweet time!

The Abridged
Atlas of Ice Cream History

1	Ancient Persian Yakhchāl	**8**	Salt and Ice Freezing Technique
2	Roman Emperor Nero's Favorite Iced Treat	**9**	Nancy Johnson's Ice Cream Maker
3	Ibn Sina's *Canon of Medicine* and Sharbat	**10**	Thomas Masters's Ice Cream Maker
4	The Journey from Sharbat to Sorbetto to Sorbet to Sherbet	**11**	Ice Cream Cart Vendors
5	Antonio Latini's *The Modern Steward*	**12**	American Ice Cream Sundae
6	Monsieur Emi's *Book of Ices*	**13**	St. Louis World's Fair Waffle Cone
7	Eliza Leslie's *Seventy-Five Receipts for Pastry, Cakes and Sweetmeats*	**14**	Iranian Bastani Sonnati
		15	Korean Bingsu
		16	Japanese American Mochi Ice Cream

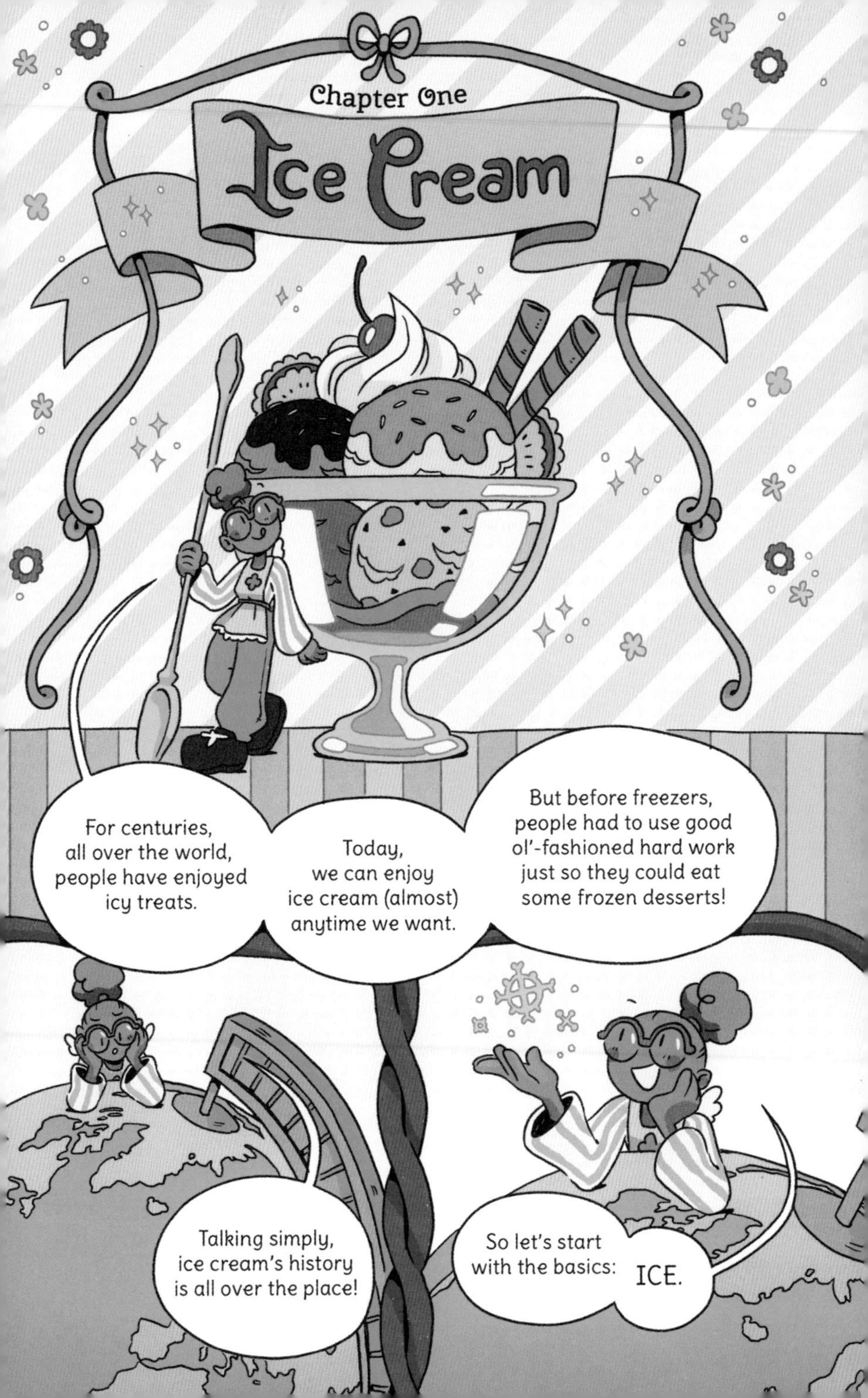
Chapter One
Ice Cream
For centuries, all over the world, people have enjoyed icy treats.
Today, we can enjoy ice cream (almost) anytime we want.
But before freezers, people had to use good ol'-fashioned hard work just so they could eat some frozen desserts!
Talking simply, ice cream's history is all over the place!
So let's start with the basics:
ICE.

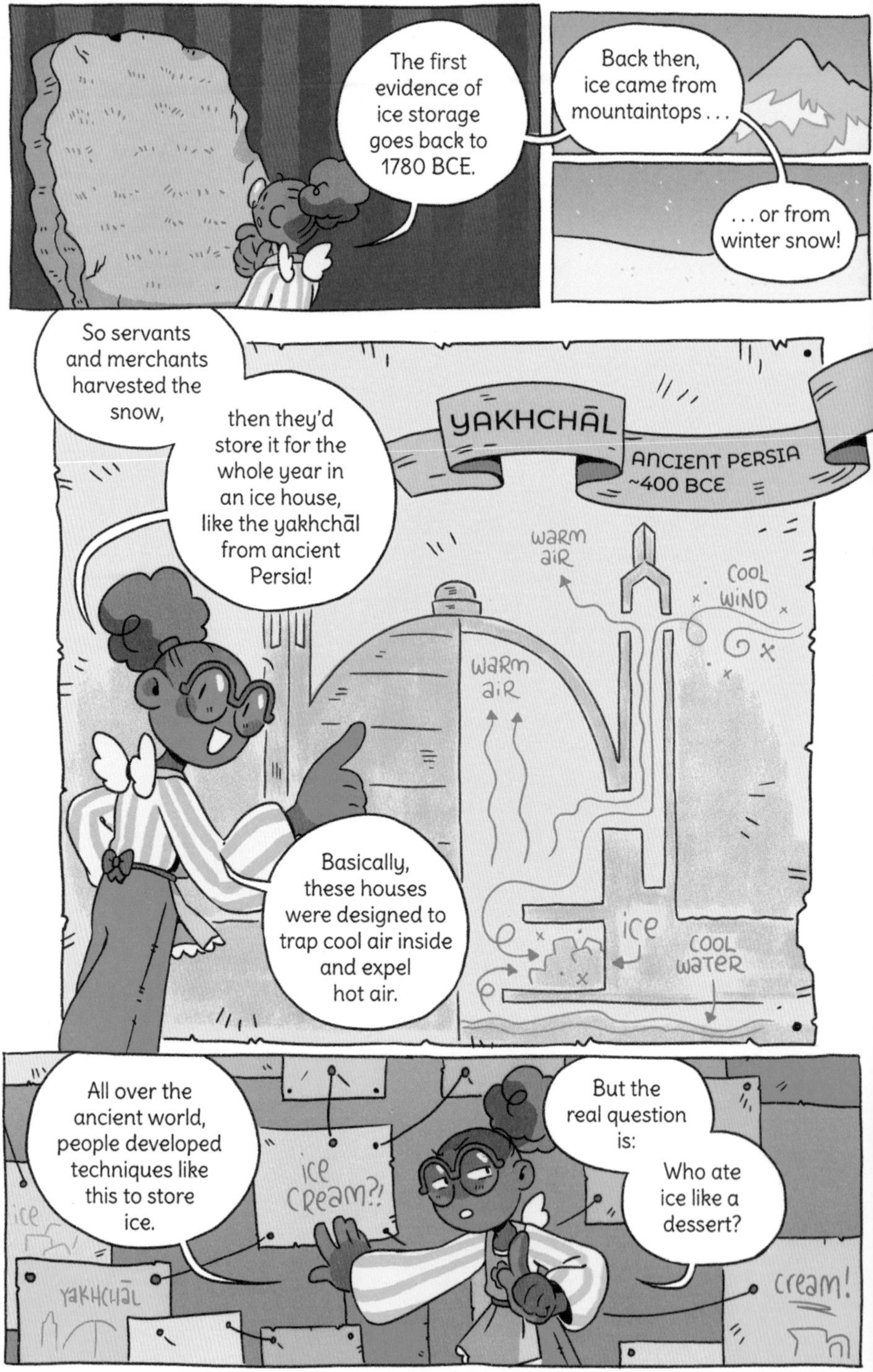

The first evidence of ice storage goes back to 1780 BCE.
Back then, ice came from mountaintops . . .
. . . or from winter snow!
So servants and merchants harvested the snow,
then they'd store it for the whole year in an ice house, like the yakhchāl from ancient Persia!
YAKHCHĀL
ANCIENT PERSIA ~400 BCE
WARM AIR
COOL WIND
WARM AIR
ICE
COOL WATER
Basically, these houses were designed to trap cool air inside and expel hot air.
All over the ancient world, people developed techniques like this to store ice.
ICE CREAM?!
YAKHCHĀL
But the real question is:
Who ate ice like a dessert?
CREAM!

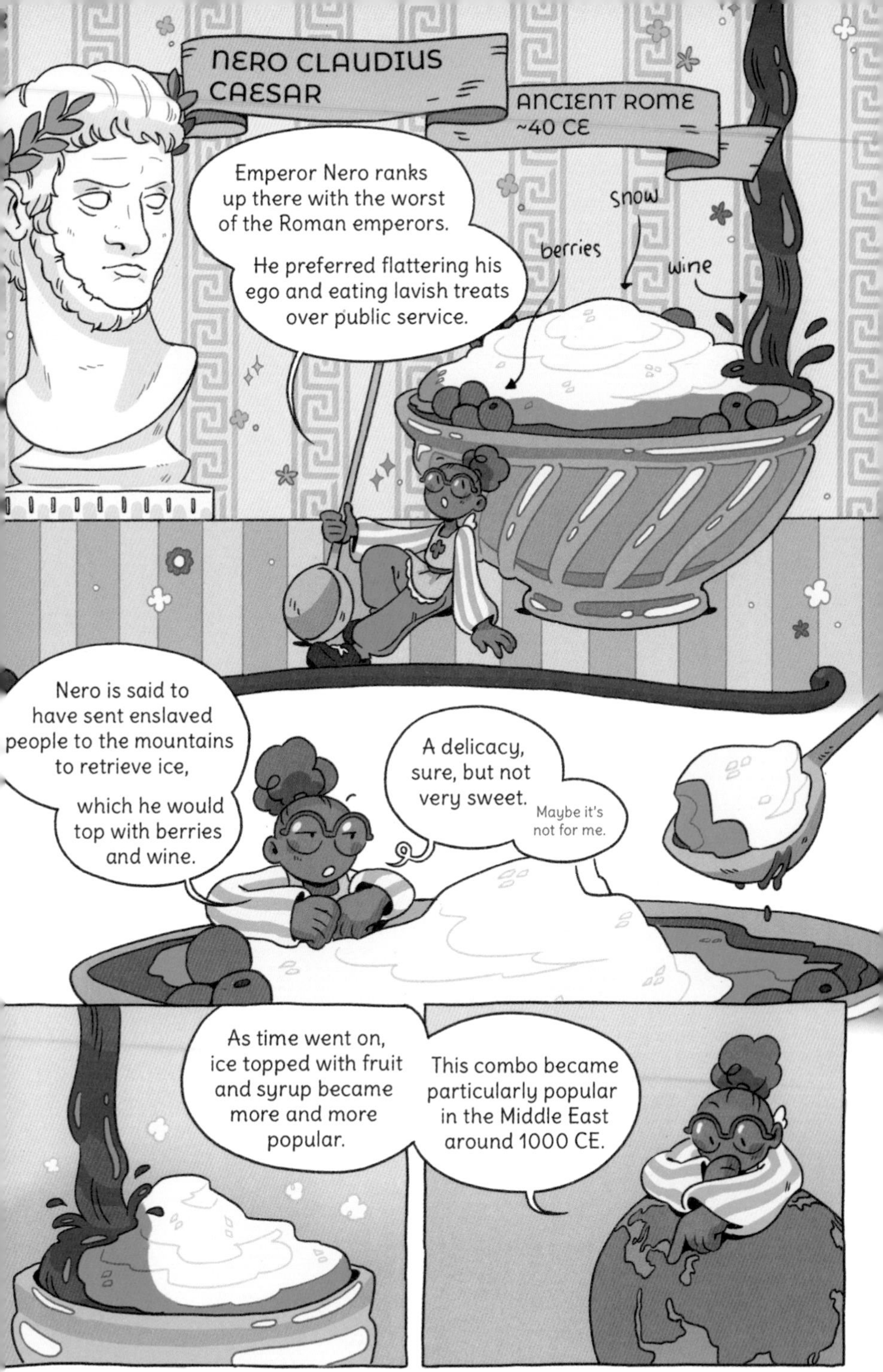
NERO CLAUDIUS CAESAR
ANCIENT ROME ~40 CE
Emperor Nero ranks up there with the worst of the Roman emperors.
He preferred flattering his ego and eating lavish treats over public service.
snow
berries
wine
Nero is said to have sent enslaved people to the mountains to retrieve ice,
which he would top with berries and wine.
A delicacy, sure, but not very sweet.
Maybe it's not for me.
As time went on, ice topped with fruit and syrup became more and more popular.
This combo became particularly popular in the Middle East around 1000 CE.

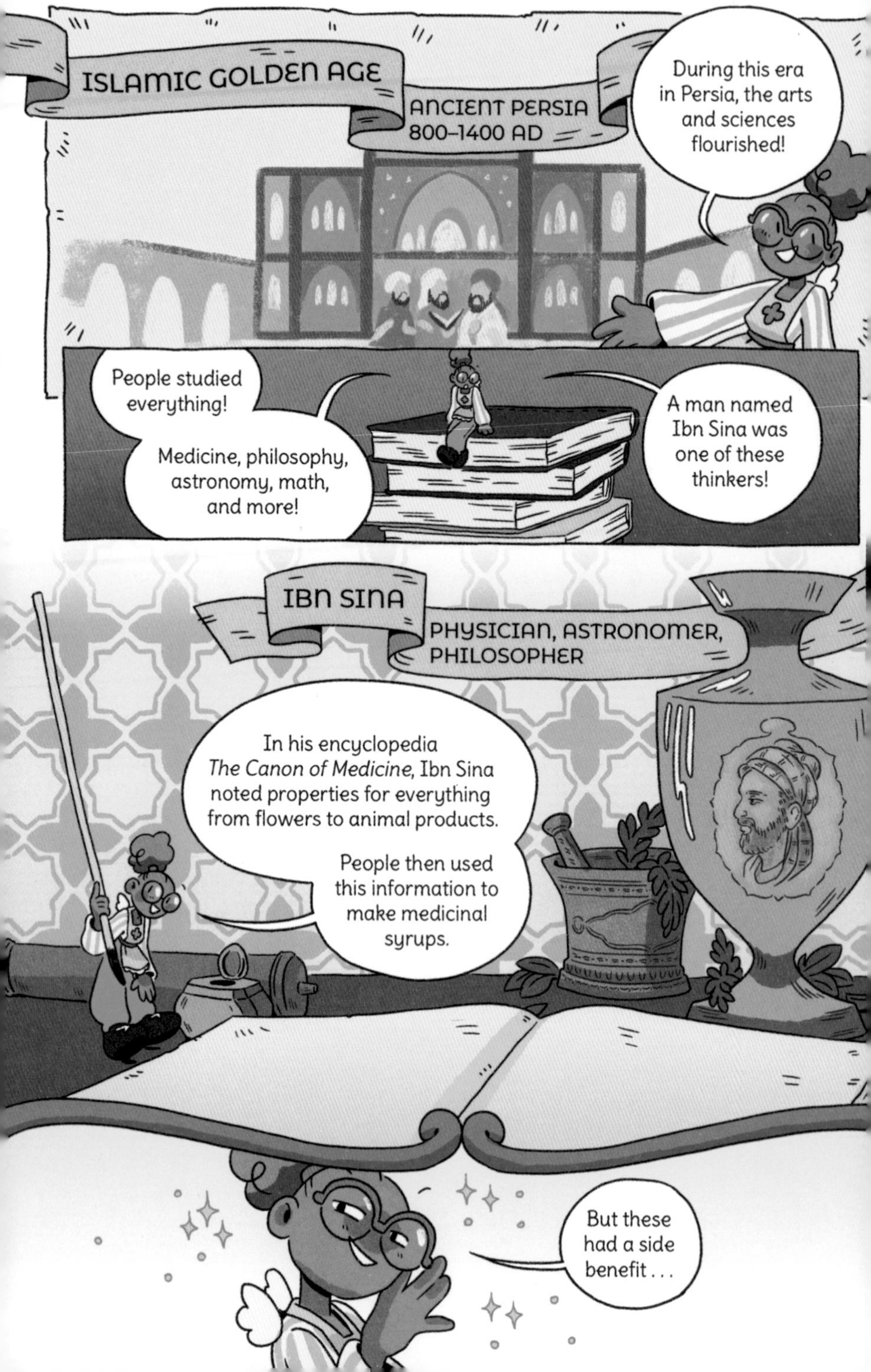
ISLAMIC GOLDEN AGE
ANCIENT PERSIA
800–1400 AD
During this era in Persia, the arts and sciences flourished!
People studied everything!
Medicine, philosophy, astronomy, math, and more!
A man named Ibn Sina was one of these thinkers!
IBN SINA
PHYSICIAN, ASTRONOMER, PHILOSOPHER
In his encyclopedia *The Canon of Medicine*, Ibn Sina noted properties for everything from flowers to animal products.
People then used this information to make medicinal syrups.
But these had a side benefit . . .

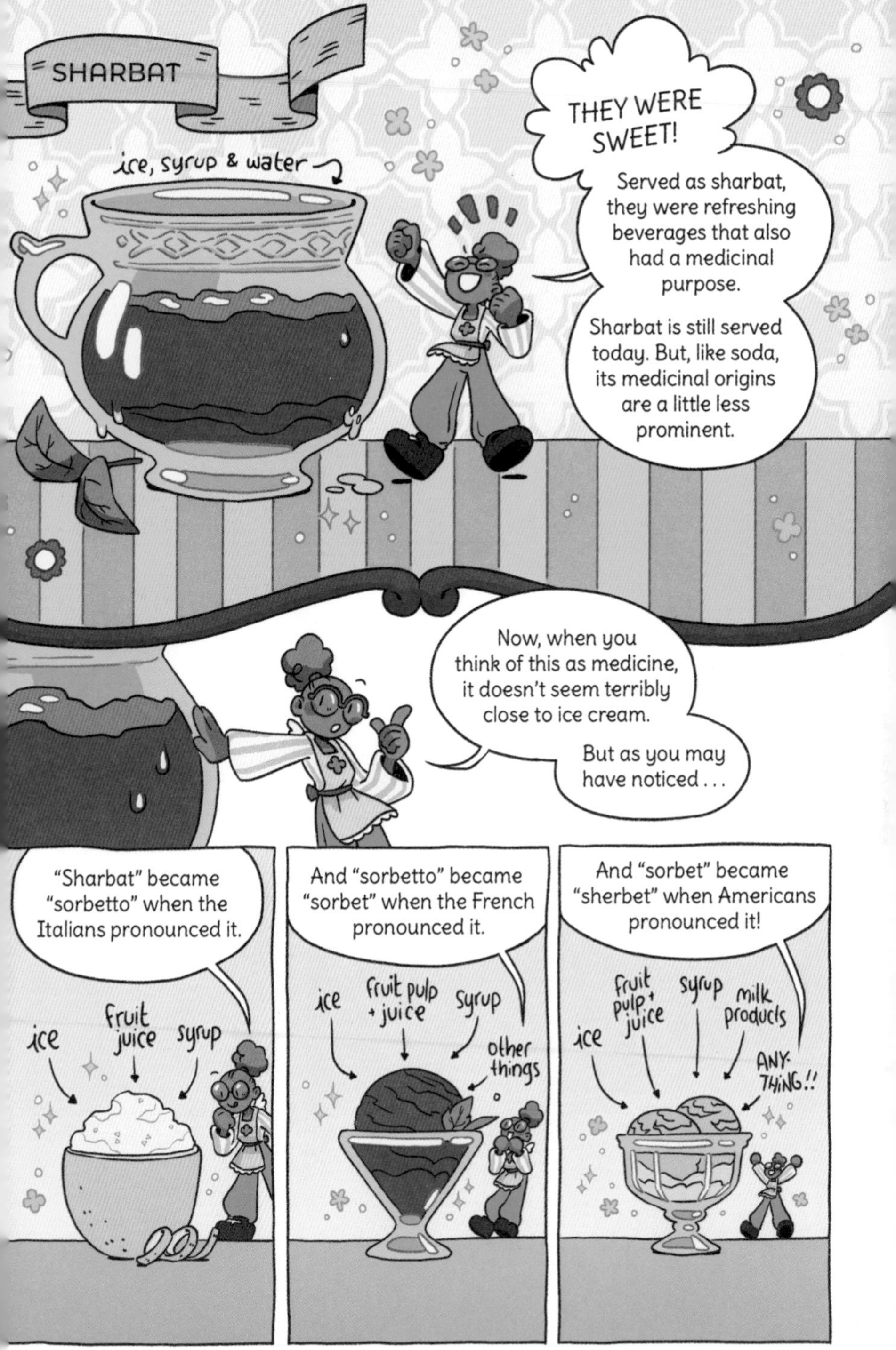
SHARBAT
ice, syrup & water
THEY WERE SWEET!
Served as sharbat, they were refreshing beverages that also had a medicinal purpose.
Sharbat is still served today. But, like soda, its medicinal origins are a little less prominent.
Now, when you think of this as medicine, it doesn't seem terribly close to ice cream.
But as you may have noticed . . .
"Sharbat" became "sorbetto" when the Italians pronounced it.
ice
fruit juice
syrup
And "sorbetto" became "sorbet" when the French pronounced it.
ice
fruit pulp + juice
syrup
other things
And "sorbet" became "sherbet" when Americans pronounced it!
ice
fruit pulp + juice
syrup
milk products
ANY-THING!!

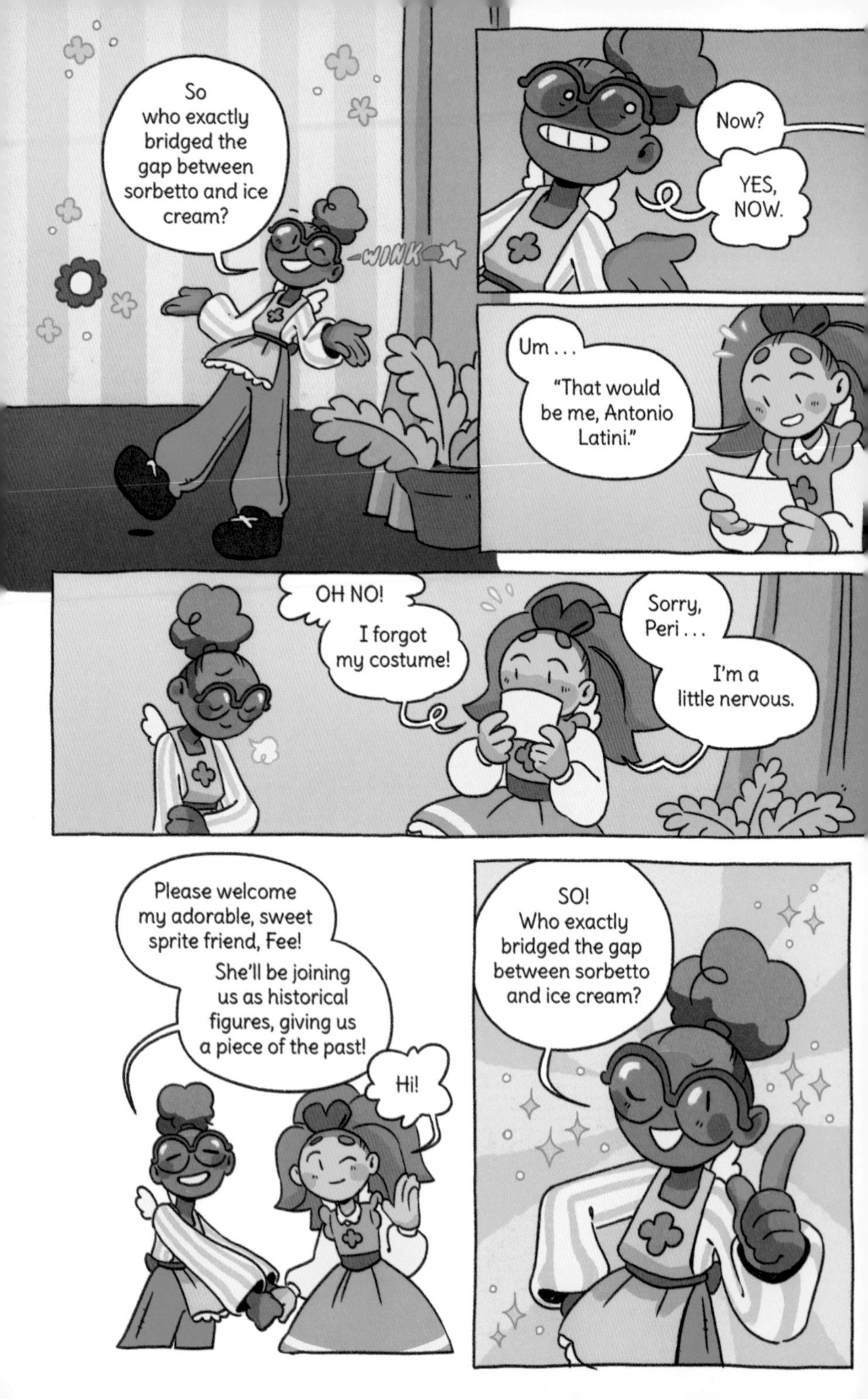

So who exactly bridged the gap between sorbetto and ice cream?
WINK
Now?
YES, NOW.
Um . . .
"That would be me, Antonio Latini."
OH NO!
I forgot my costume!
Sorry, Peri . . .
I'm a little nervous.
Please welcome my adorable, sweet sprite friend, Fee!
She'll be joining us as historical figures, giving us a piece of the past!
Hi!
SO! Who exactly bridged the gap between sorbetto and ice cream?

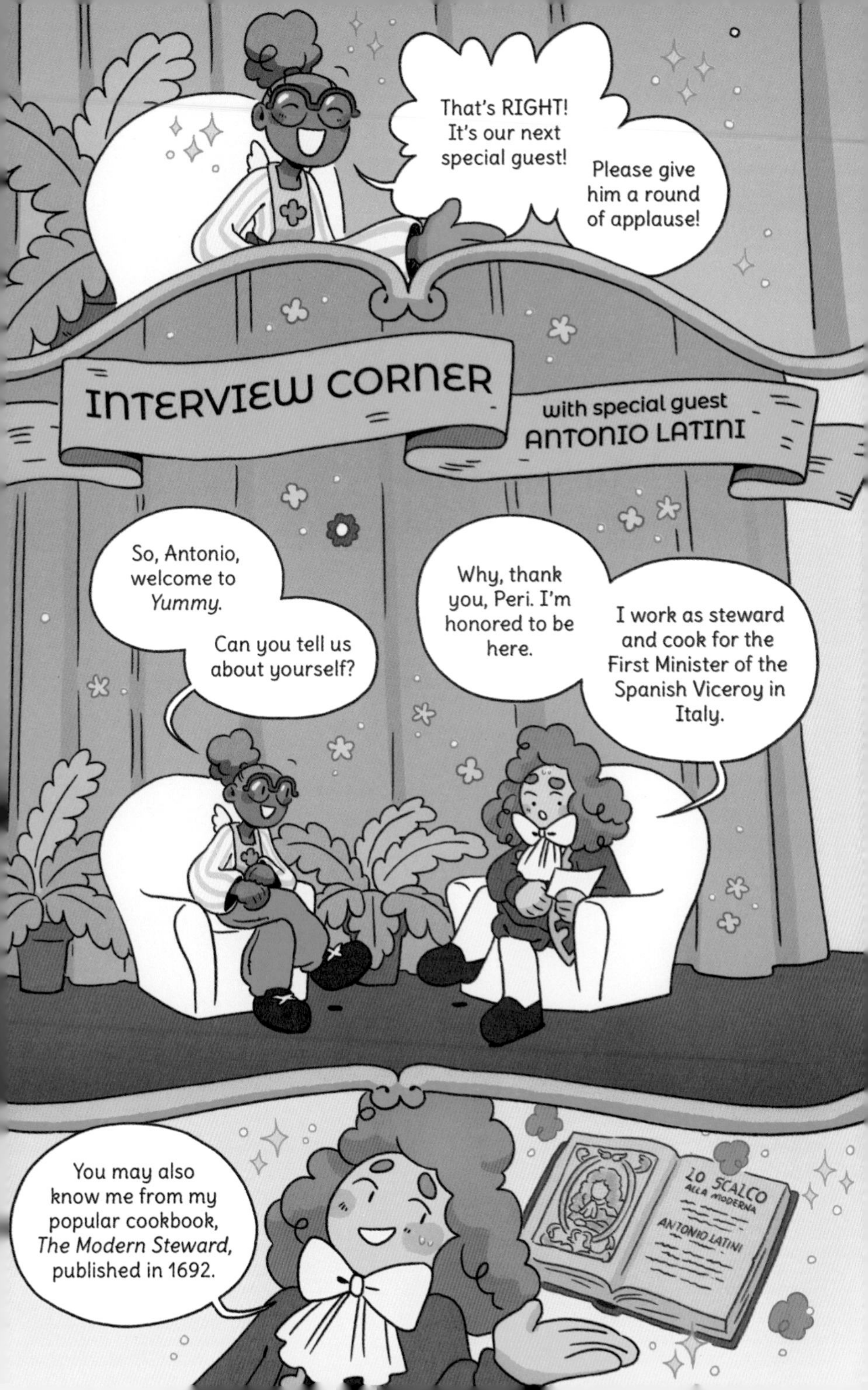
That's RIGHT! It's our next special guest!
Please give him a round of applause!
INTERVIEW CORNER
with special guest ANTONIO LATINI
So, Antonio, welcome to *Yummy*.
Can you tell us about yourself?
Why, thank you, Peri. I'm honored to be here.
I work as steward and cook for the First Minister of the Spanish Viceroy in Italy.
You may also know me from my popular cookbook, *The Modern Steward*, published in 1692.
LO SCALCO ALLA MODERNA
ANTONIO LATINI

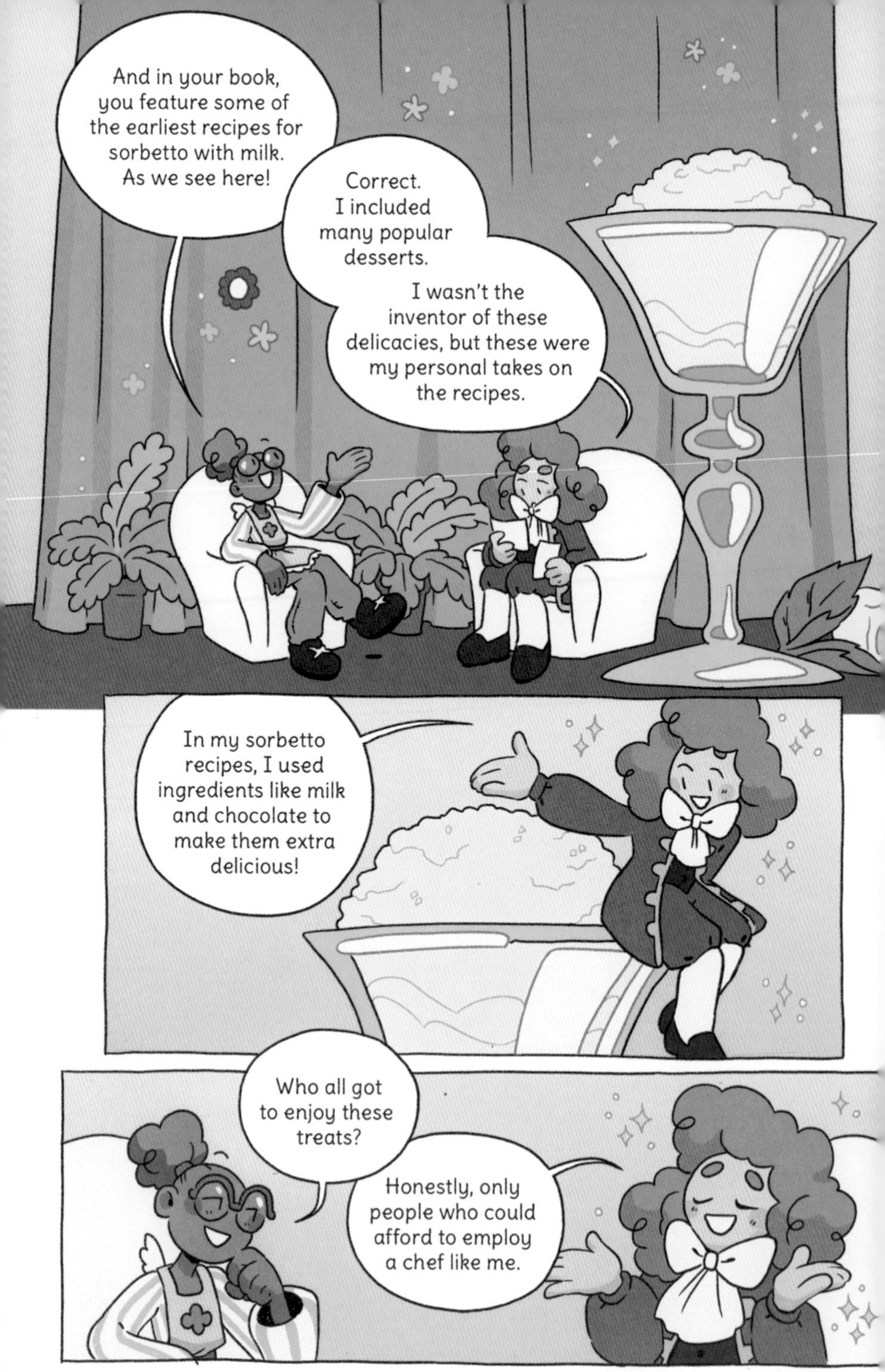
And in your book, you feature some of the earliest recipes for sorbetto with milk. As we see here!
Correct. I included many popular desserts.
I wasn't the inventor of these delicacies, but these were my personal takes on the recipes.
In my sorbetto recipes, I used ingredients like milk and chocolate to make them extra delicious!
Who all got to enjoy these treats?
Honestly, only people who could afford to employ a chef like me.

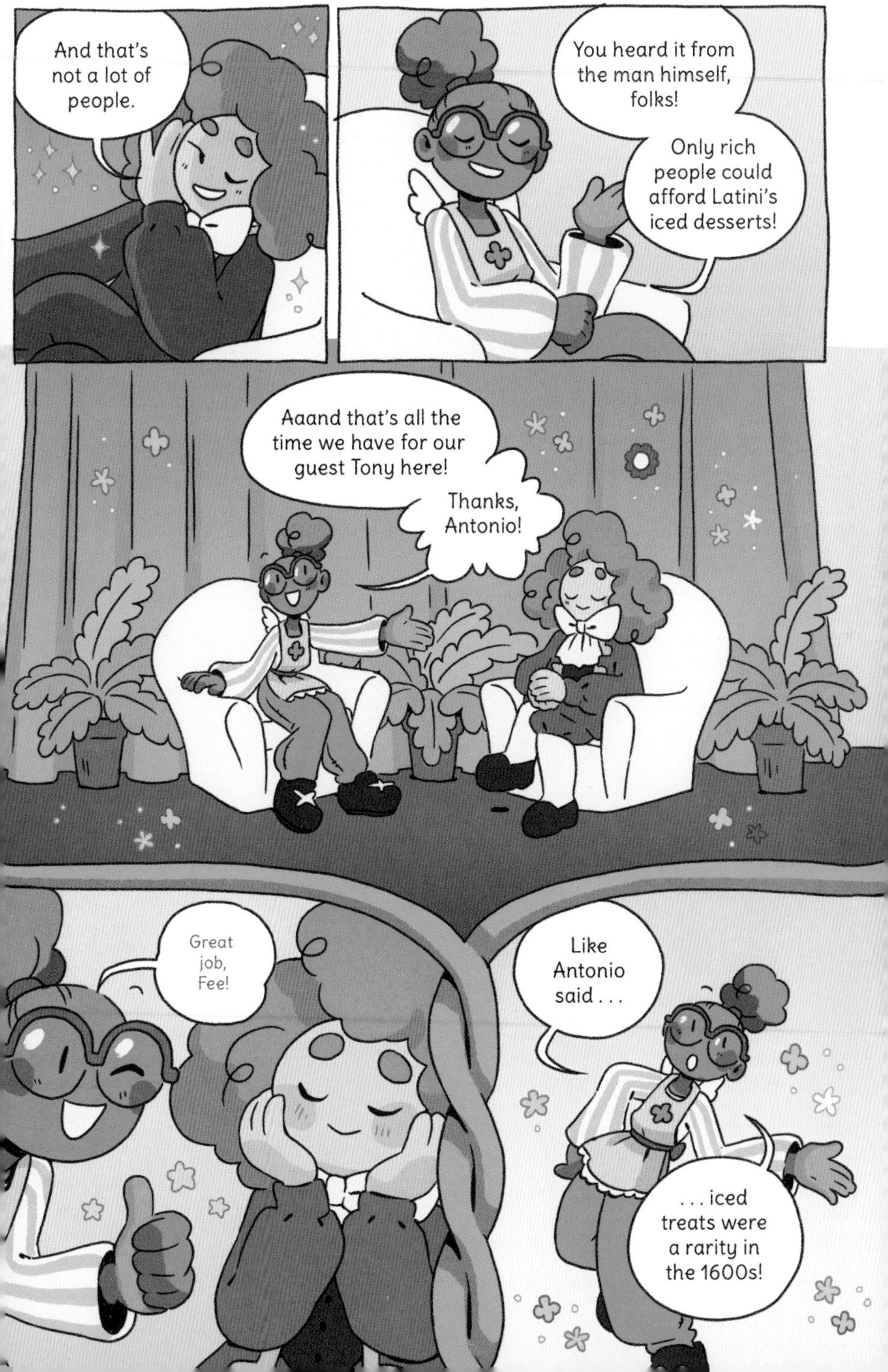
And that's not a lot of people.
You heard it from the man himself, folks!
Only rich people could afford Latini's iced desserts!
Aaand that's all the time we have for our guest Tony here!
Thanks, Antonio!
Great job, Fee!
Like Antonio said . . .
. . . iced treats were a rarity in the 1600s!

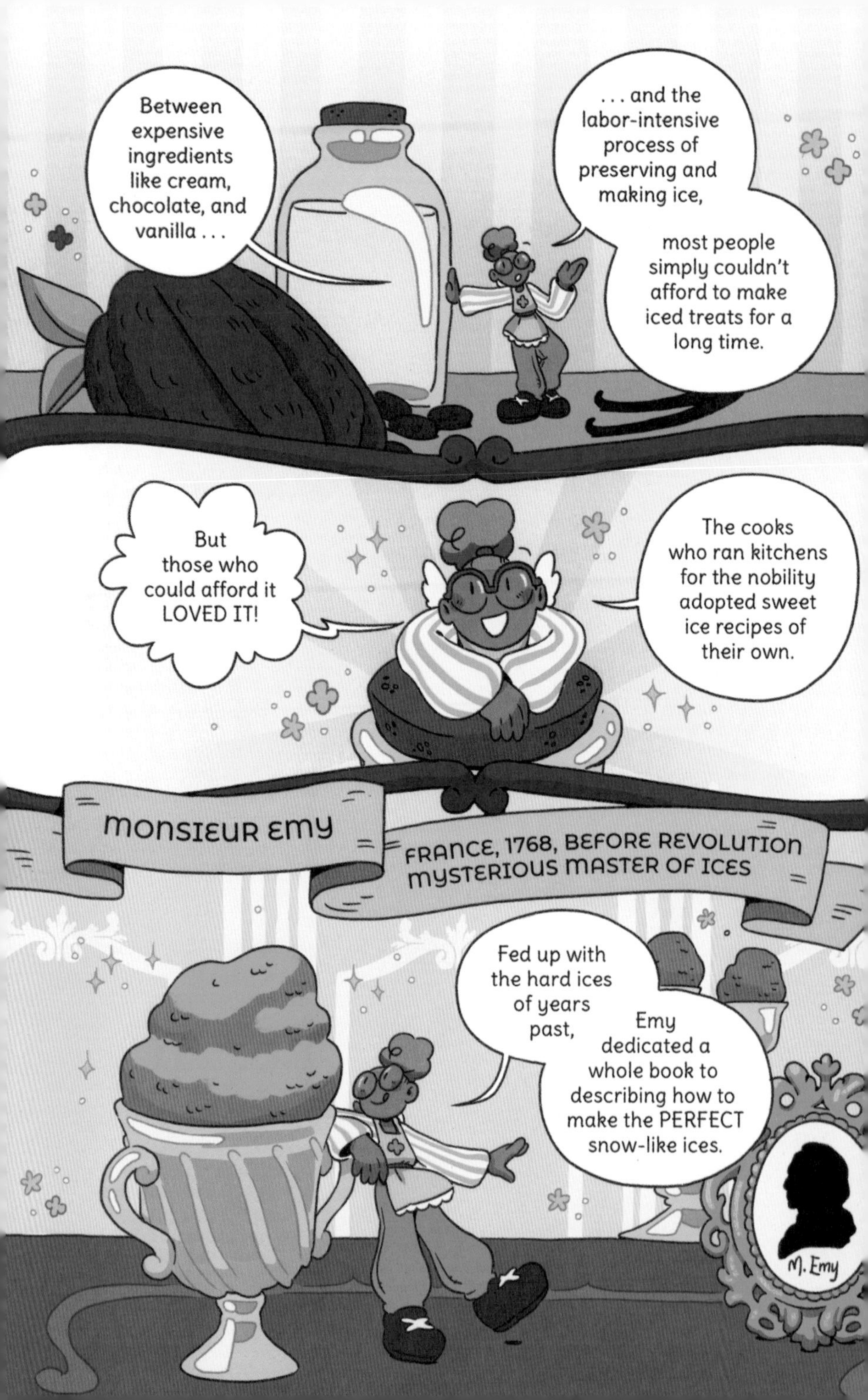
Between expensive ingredients like cream, chocolate, and vanilla . . .
. . . and the labor-intensive process of preserving and making ice,
most people simply couldn't afford to make iced treats for a long time.
But those who could afford it LOVED IT!
The cooks who ran kitchens for the nobility adopted sweet ice recipes of their own.
MONSIEUR EMY
FRANCE, 1768, BEFORE REVOLUTION
MYSTERIOUS MASTER OF ICES
Fed up with the hard ices of years past,
Emy dedicated a whole book to describing how to make the PERFECT snow-like ices.
M. Emy

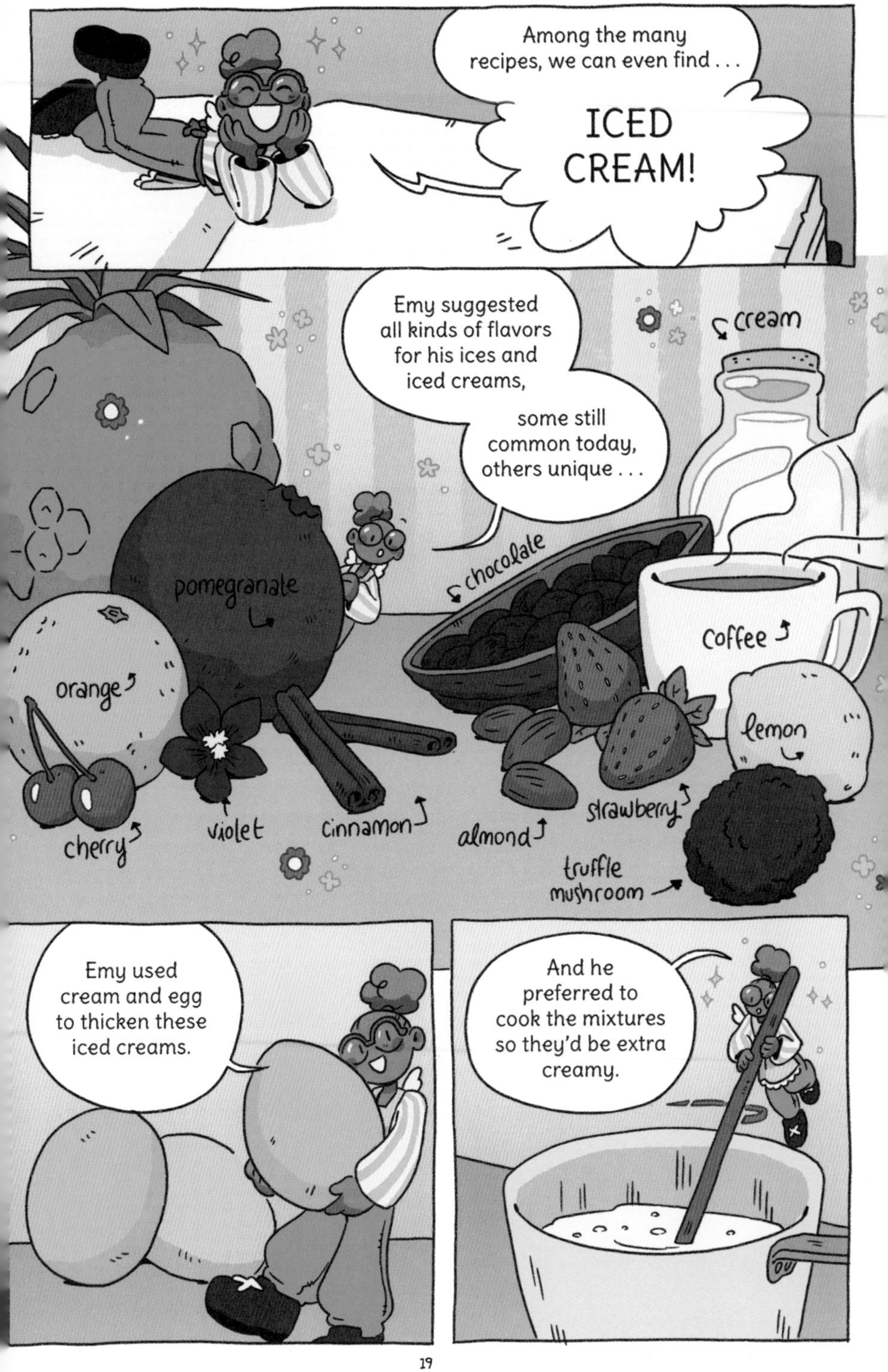
Among the many recipes, we can even find . . .
ICED CREAM!
Emy suggested all kinds of flavors for his ices and iced creams,
some still common today, others unique . . .
cream
chocolate
pomegranate
coffee
orange
lemon
cherry
violet
cinnamon
almond
strawberry
truffle mushroom
Emy used cream and egg to thicken these iced creams.
And he preferred to cook the mixtures so they'd be extra creamy.

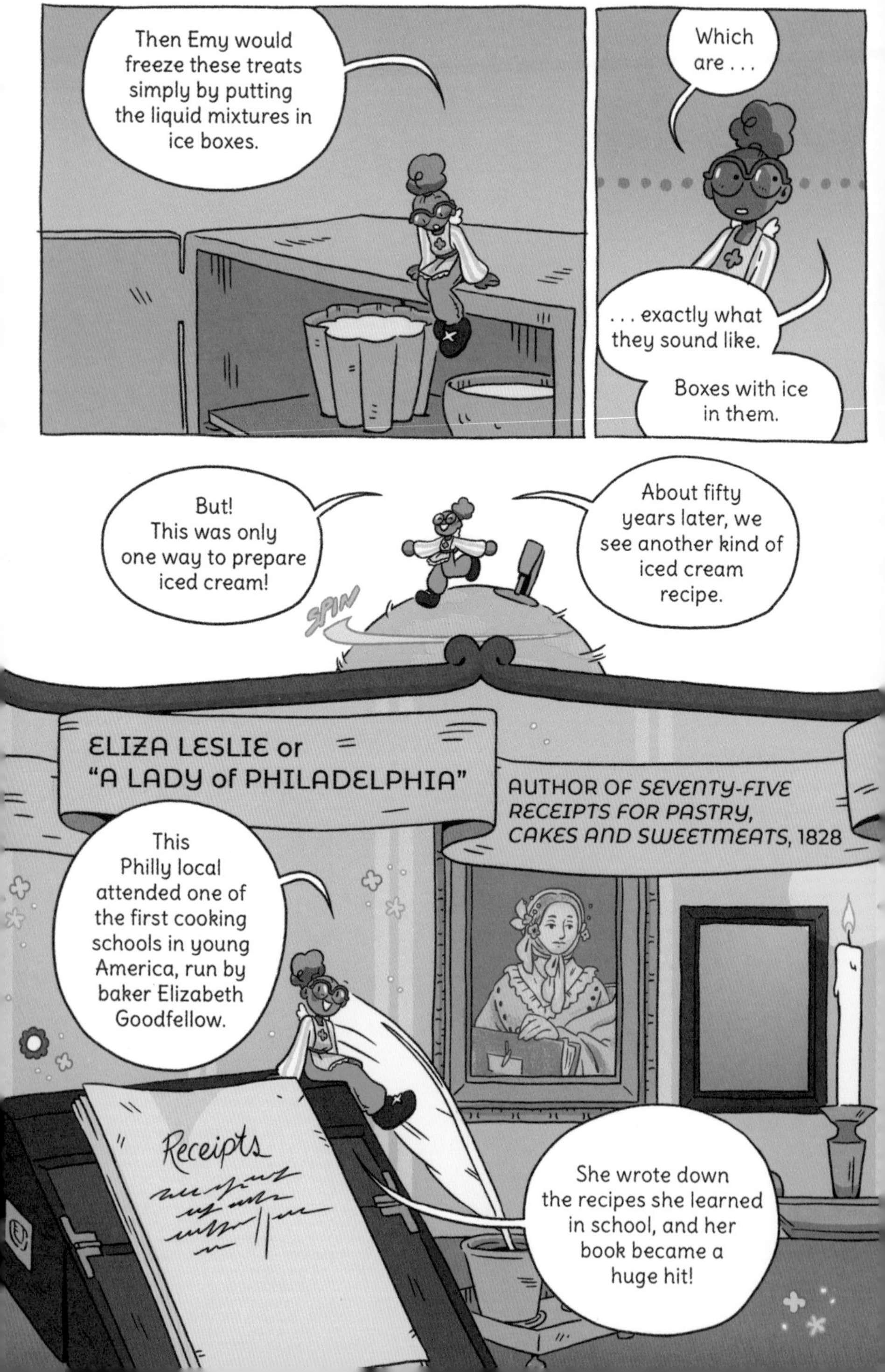
Then Emy would freeze these treats simply by putting the liquid mixtures in ice boxes.
Which are . . .
. . . exactly what they sound like.
Boxes with ice in them.
But! This was only one way to prepare iced cream!
SPIN
About fifty years later, we see another kind of iced cream recipe.
ELIZA LESLIE or "A LADY of PHILADELPHIA"
AUTHOR OF *SEVENTY-FIVE RECEIPTS FOR PASTRY, CAKES AND SWEETMEATS*, 1828
This Philly local attended one of the first cooking schools in young America, run by baker Elizabeth Goodfellow.
Receipts
She wrote down the recipes she learned in school, and her book became a huge hit!

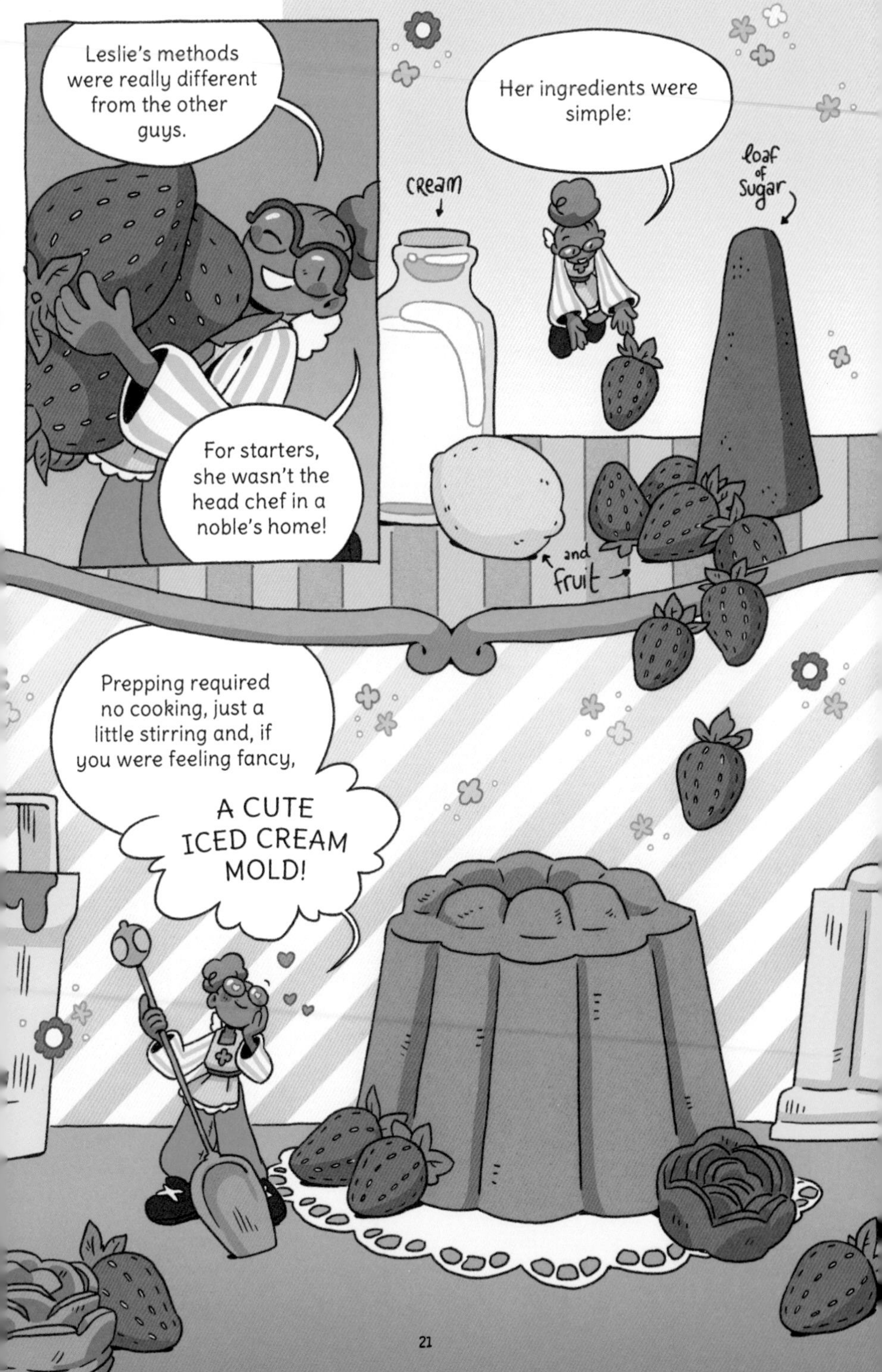
Leslie's methods were really different from the other guys.
For starters, she wasn't the head chef in a noble's home!
Her ingredients were simple:
cream
loaf of sugar
and fruit
Prepping required no cooking, just a little stirring and, if you were feeling fancy,
A CUTE ICED CREAM MOLD!

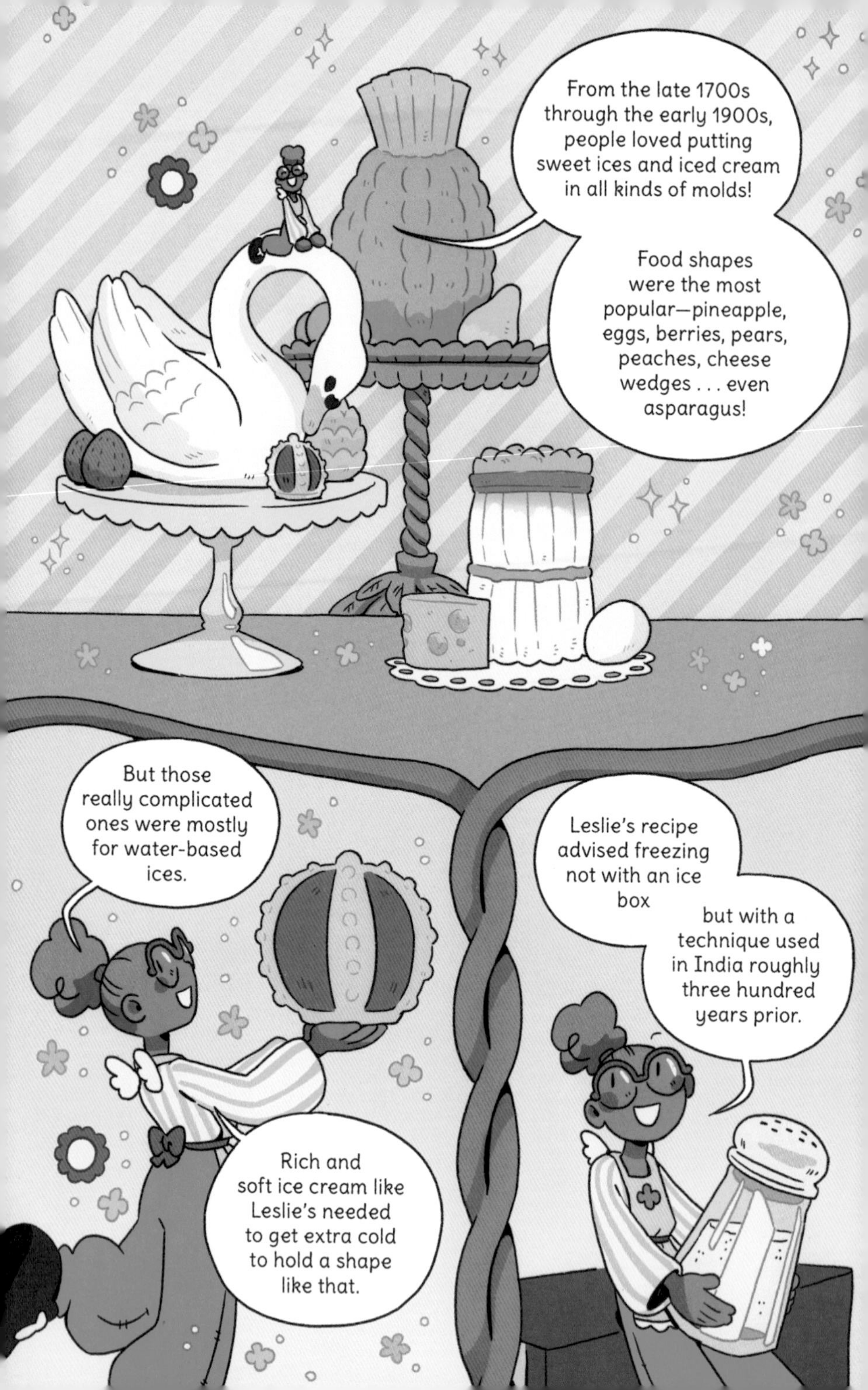
From the late 1700s through the early 1900s, people loved putting sweet ices and iced cream in all kinds of molds!
Food shapes were the most popular—pineapple, eggs, berries, pears, peaches, cheese wedges . . . even asparagus!
But those really complicated ones were mostly for water-based ices.
Rich and soft ice cream like Leslie's needed to get extra cold to hold a shape like that.
Leslie's recipe advised freezing not with an ice box
but with a technique used in India roughly three hundred years prior.

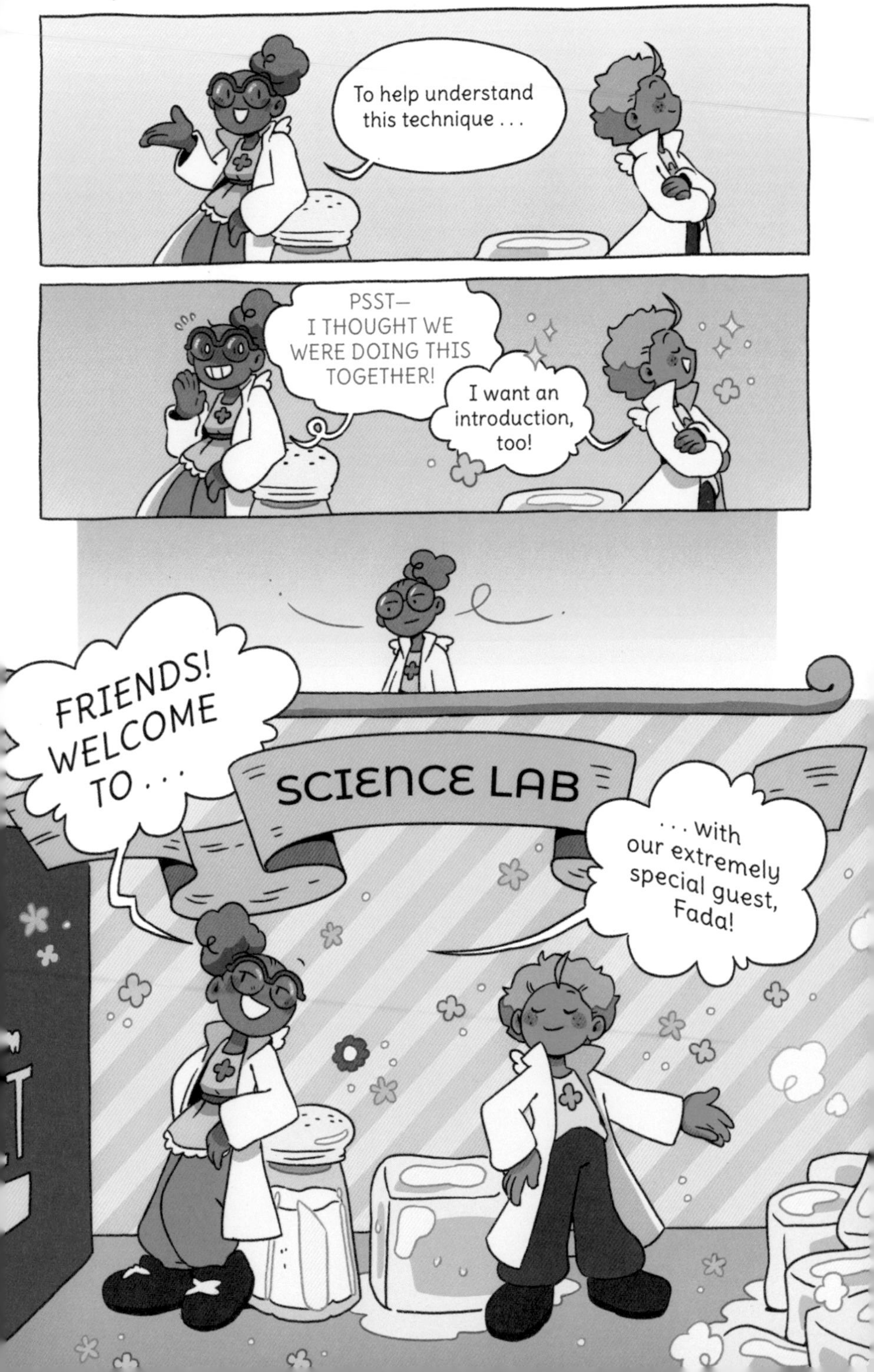
To help understand this technique . . .
PSST— I THOUGHT WE WERE DOING THIS TOGETHER!
I want an introduction, too!
FRIENDS! WELCOME TO . . .
SCIENCE LAB
. . . with our extremely special guest, Fada!

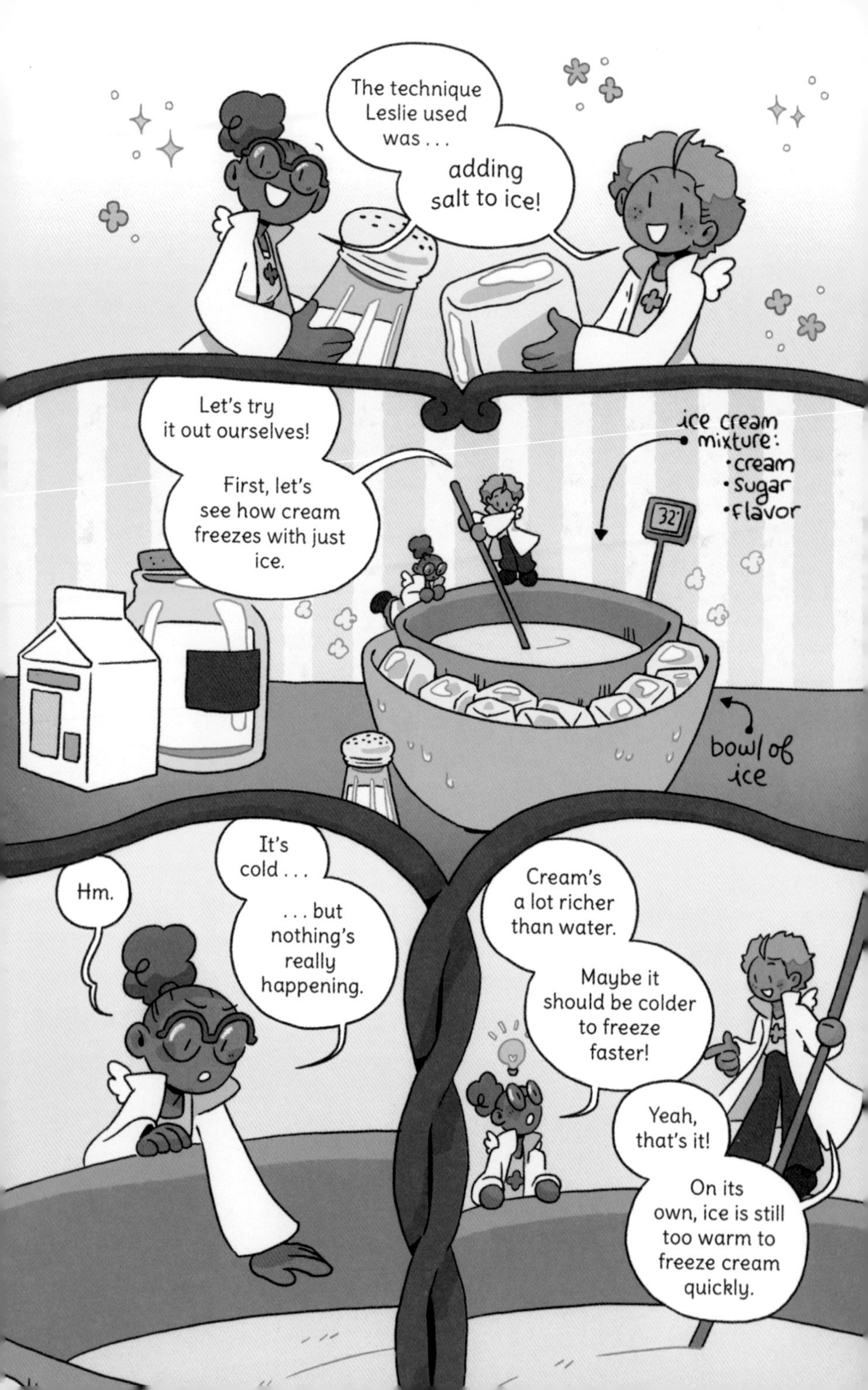

The technique Leslie used was . . .
adding salt to ice!
Let's try it out ourselves!
First, let's see how cream freezes with just ice.
ice cream mixture:
•cream
•sugar
•flavor
32°
bowl of ice
Hm.
It's cold . . .
. . . but nothing's really happening.
Cream's a lot richer than water.
Maybe it should be colder to freeze faster!
Yeah, that's it!
On its own, ice is still too warm to freeze cream quickly.

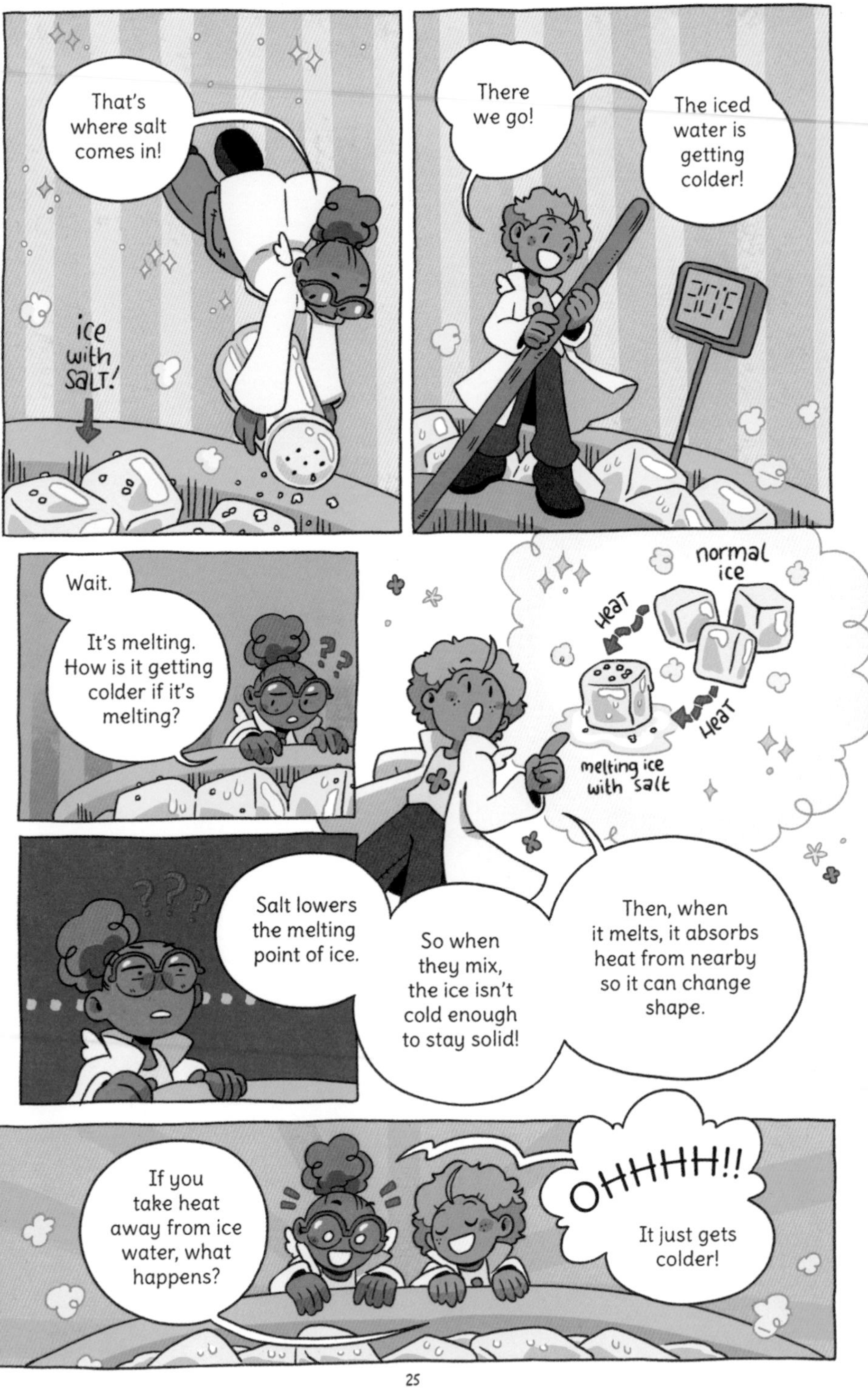
That's where salt comes in!
ice with SALT!
There we go!
The iced water is getting colder!
30°F
Wait.
It's melting. How is it getting colder if it's melting?
normal ice
HEAT
HEAT
melting ice with salt
Salt lowers the melting point of ice.
So when they mix, the ice isn't cold enough to stay solid!
Then, when it melts, it absorbs heat from nearby so it can change shape.
If you take heat away from ice water, what happens?
OHHHHH!!
It just gets colder!

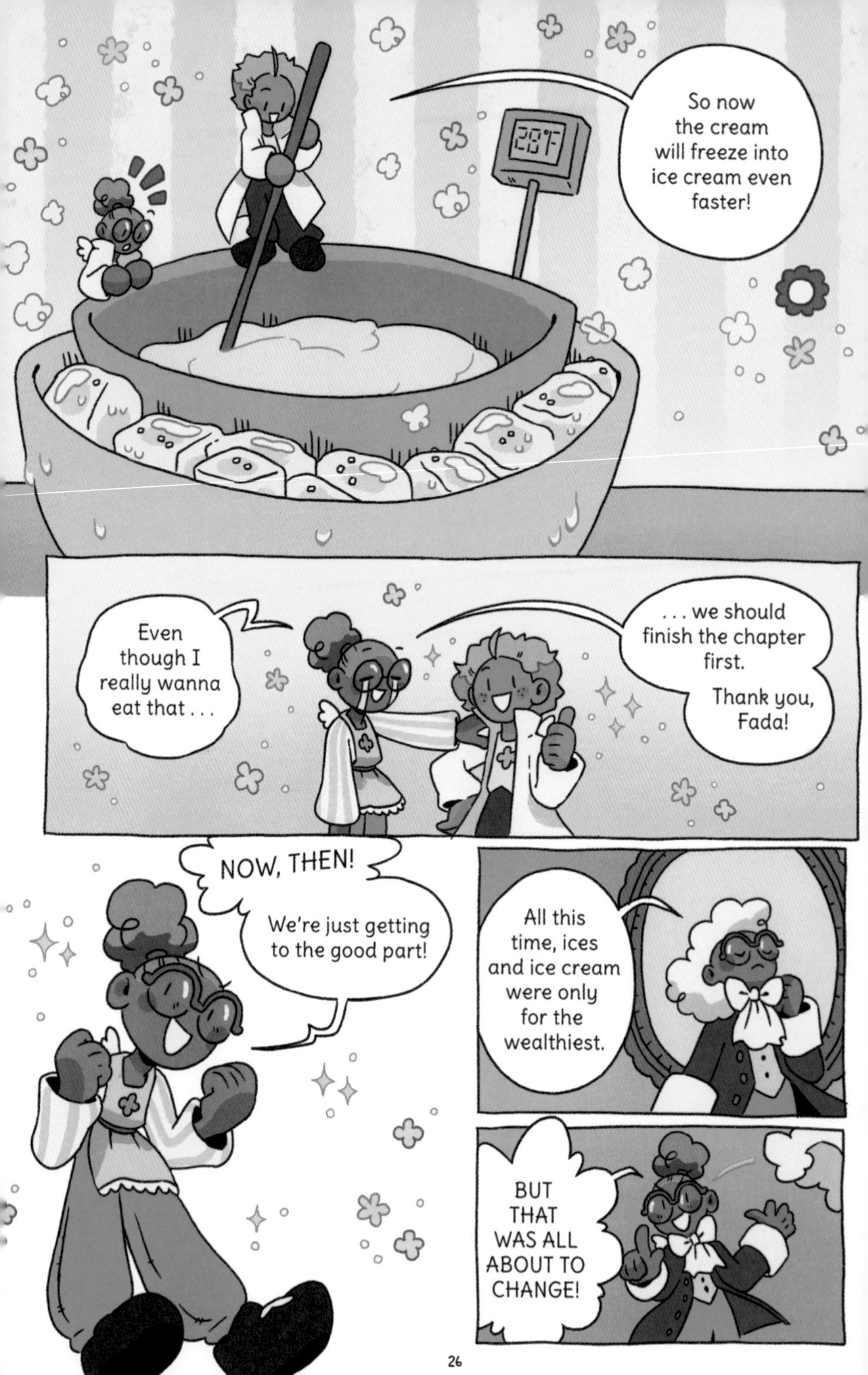
28°F
So now the cream will freeze into ice cream even faster!
Even though I really wanna eat that . . .
. . . we should finish the chapter first.
Thank you, Fada!
NOW, THEN!
We're just getting to the good part!
All this time, ices and ice cream were only for the wealthiest.
BUT THAT WAS ALL ABOUT TO CHANGE!

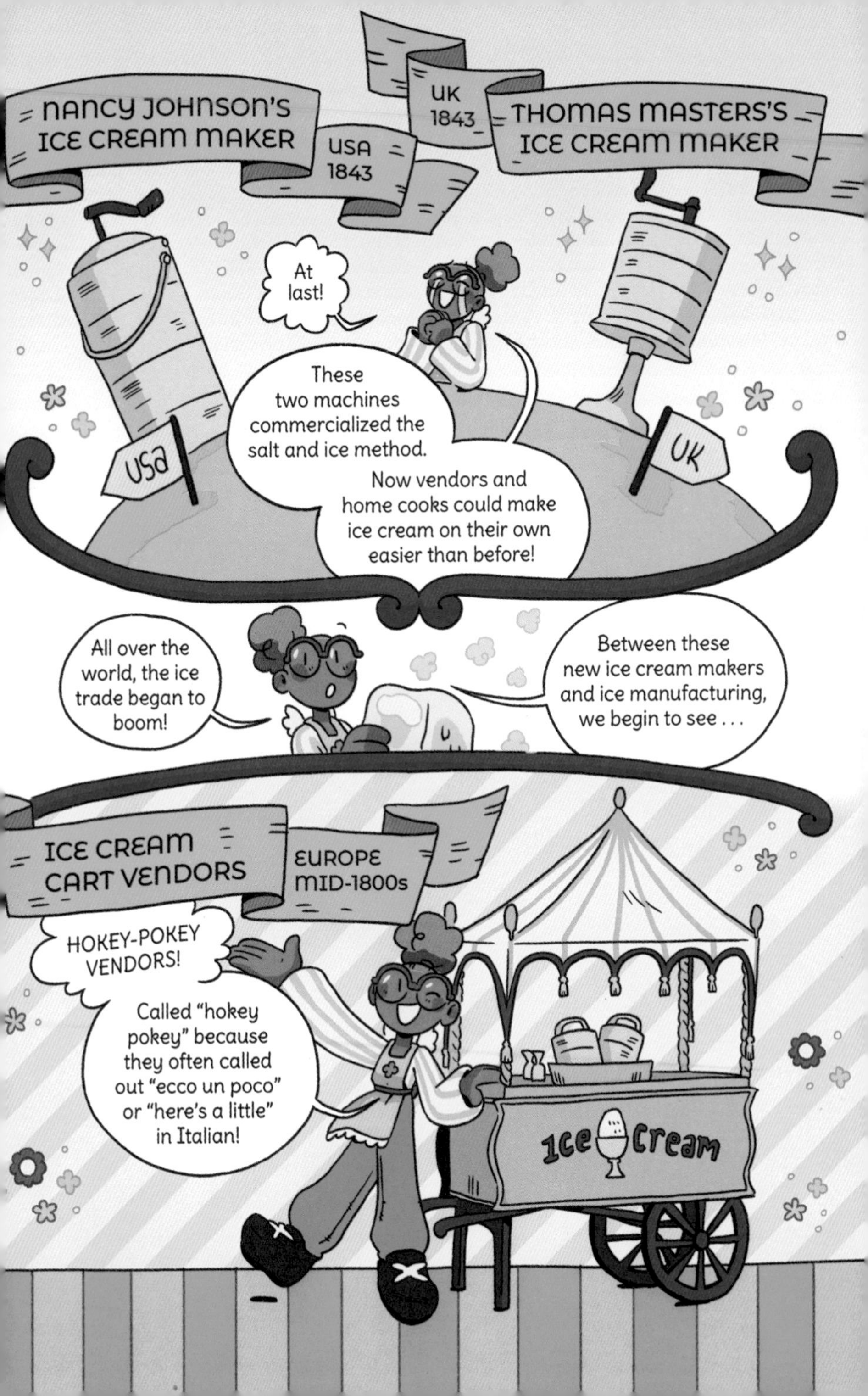
NANCY JOHNSON'S ICE CREAM MAKER
USA 1843
UK 1843
THOMAS MASTERS'S ICE CREAM MAKER
At last!
These two machines commercialized the salt and ice method.
Now vendors and home cooks could make ice cream on their own easier than before!
USA
UK
All over the world, the ice trade began to boom!
Between these new ice cream makers and ice manufacturing, we begin to see . . .
ICE CREAM CART VENDORS
EUROPE MID-1800s
HOKEY-POKEY VENDORS!
Called "hokey pokey" because they often called out "ecco un poco" or "here's a little" in Italian!
Ice Cream

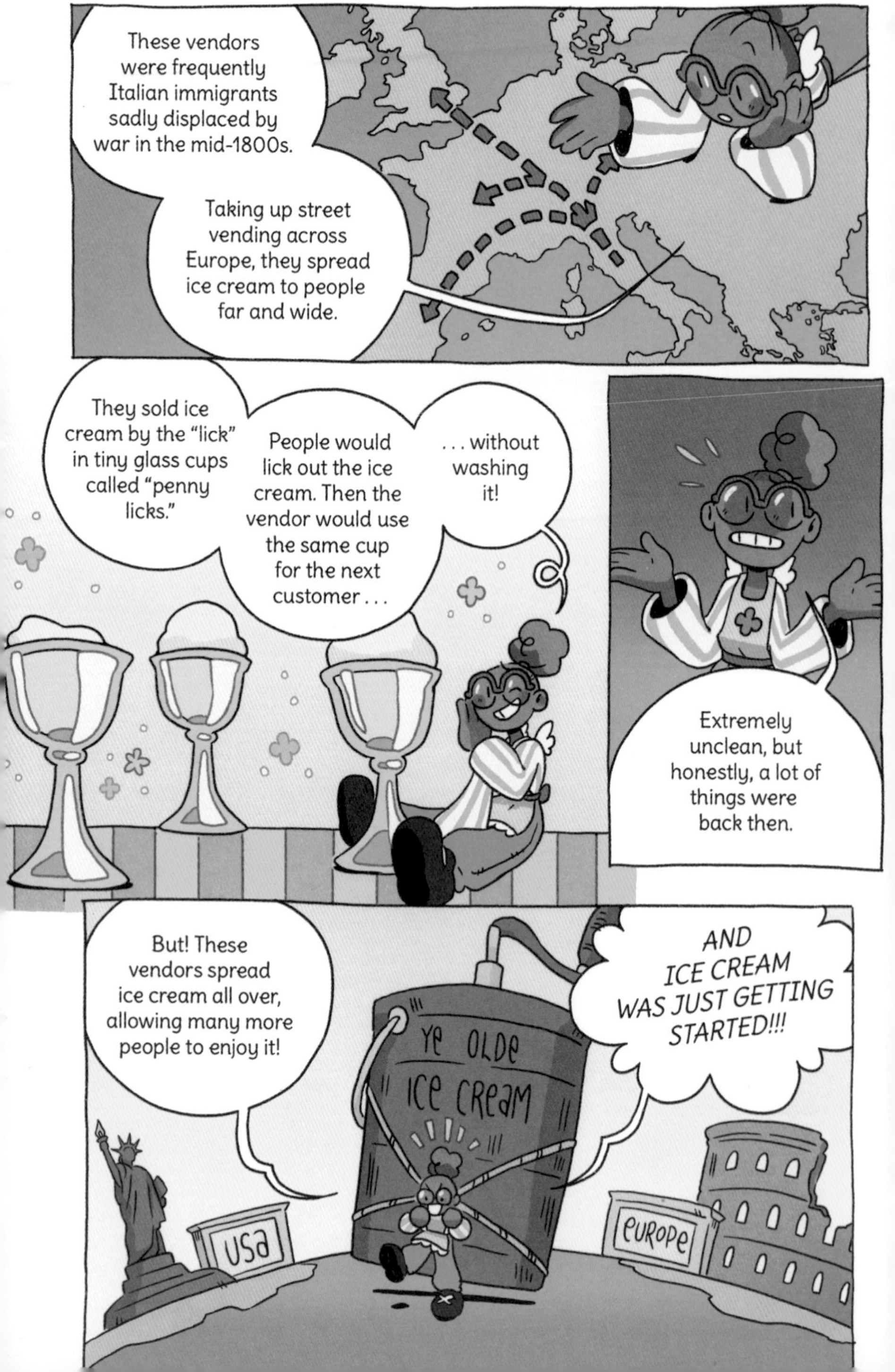
These vendors were frequently Italian immigrants sadly displaced by war in the mid-1800s.
Taking up street vending across Europe, they spread ice cream to people far and wide.
They sold ice cream by the "lick" in tiny glass cups called "penny licks."
People would lick out the ice cream. Then the vendor would use the same cup for the next customer . . .
. . . without washing it!
Extremely unclean, but honestly, a lot of things were back then.
But! These vendors spread ice cream all over, allowing many more people to enjoy it!
YE OLDE ICE CREAM
USA
EUROPE
AND ICE CREAM WAS JUST GETTING STARTED!!!

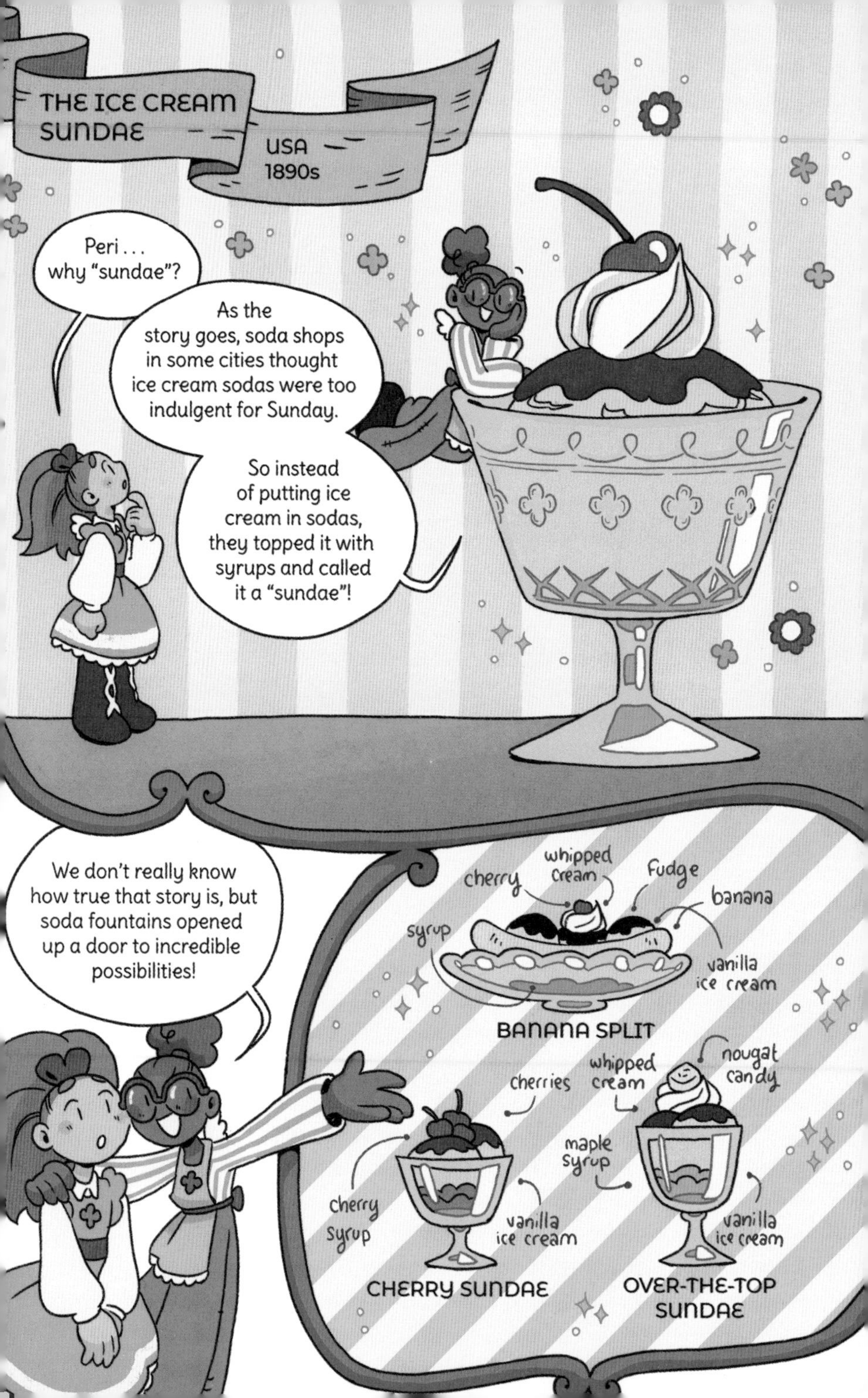

THE ICE CREAM SUNDAE
USA 1890s
Peri . . . why "sundae"?
As the story goes, soda shops in some cities thought ice cream sodas were too indulgent for Sunday.
So instead of putting ice cream in sodas, they topped it with syrups and called it a "sundae"!
We don't really know how true that story is, but soda fountains opened up a door to incredible possibilities!
cherry
whipped cream
fudge
banana
syrup
vanilla ice cream
BANANA SPLIT
cherries
whipped cream
nougat candy
maple syrup
cherry syrup
vanilla ice cream
vanilla ice cream
CHERRY SUNDAE
OVER-THE-TOP SUNDAE

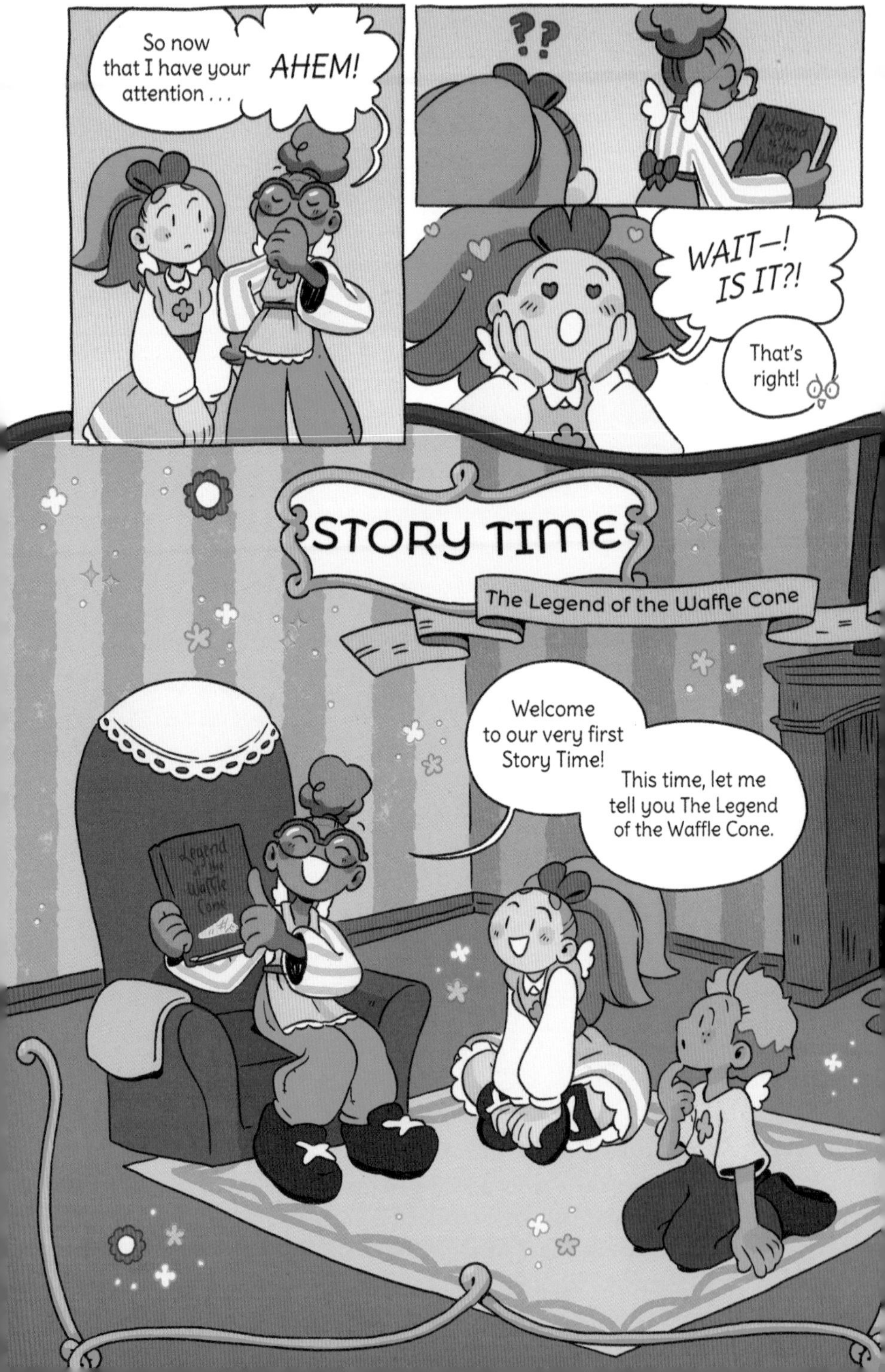
So now that I have your attention . . .
AHEM!
??
WAIT—! IS IT?!
That's right!
STORY TIME
The Legend of the Waffle Cone
Legend of the Waffle Cone
Welcome to our very first Story Time!
This time, let me tell you The Legend of the Waffle Cone.

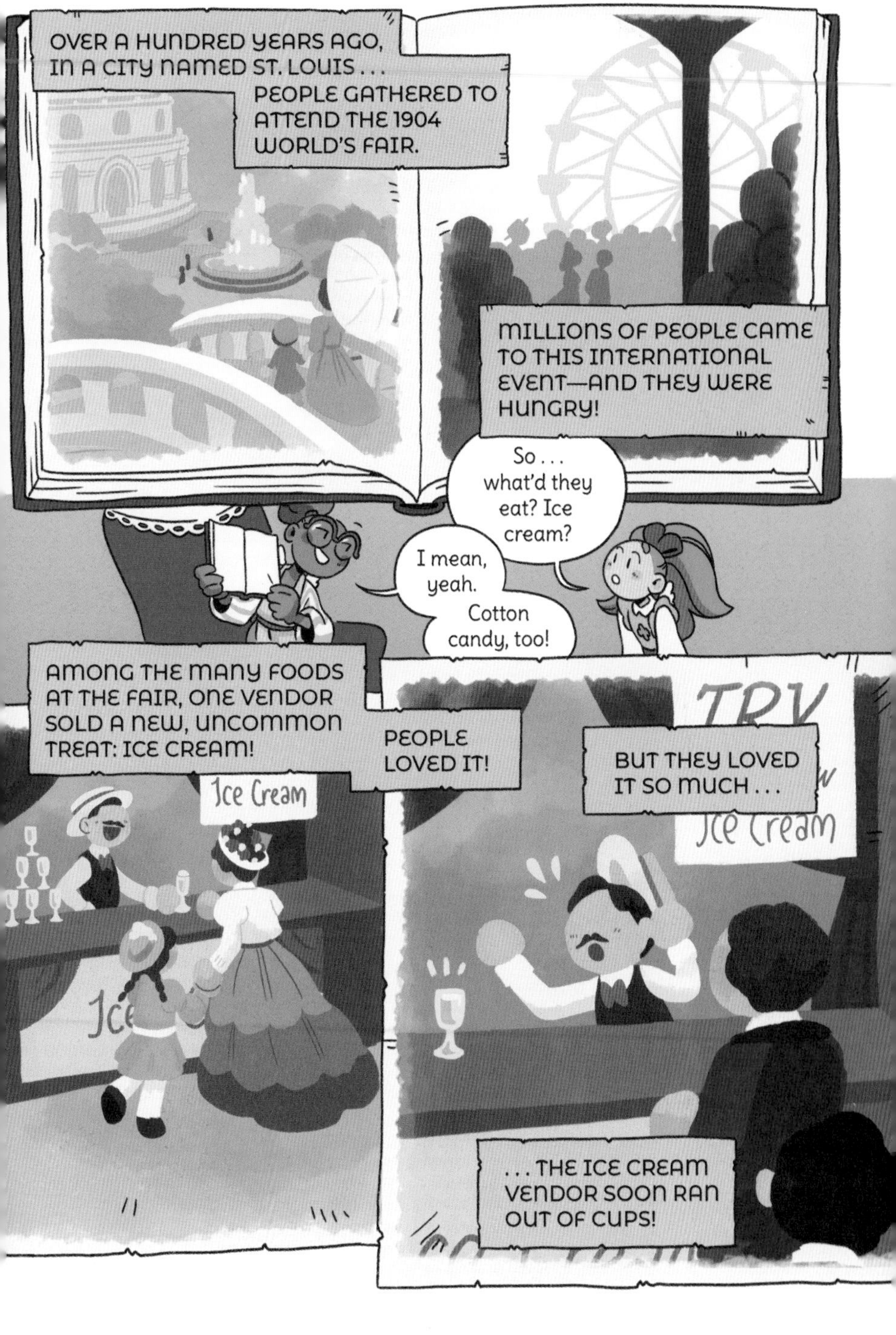

OVER A HUNDRED YEARS AGO, IN A CITY NAMED ST. LOUIS . . .
PEOPLE GATHERED TO ATTEND THE 1904 WORLD'S FAIR.
MILLIONS OF PEOPLE CAME TO THIS INTERNATIONAL EVENT—AND THEY WERE HUNGRY!
So . . . what'd they eat? Ice cream?
I mean, yeah.
Cotton candy, too!
AMONG THE MANY FOODS AT THE FAIR, ONE VENDOR SOLD A NEW, UNCOMMON TREAT: ICE CREAM!
Ice Cream
PEOPLE LOVED IT!
TRY
Ice Cream
BUT THEY LOVED IT SO MUCH . . .
. . . THE ICE CREAM VENDOR SOON RAN OUT OF CUPS!

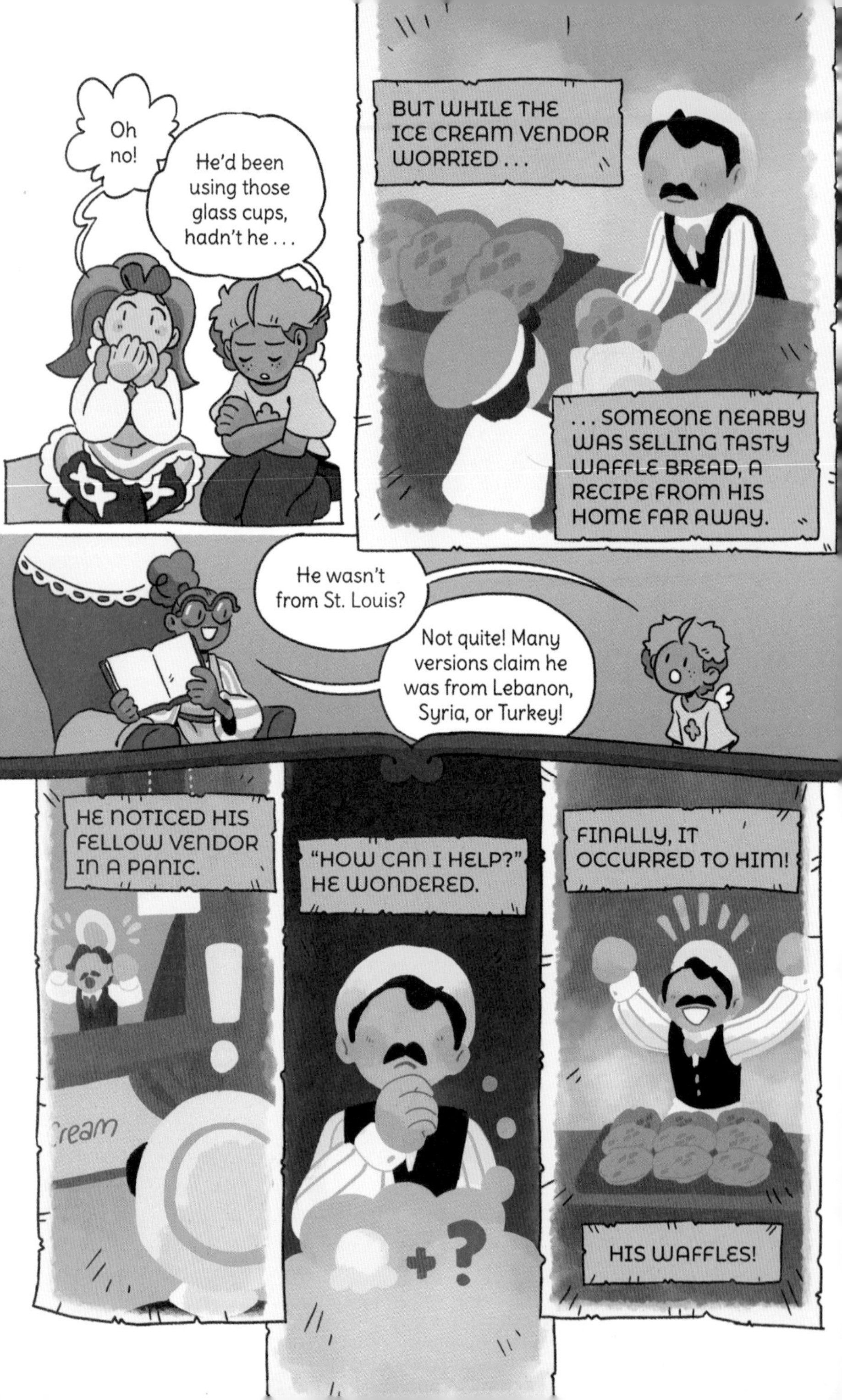
Oh no!
He'd been using those glass cups, hadn't he . . .
BUT WHILE THE ICE CREAM VENDOR WORRIED . . .
. . . SOMEONE NEARBY WAS SELLING TASTY WAFFLE BREAD, A RECIPE FROM HIS HOME FAR AWAY.
He wasn't from St. Louis?
Not quite! Many versions claim he was from Lebanon, Syria, or Turkey!
HE NOTICED HIS FELLOW VENDOR IN A PANIC.
Cream
"HOW CAN I HELP?" HE WONDERED.
FINALLY, IT OCCURRED TO HIM!
HIS WAFFLES!

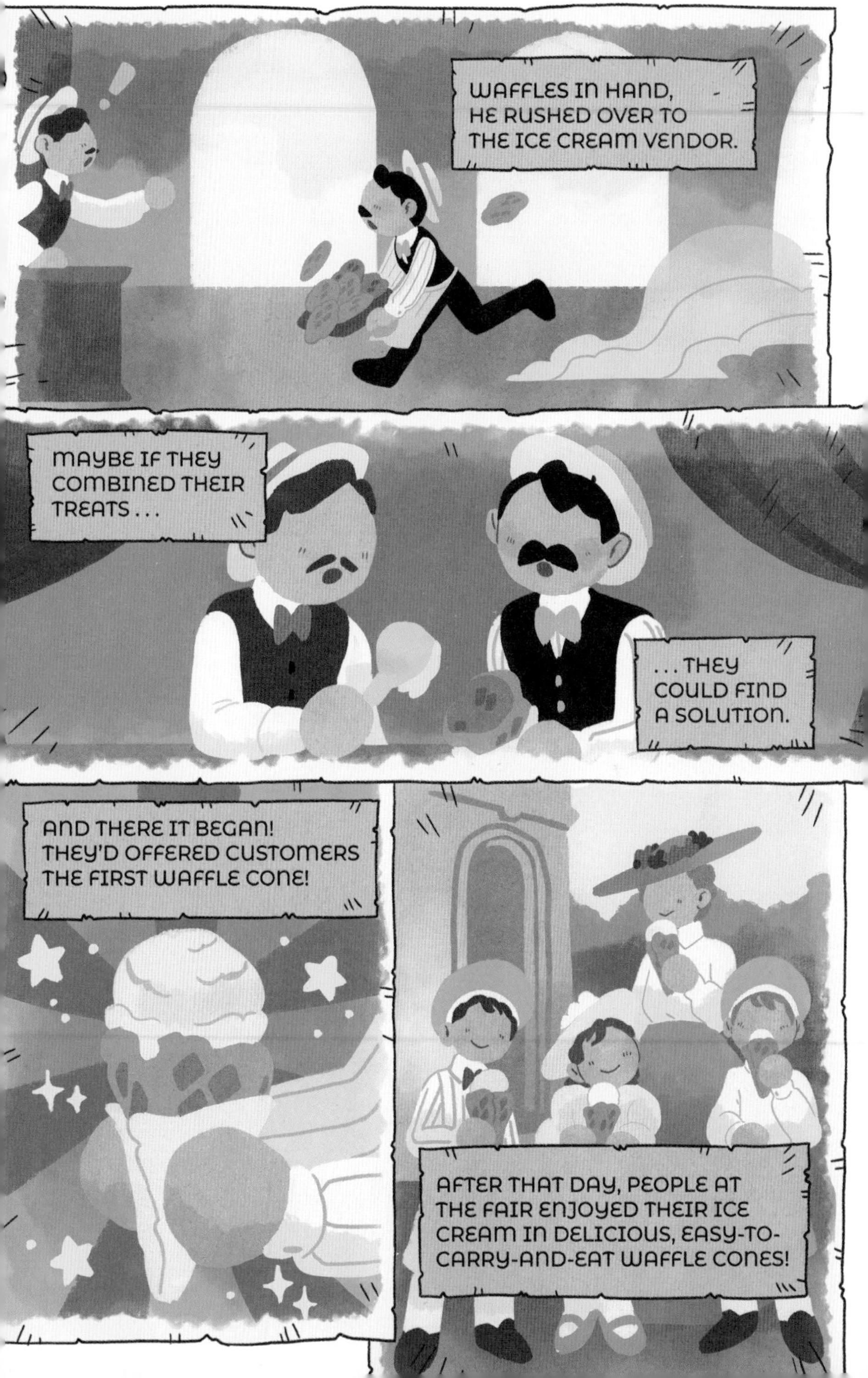
WAFFLES IN HAND, HE RUSHED OVER TO THE ICE CREAM VENDOR.
MAYBE IF THEY COMBINED THEIR TREATS . . .
. . . THEY COULD FIND A SOLUTION.
AND THERE IT BEGAN! THEY'D OFFERED CUSTOMERS THE FIRST WAFFLE CONE!
AFTER THAT DAY, PEOPLE AT THE FAIR ENJOYED THEIR ICE CREAM IN DELICIOUS, EASY-TO-CARRY-AND-EAT WAFFLE CONES!

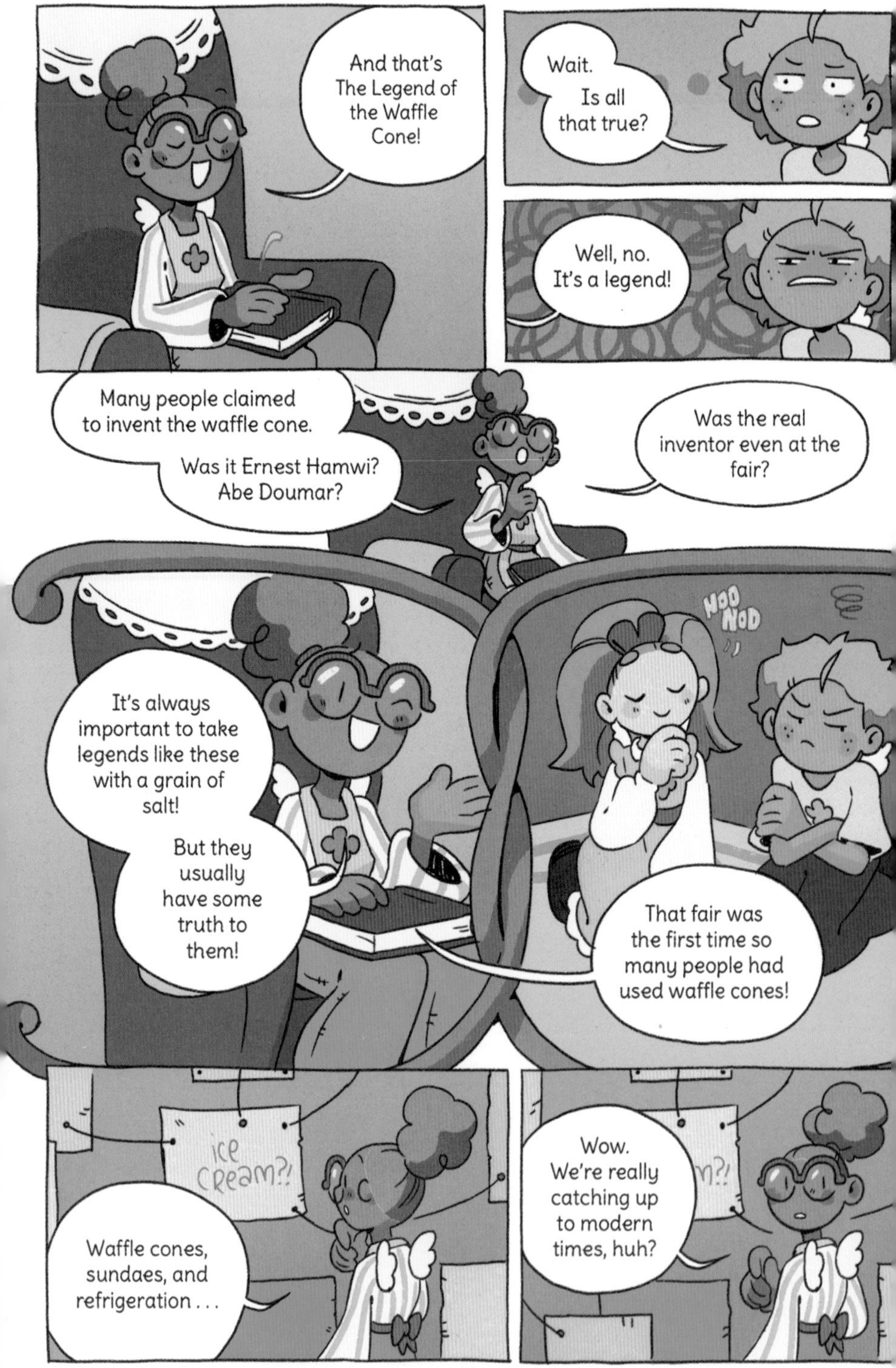

And that's The Legend of the Waffle Cone!
Wait.
Is all that true?
Well, no. It's a legend!
Many people claimed to invent the waffle cone.
Was it Ernest Hamwi? Abe Doumar?
Was the real inventor even at the fair?
NOD NOD
It's always important to take legends like these with a grain of salt!
But they usually have some truth to them!
That fair was the first time so many people had used waffle cones!
ICE CREAM?!
Waffle cones, sundaes, and refrigeration . . .
Wow. We're really catching up to modern times, huh?

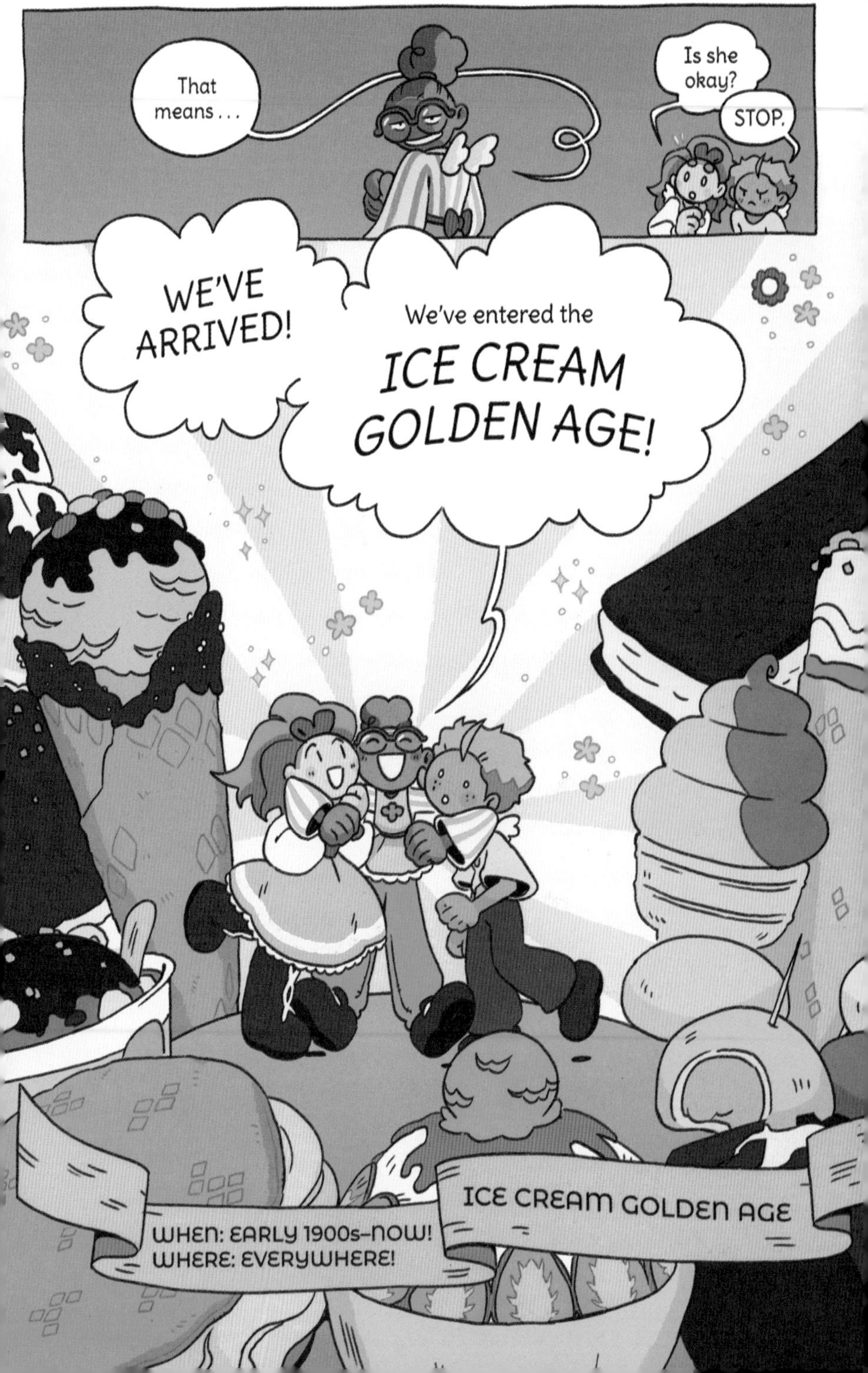

That means . . .
Is she okay?
STOP.
WE'VE ARRIVED!
We've entered the ICE CREAM GOLDEN AGE!
ICE CREAM GOLDEN AGE
WHEN: EARLY 1900s–NOW!
WHERE: EVERYWHERE!

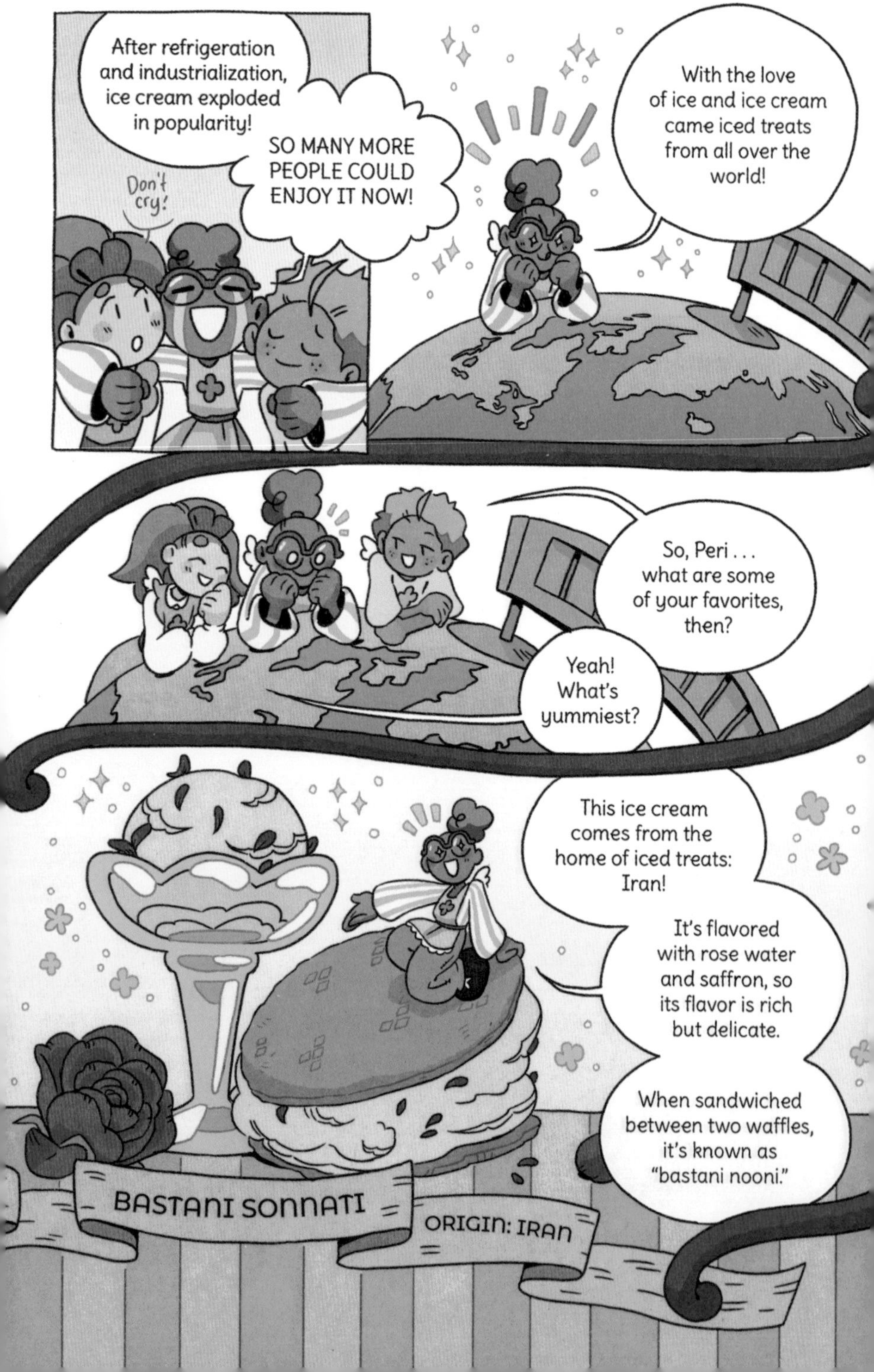

After refrigeration and industrialization, ice cream exploded in popularity!
SO MANY MORE PEOPLE COULD ENJOY IT NOW!
Don't cry!
With the love of ice and ice cream came iced treats from all over the world!
So, Peri . . . what are some of your favorites, then?
Yeah! What's yummiest?
This ice cream comes from the home of iced treats: Iran!
It's flavored with rose water and saffron, so its flavor is rich but delicate.
When sandwiched between two waffles, it's known as "bastani nooni."
BASTANI SONNATI
ORIGIN: IRAN

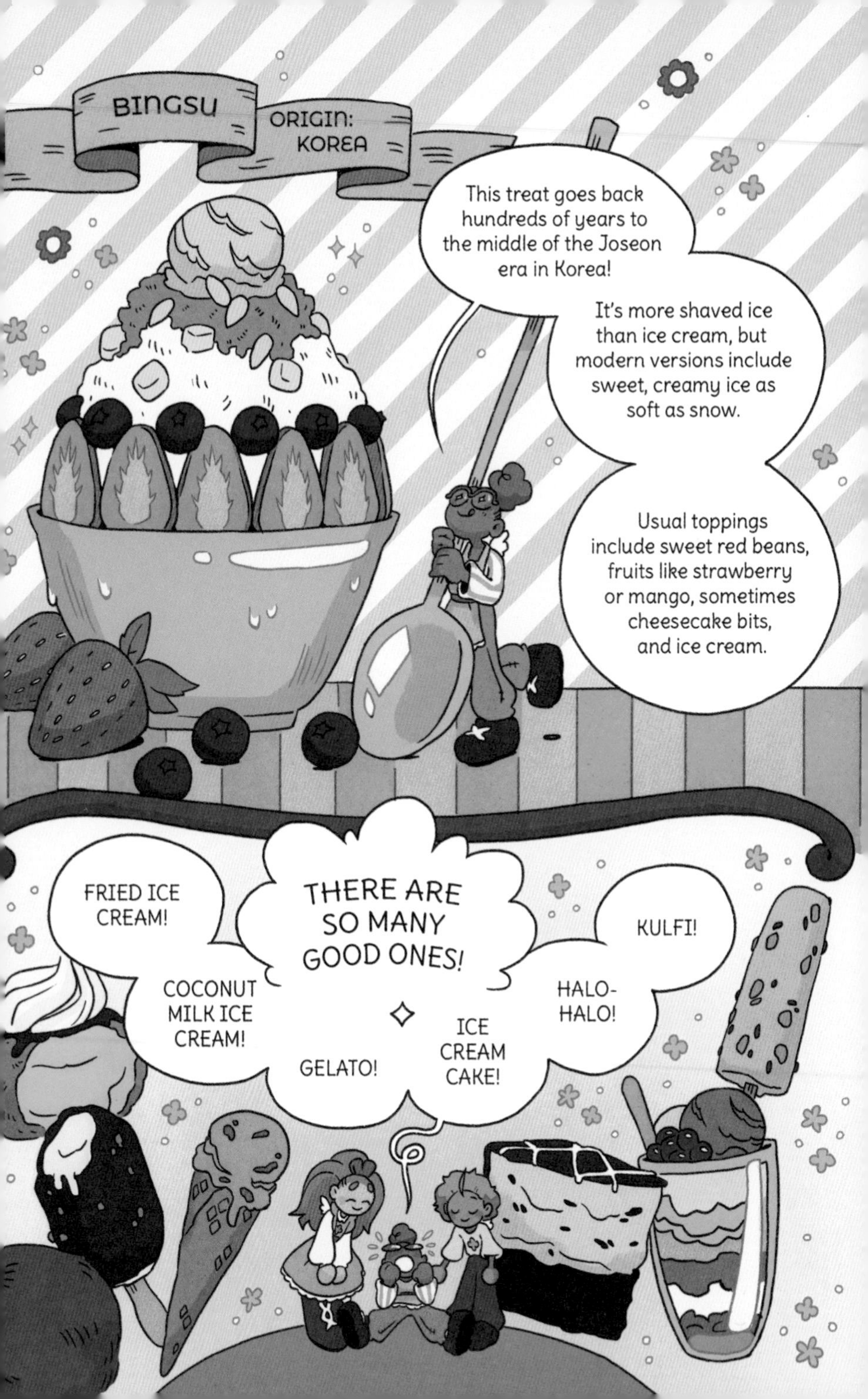

BINGSU
ORIGIN: KOREA
This treat goes back hundreds of years to the middle of the Joseon era in Korea!
It's more shaved ice than ice cream, but modern versions include sweet, creamy ice as soft as snow.
Usual toppings include sweet red beans, fruits like strawberry or mango, sometimes cheesecake bits, and ice cream.
FRIED ICE CREAM!
THERE ARE SO MANY GOOD ONES!
KULFI!
COCONUT MILK ICE CREAM!
HALO-HALO!
GELATO!
ICE CREAM CAKE!

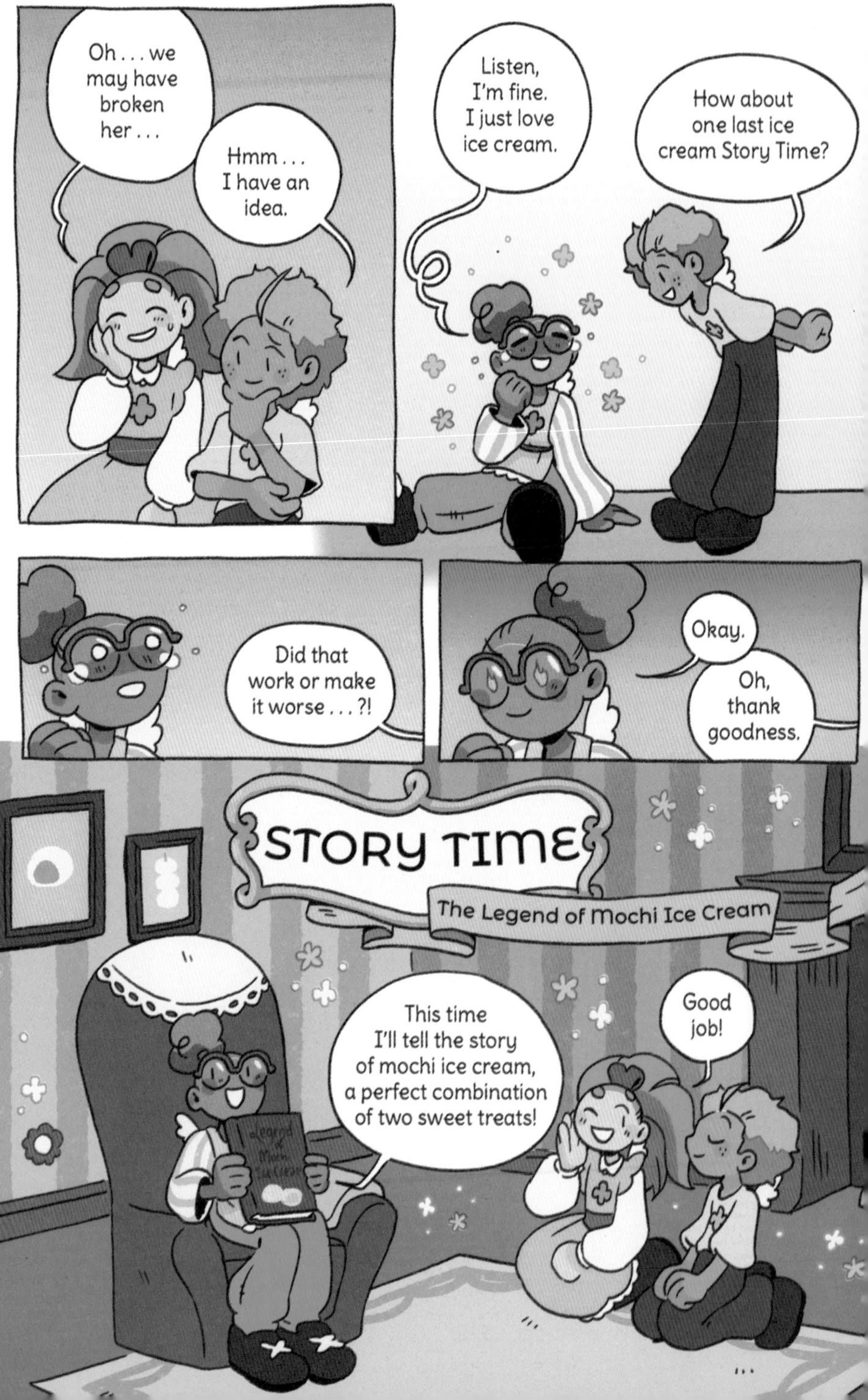
Oh . . . we may have broken her . . .
Hmm . . . I have an idea.
Listen, I'm fine. I just love ice cream.
How about one last ice cream Story Time?
Did that work or make it worse . . . ?!
Okay.
Oh, thank goodness.
STORY TIME
The Legend of Mochi Ice Cream
This time I'll tell the story of mochi ice cream, a perfect combination of two sweet treats!
Good job!

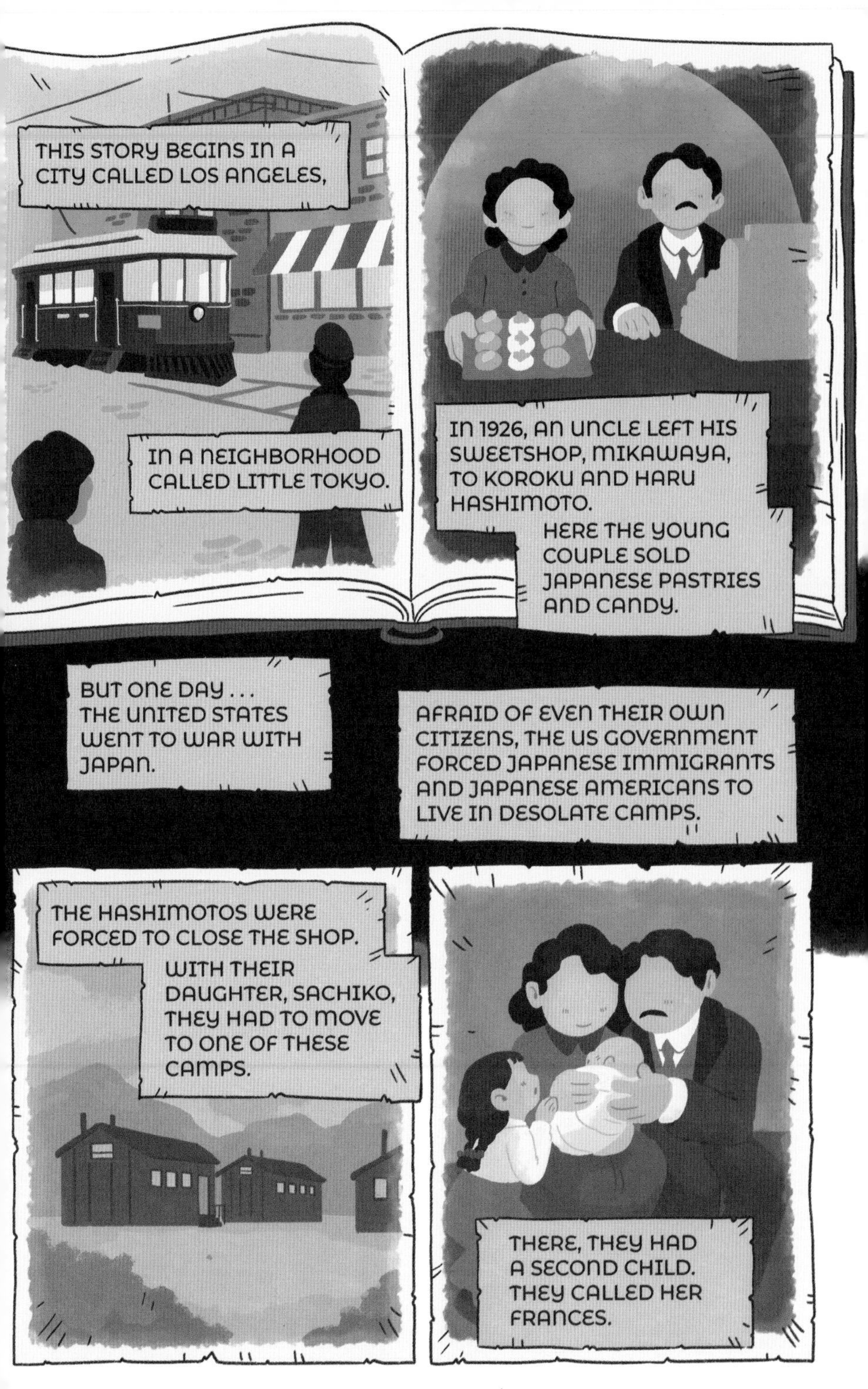
THIS STORY BEGINS IN A CITY CALLED LOS ANGELES,
IN A NEIGHBORHOOD CALLED LITTLE TOKYO.
IN 1926, AN UNCLE LEFT HIS SWEETSHOP, MIKAWAYA, TO KOROKU AND HARU HASHIMOTO.
HERE THE YOUNG COUPLE SOLD JAPANESE PASTRIES AND CANDY.
BUT ONE DAY . . . THE UNITED STATES WENT TO WAR WITH JAPAN.
AFRAID OF EVEN THEIR OWN CITIZENS, THE US GOVERNMENT FORCED JAPANESE IMMIGRANTS AND JAPANESE AMERICANS TO LIVE IN DESOLATE CAMPS.
THE HASHIMOTOS WERE FORCED TO CLOSE THE SHOP.
WITH THEIR DAUGHTER, SACHIKO, THEY HAD TO MOVE TO ONE OF THESE CAMPS.
THERE, THEY HAD A SECOND CHILD. THEY CALLED HER FRANCES.

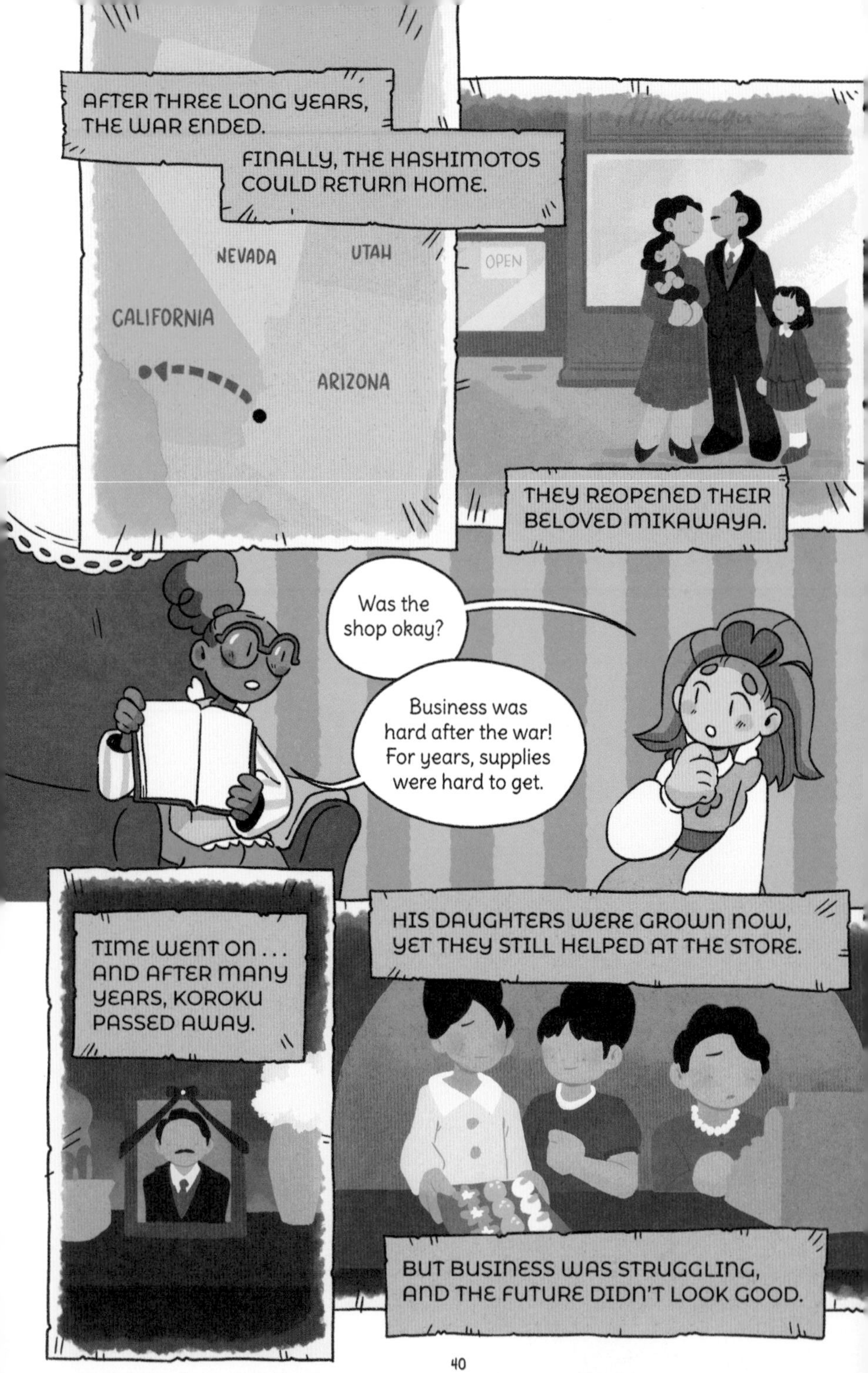
AFTER THREE LONG YEARS, THE WAR ENDED.
FINALLY, THE HASHIMOTOS COULD RETURN HOME.
NEVADA
UTAH
CALIFORNIA
ARIZONA
OPEN
THEY REOPENED THEIR BELOVED MIKAWAYA.
Was the shop okay?
Business was hard after the war! For years, supplies were hard to get.
TIME WENT ON . . . AND AFTER MANY YEARS, KOROKU PASSED AWAY.
HIS DAUGHTERS WERE GROWN NOW, YET THEY STILL HELPED AT THE STORE.
BUT BUSINESS WAS STRUGGLING, AND THE FUTURE DIDN'T LOOK GOOD.

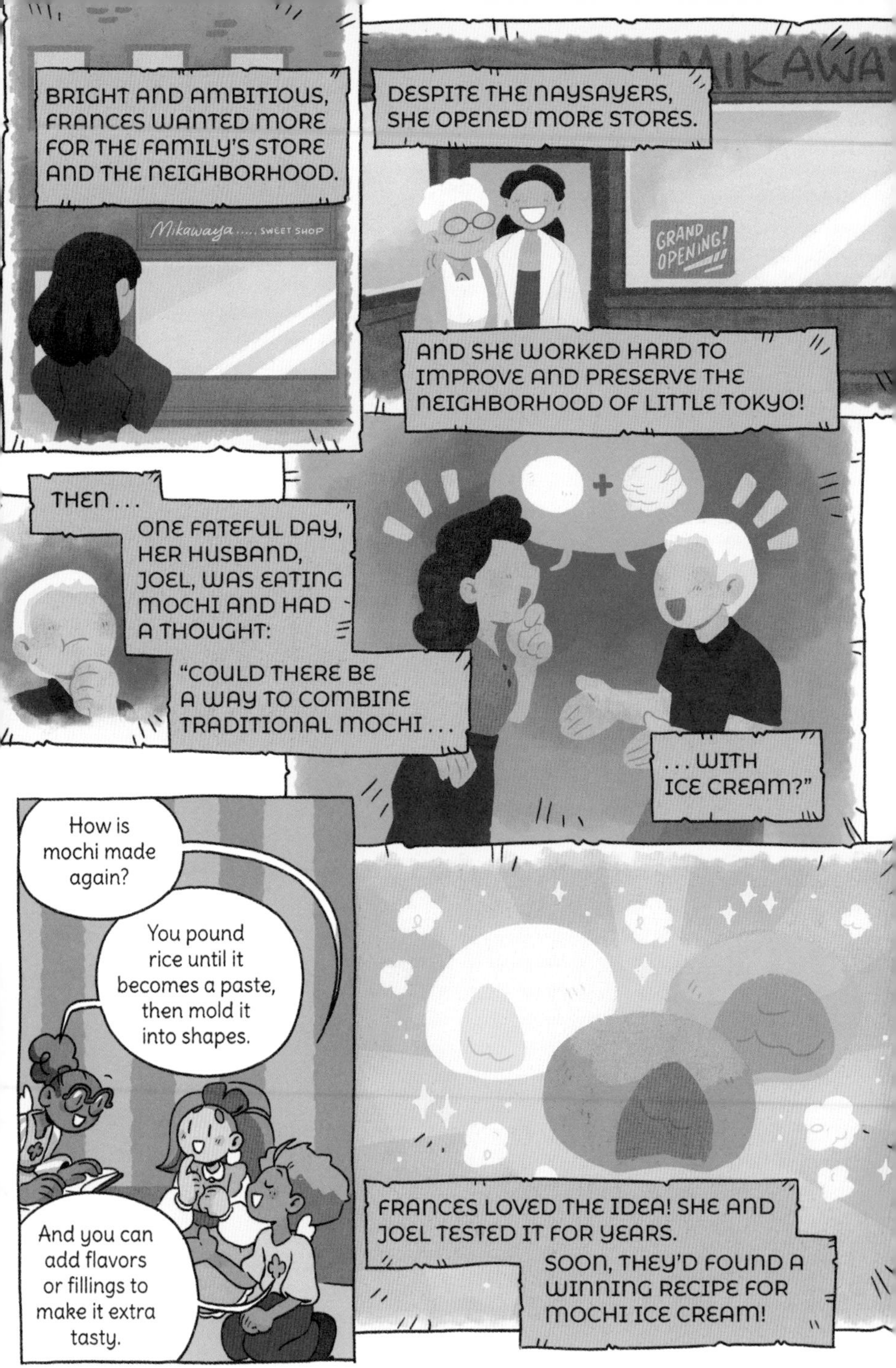

BRIGHT AND AMBITIOUS, FRANCES WANTED MORE FOR THE FAMILY'S STORE AND THE NEIGHBORHOOD.
Mikawaya ..... SWEET SHOP
DESPITE THE NAYSAYERS, SHE OPENED MORE STORES.
MIKAWA
GRAND OPENING!
AND SHE WORKED HARD TO IMPROVE AND PRESERVE THE NEIGHBORHOOD OF LITTLE TOKYO!
THEN . . .
ONE FATEFUL DAY, HER HUSBAND, JOEL, WAS EATING MOCHI AND HAD A THOUGHT:
"COULD THERE BE A WAY TO COMBINE TRADITIONAL MOCHI . . .
. . . WITH ICE CREAM?"
How is mochi made again?
You pound rice until it becomes a paste, then mold it into shapes.
And you can add flavors or fillings to make it extra tasty.
FRANCES LOVED THE IDEA! SHE AND JOEL TESTED IT FOR YEARS.
SOON, THEY'D FOUND A WINNING RECIPE FOR MOCHI ICE CREAM!

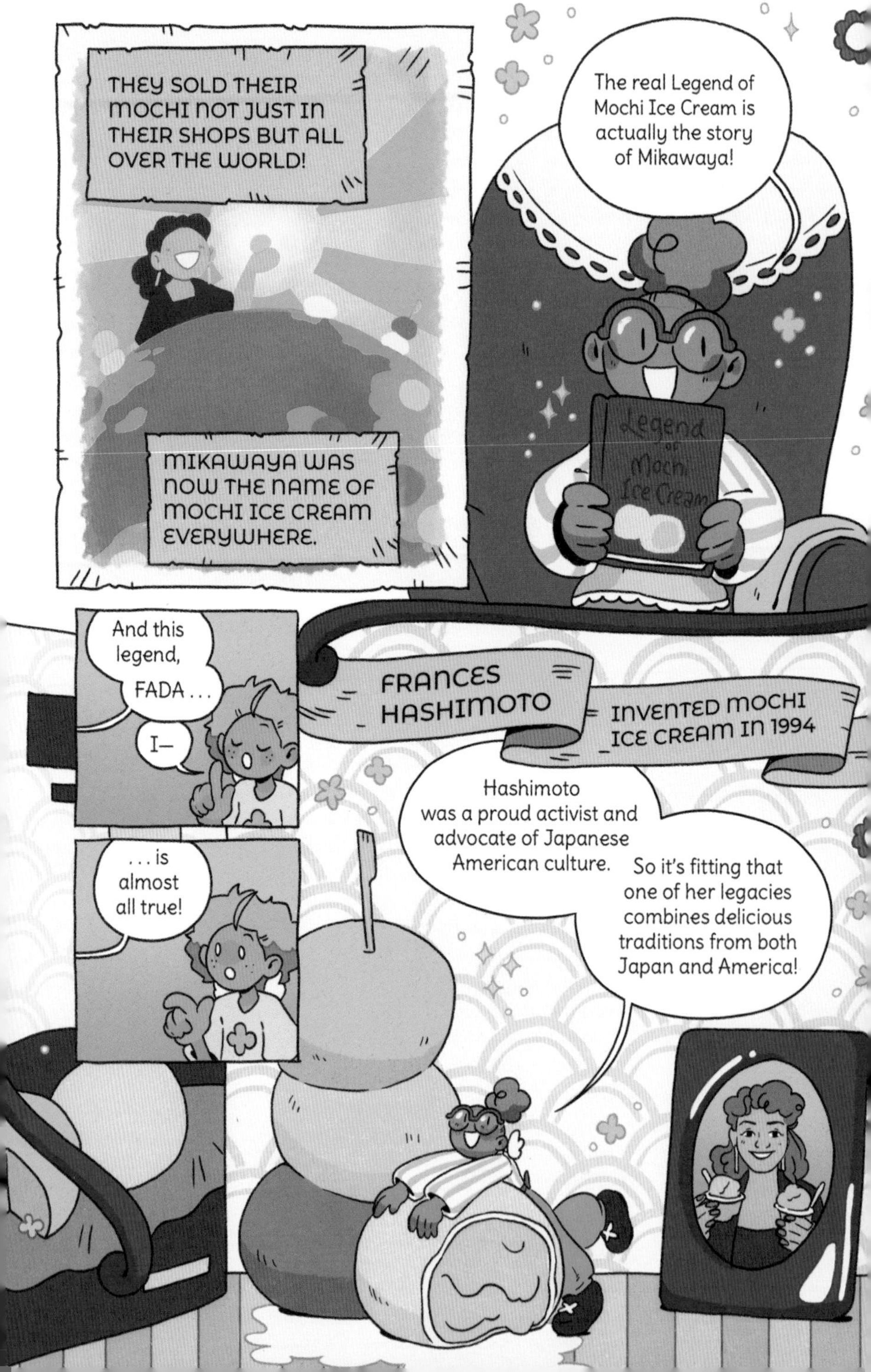
THEY SOLD THEIR MOCHI NOT JUST IN THEIR SHOPS BUT ALL OVER THE WORLD!
MIKAWAYA WAS NOW THE NAME OF MOCHI ICE CREAM EVERYWHERE.
The real Legend of Mochi Ice Cream is actually the story of Mikawaya!
Legend of Mochi Ice Cream
And this legend,
FADA . . .
I—
. . . is almost all true!
FRANCES HASHIMOTO
INVENTED MOCHI ICE CREAM IN 1994
Hashimoto was a proud activist and advocate of Japanese American culture.
So it's fitting that one of her legacies combines delicious traditions from both Japan and America!

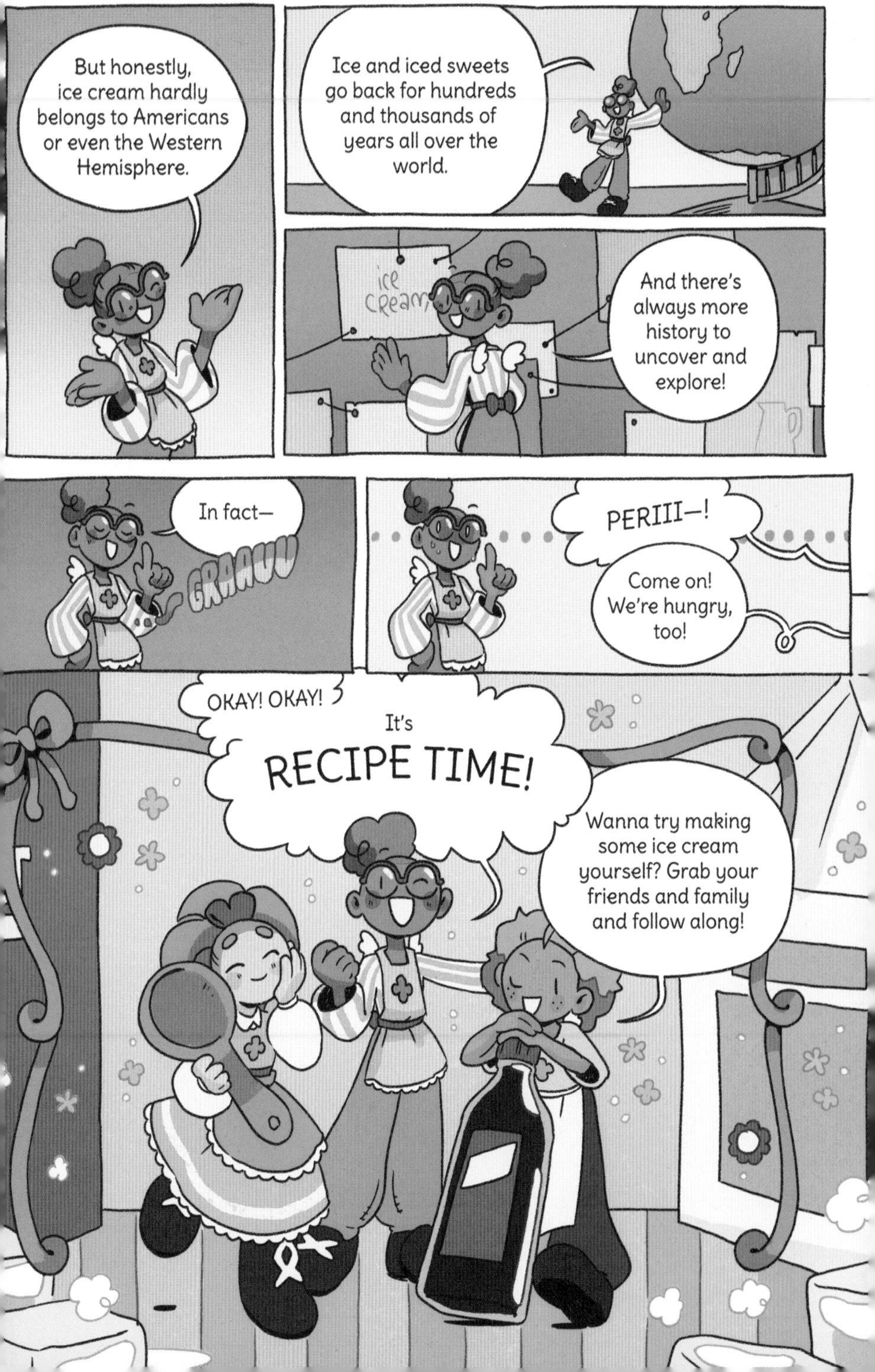

But honestly, ice cream hardly belongs to Americans or even the Western Hemisphere.
Ice and iced sweets go back for hundreds and thousands of years all over the world.
ice cream
And there's always more history to uncover and explore!
In fact—
GRAAUU
PERIII—!
Come on! We're hungry, too!
OKAY! OKAY!
It's RECIPE TIME!
Wanna try making some ice cream yourself? Grab your friends and family and follow along!

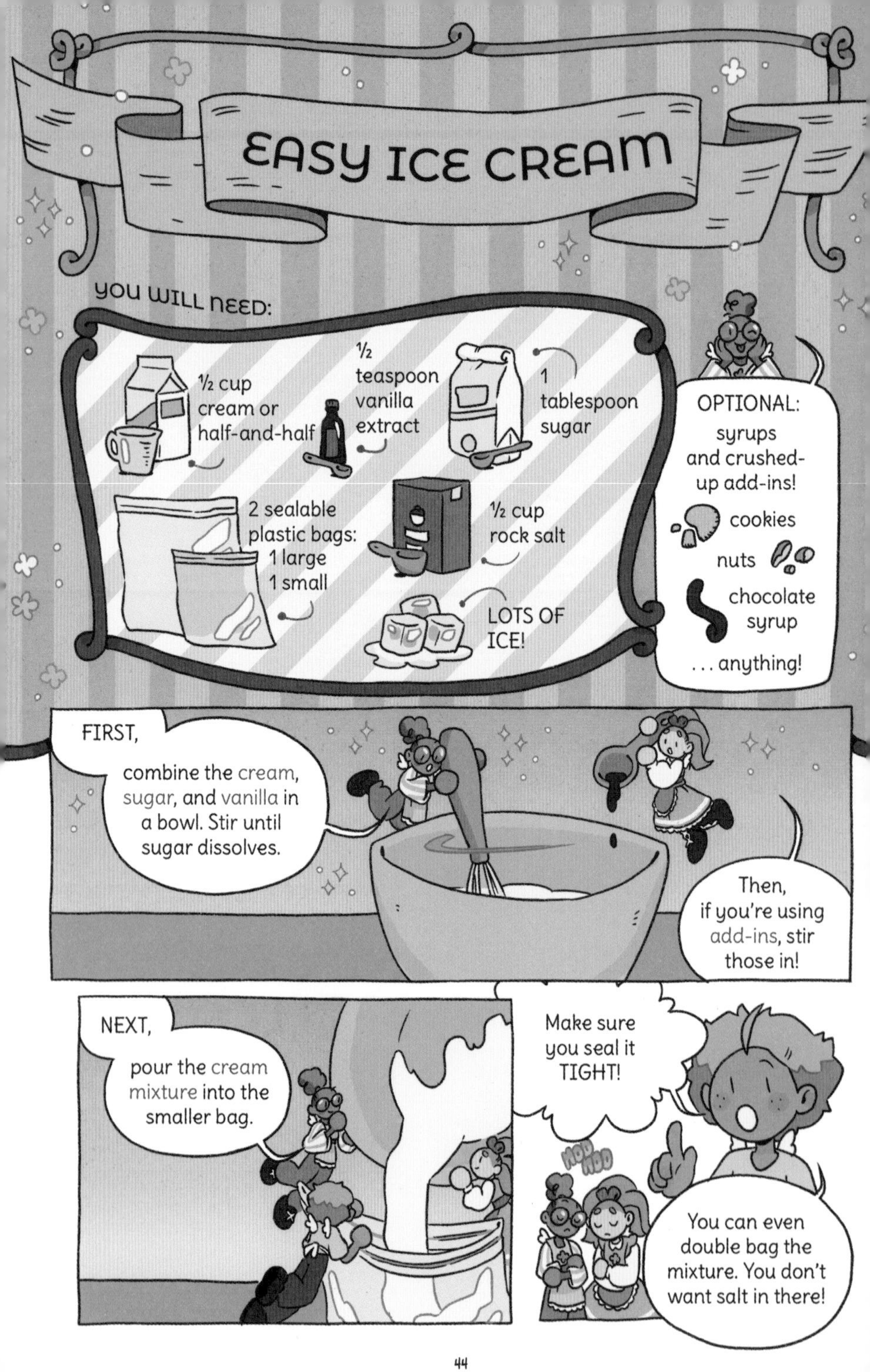

EASY ICE CREAM
YOU WILL NEED:
½ cup cream or half-and-half
½ teaspoon vanilla extract
1 tablespoon sugar
2 sealable plastic bags: 1 large 1 small
½ cup rock salt
LOTS OF ICE!
OPTIONAL: syrups and crushed-up add-ins!
cookies
nuts
chocolate syrup
. . . anything!
FIRST,
combine the cream, sugar, and vanilla in a bowl. Stir until sugar dissolves.
Then, if you're using add-ins, stir those in!
NEXT,
pour the cream mixture into the smaller bag.
Make sure you seal it TIGHT!
NOD NOD
You can even double bag the mixture. You don't want salt in there!

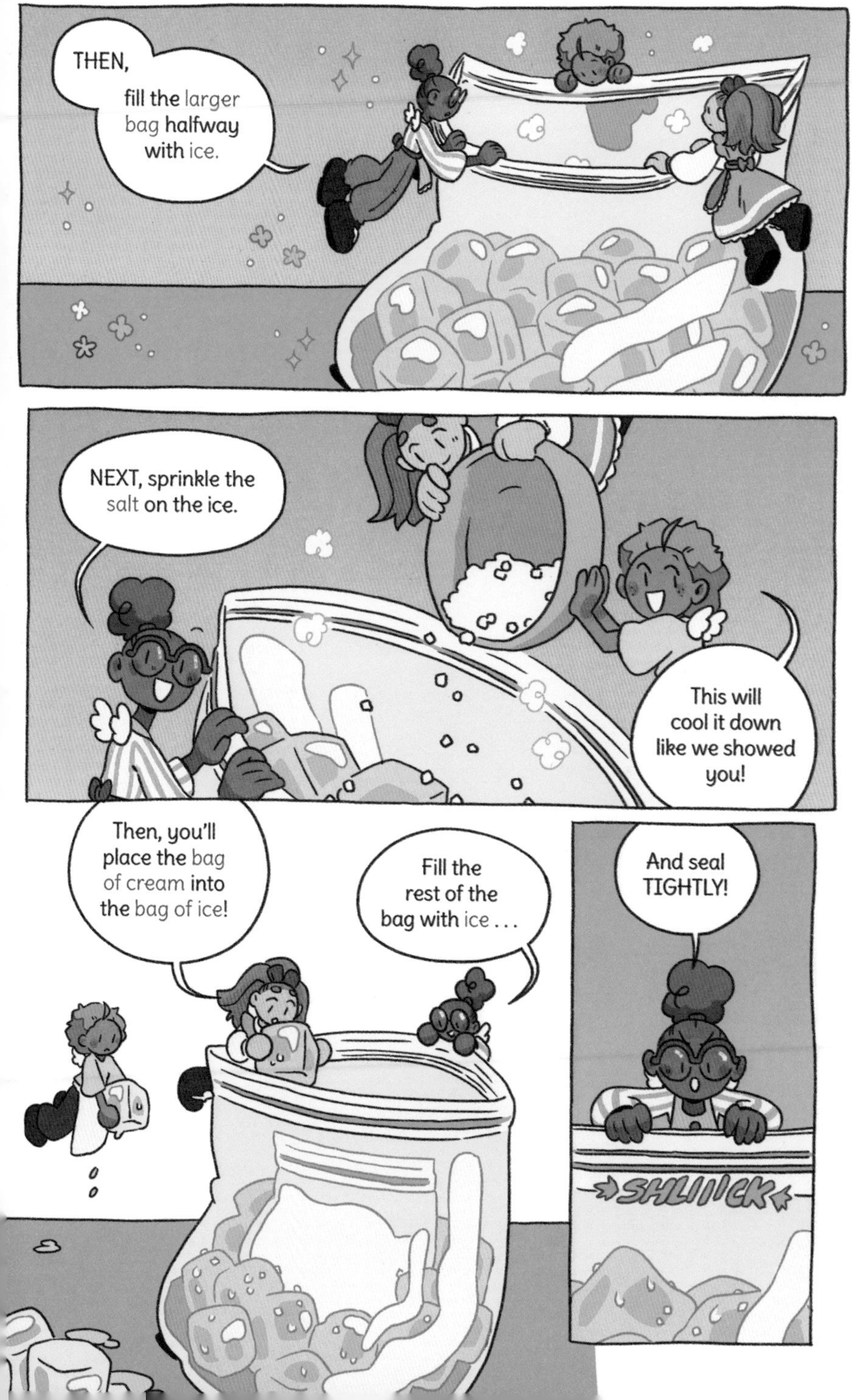
THEN, fill the larger bag halfway with ice.
NEXT, sprinkle the salt on the ice.
This will cool it down like we showed you!
Then, you'll place the bag of cream into the bag of ice!
Fill the rest of the bag with ice . . .
And seal TIGHTLY!
SHLIIICK

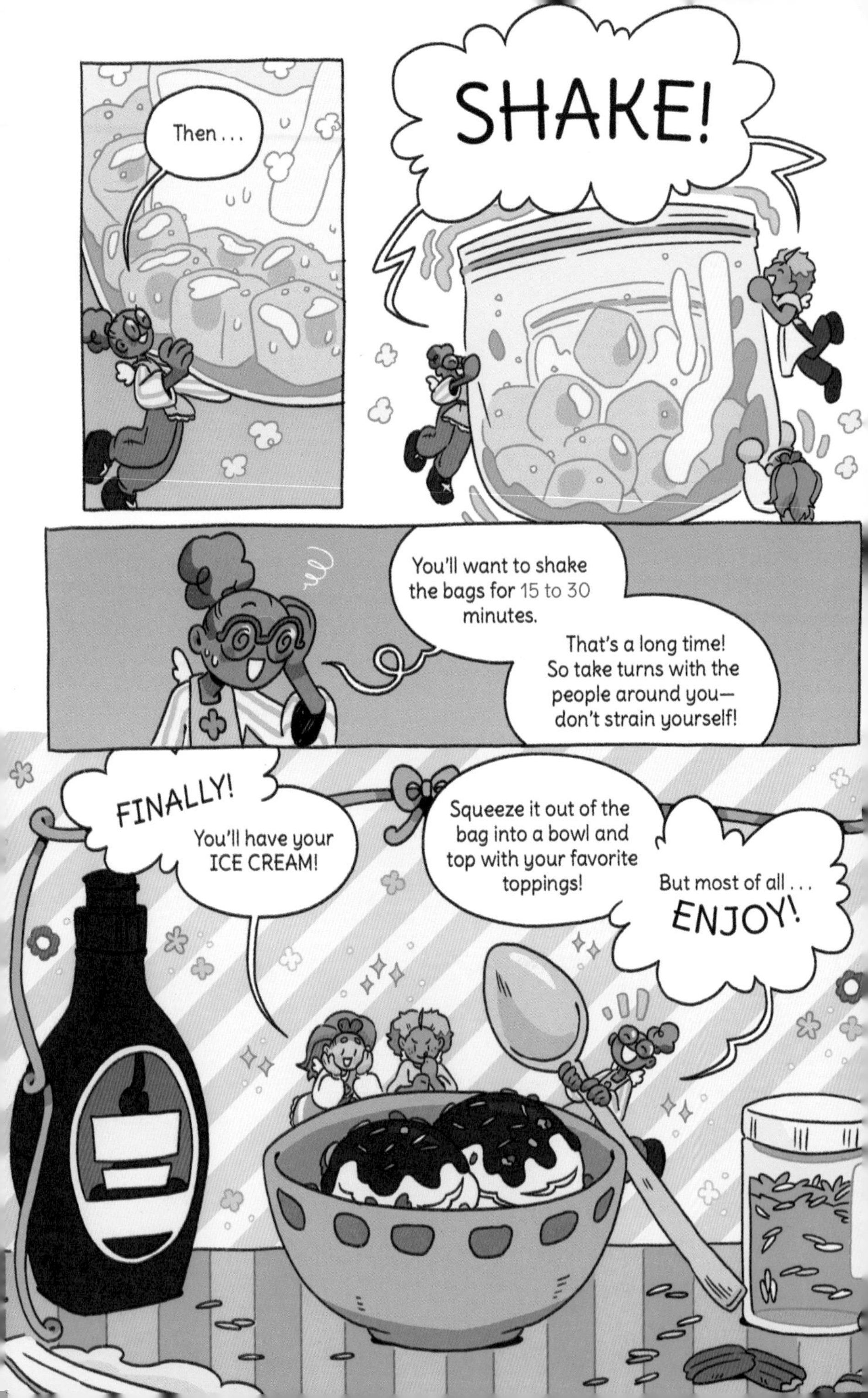
Then . . .
SHAKE!
You'll want to shake the bags for 15 to 30 minutes.
That's a long time! So take turns with the people around you—don't strain yourself!
FINALLY!
You'll have your ICE CREAM!
Squeeze it out of the bag into a bowl and top with your favorite toppings!
But most of all . . .
ENJOY!

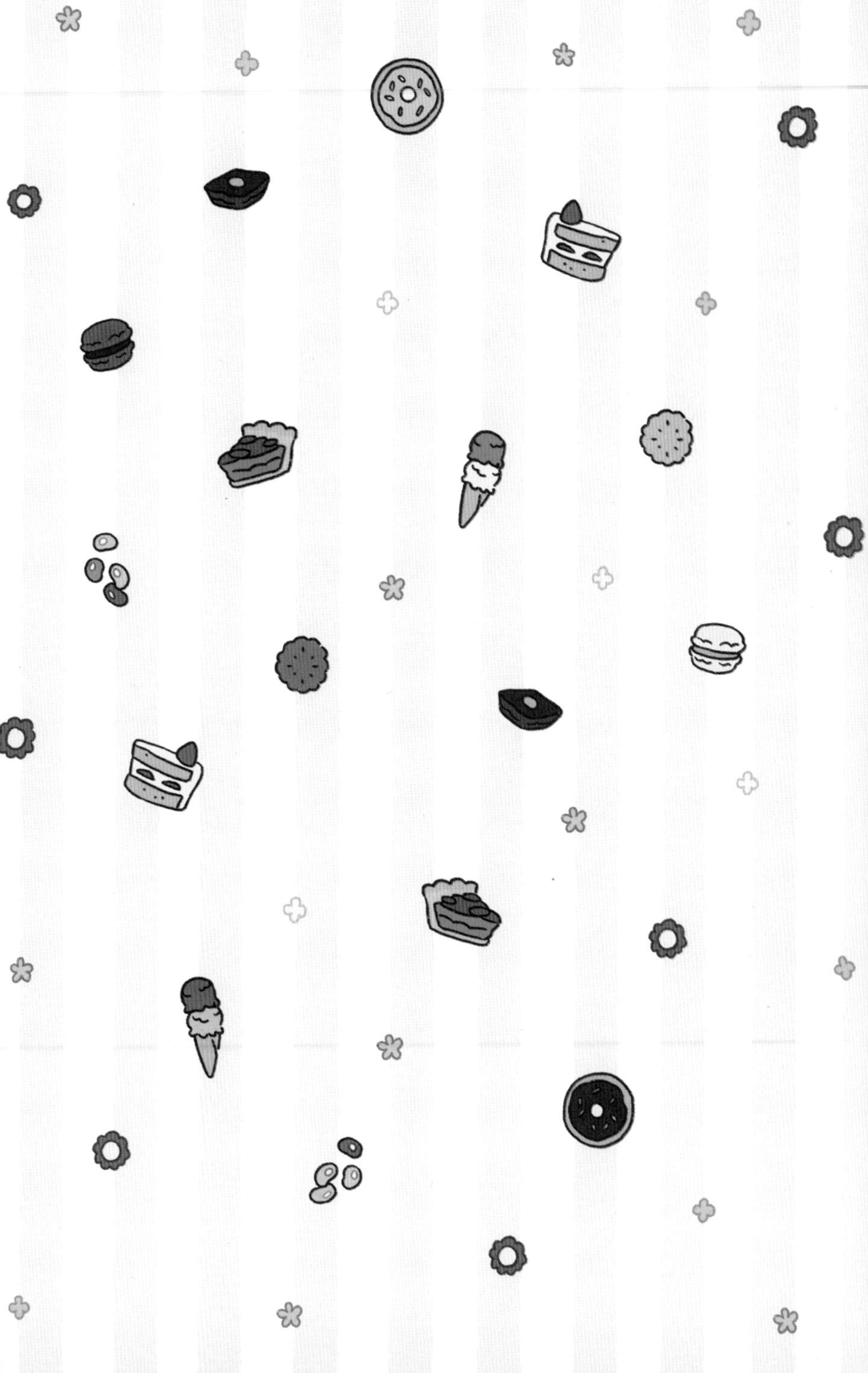

The Abridged
Atlas of Cake History

1. Prehistoric Egyptian Sweet Bread
2. Ethiopian and Eritian Himbasha/Ambasha
3. Ancient Greek Plakous
4. Ancient Roman Placenta
5. Chinese Mooncakes
6. Martino da Como's *The Art of Cooking*
7. Origin of Refined Sugar
8. Origin of Cinnamon
9. Origin of Chocolate and Vanilla
10. German Gugelhupf
11. Western European Pound Cake
12. Spanish Sponge Cake
13. Japanese Castella Cake
14. Indonesian, Singaporean, and Southeast Asian Pandan Cake
15. Austrian Chocolate Torte
16. Fannie Farmer's *Boston Cooking-School Cook Book*
17. Baking Soda and Baking Powder
18. Boxed and Canned Cake Mixes
19. John A. Adams's Red Velvet Cake

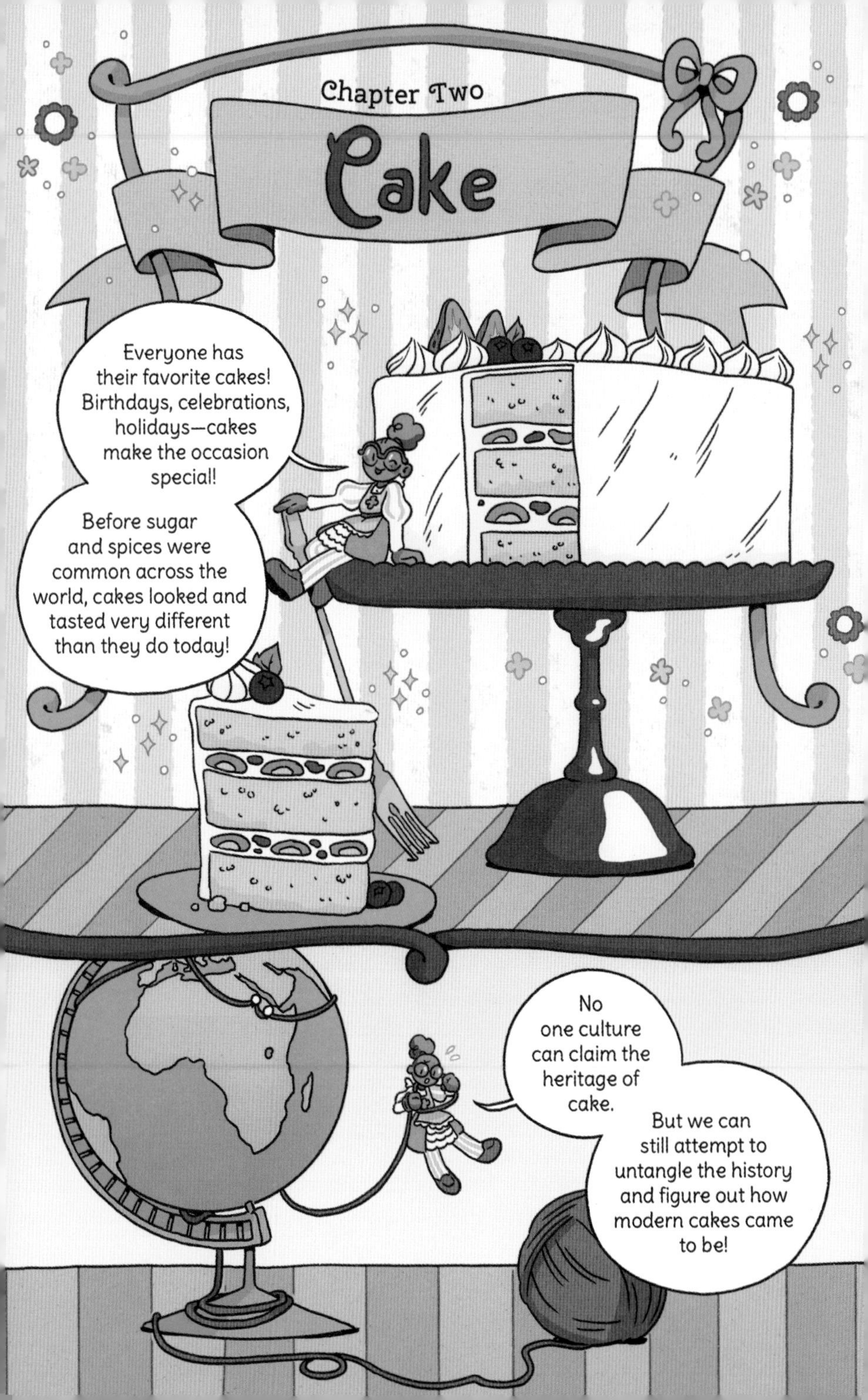
Chapter Two
Cake
Everyone has their favorite cakes! Birthdays, celebrations, holidays—cakes make the occasion special!
Before sugar and spices were common across the world, cakes looked and tasted very different than they do today!
No one culture can claim the heritage of cake.
But we can still attempt to untangle the history and figure out how modern cakes came to be!

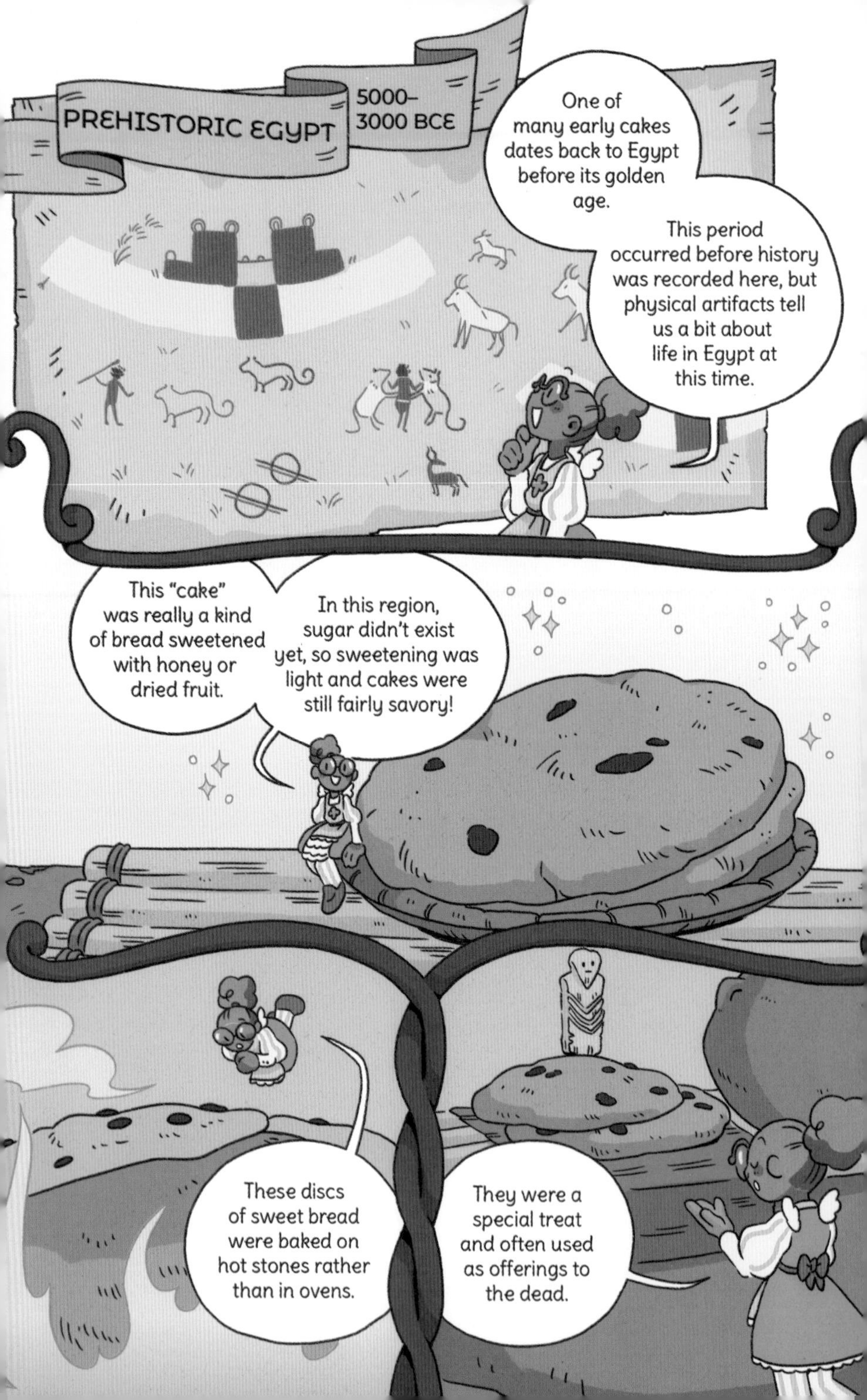
PREHISTORIC EGYPT
5000–3000 BCE
One of many early cakes dates back to Egypt before its golden age.
This period occurred before history was recorded here, but physical artifacts tell us a bit about life in Egypt at this time.
This "cake" was really a kind of bread sweetened with honey or dried fruit.
In this region, sugar didn't exist yet, so sweetening was light and cakes were still fairly savory!
These discs of sweet bread were baked on hot stones rather than in ovens.
They were a special treat and often used as offerings to the dead.

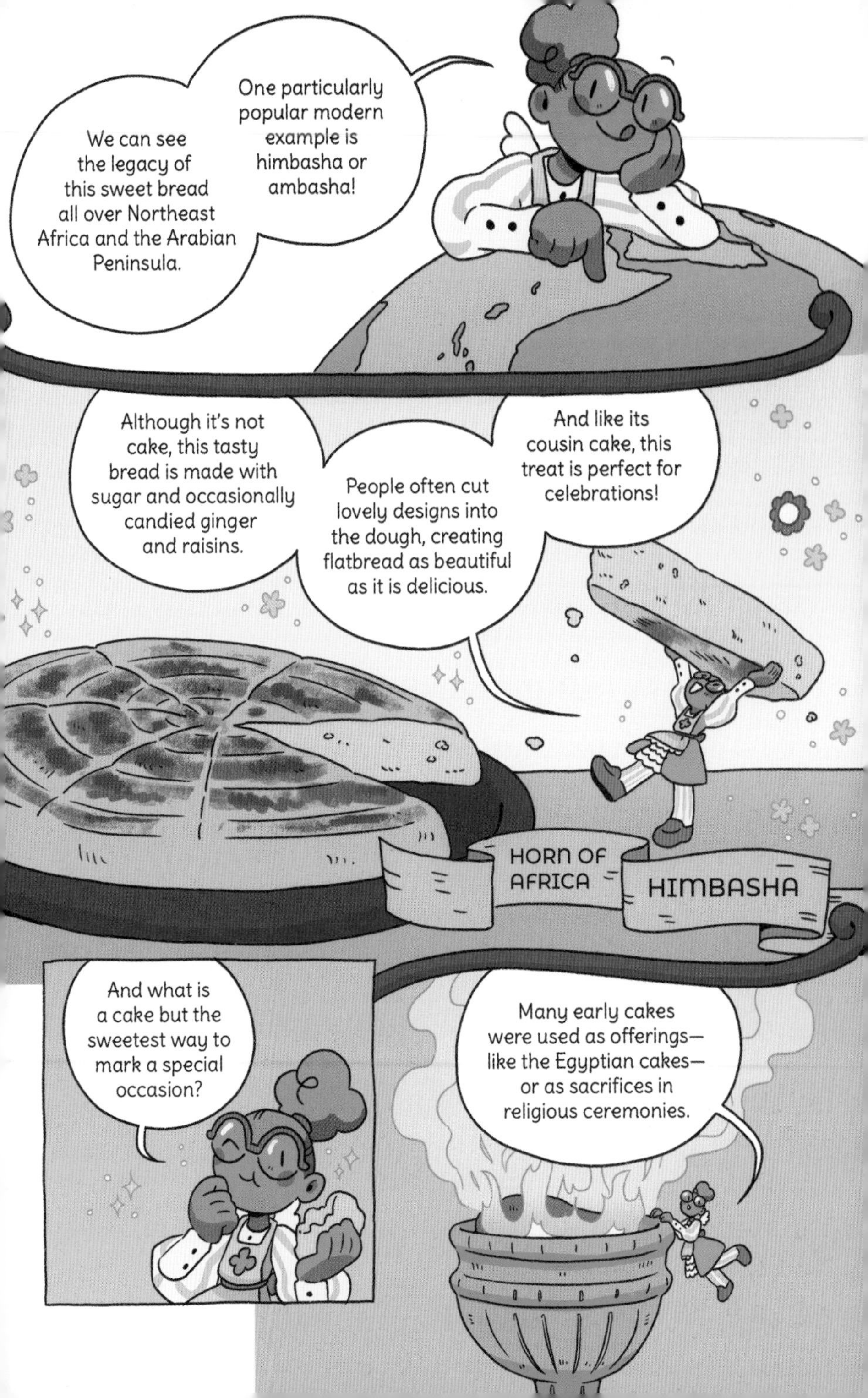
We can see the legacy of this sweet bread all over Northeast Africa and the Arabian Peninsula.
One particularly popular modern example is himbasha or ambasha!
Although it's not cake, this tasty bread is made with sugar and occasionally candied ginger and raisins.
People often cut lovely designs into the dough, creating flatbread as beautiful as it is delicious.
And like its cousin cake, this treat is perfect for celebrations!
HORN OF AFRICA
HIMBASHA
And what is a cake but the sweetest way to mark a special occasion?
Many early cakes were used as offerings—like the Egyptian cakes—or as sacrifices in religious ceremonies.

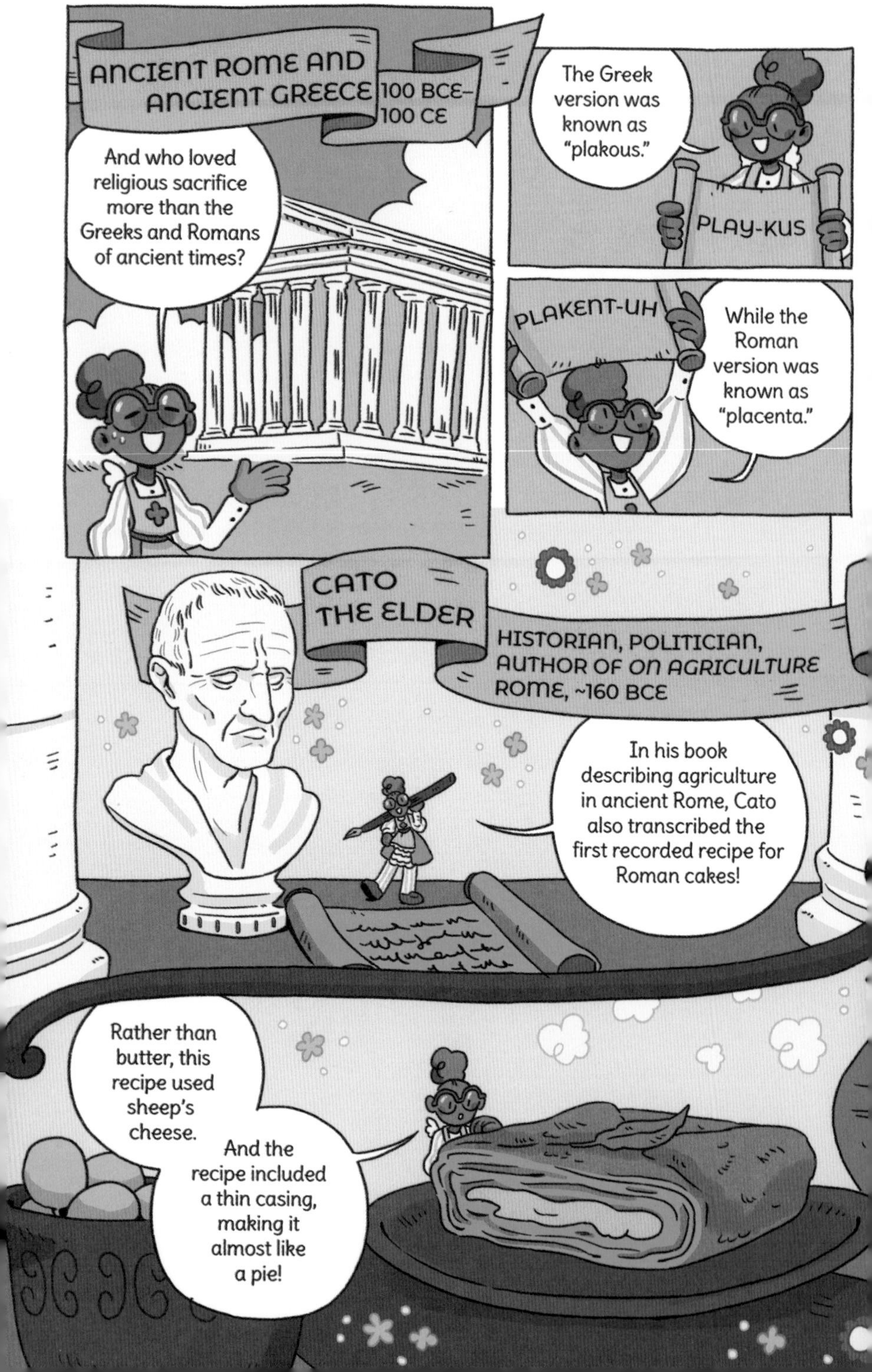
ANCIENT ROME AND ANCIENT GREECE 100 BCE–100 CE
And who loved religious sacrifice more than the Greeks and Romans of ancient times?
The Greek version was known as "plakous."
PLAY-KUS
PLAKENT-UH
While the Roman version was known as "placenta."
CATO THE ELDER
HISTORIAN, POLITICIAN, AUTHOR OF ON AGRICULTURE ROME, ~160 BCE
In his book describing agriculture in ancient Rome, Cato also transcribed the first recorded recipe for Roman cakes!
Rather than butter, this recipe used sheep's cheese.
And the recipe included a thin casing, making it almost like a pie!

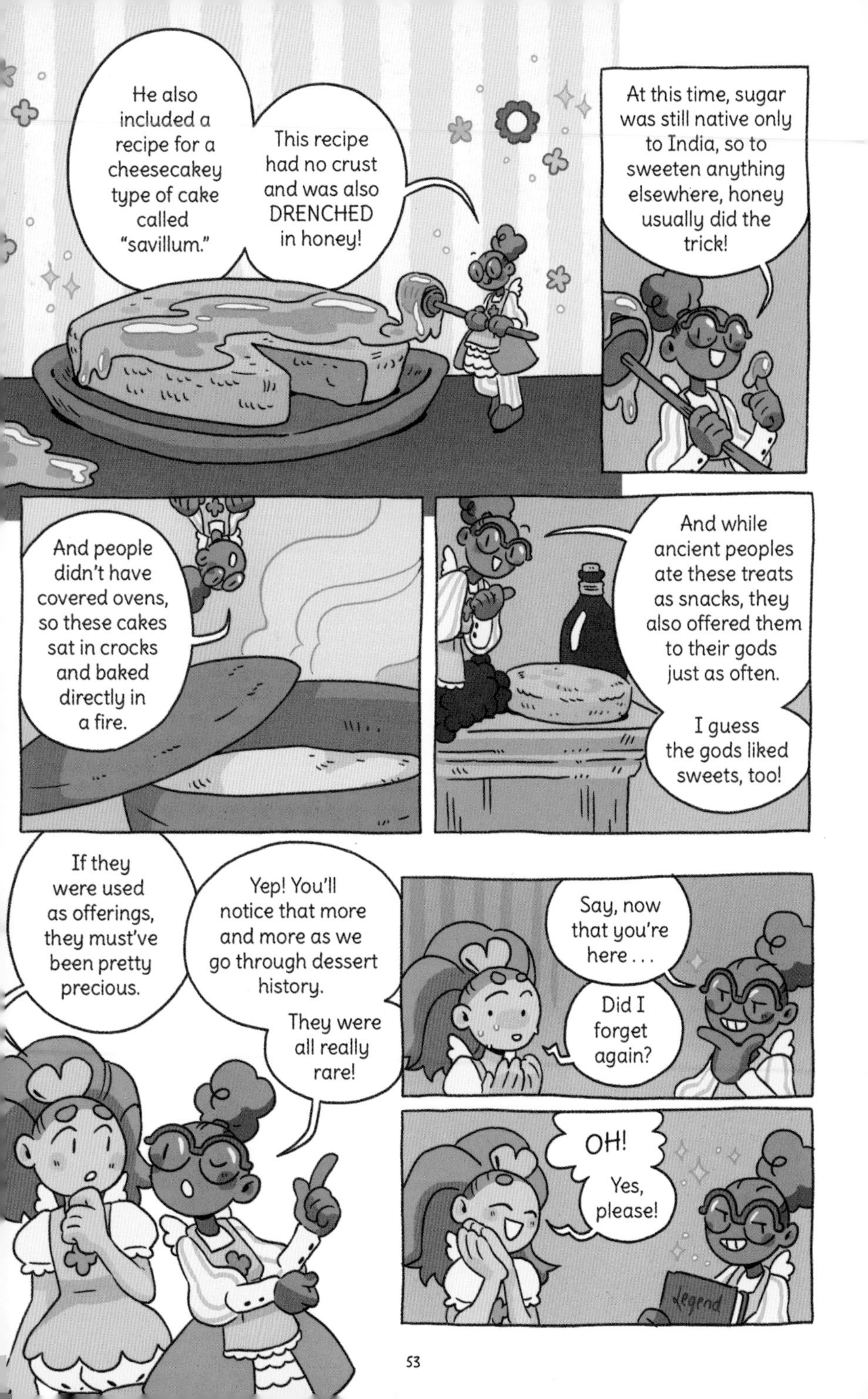

He also included a recipe for a cheesecakey type of cake called "savillum."
This recipe had no crust and was also DRENCHED in honey!
At this time, sugar was still native only to India, so to sweeten anything elsewhere, honey usually did the trick!
And people didn't have covered ovens, so these cakes sat in crocks and baked directly in a fire.
And while ancient peoples ate these treats as snacks, they also offered them to their gods just as often.
I guess the gods liked sweets, too!
If they were used as offerings, they must've been pretty precious.
Yep! You'll notice that more and more as we go through dessert history.
They were all really rare!
Say, now that you're here . . .
Did I forget again?
OH!
Yes, please!
Legend

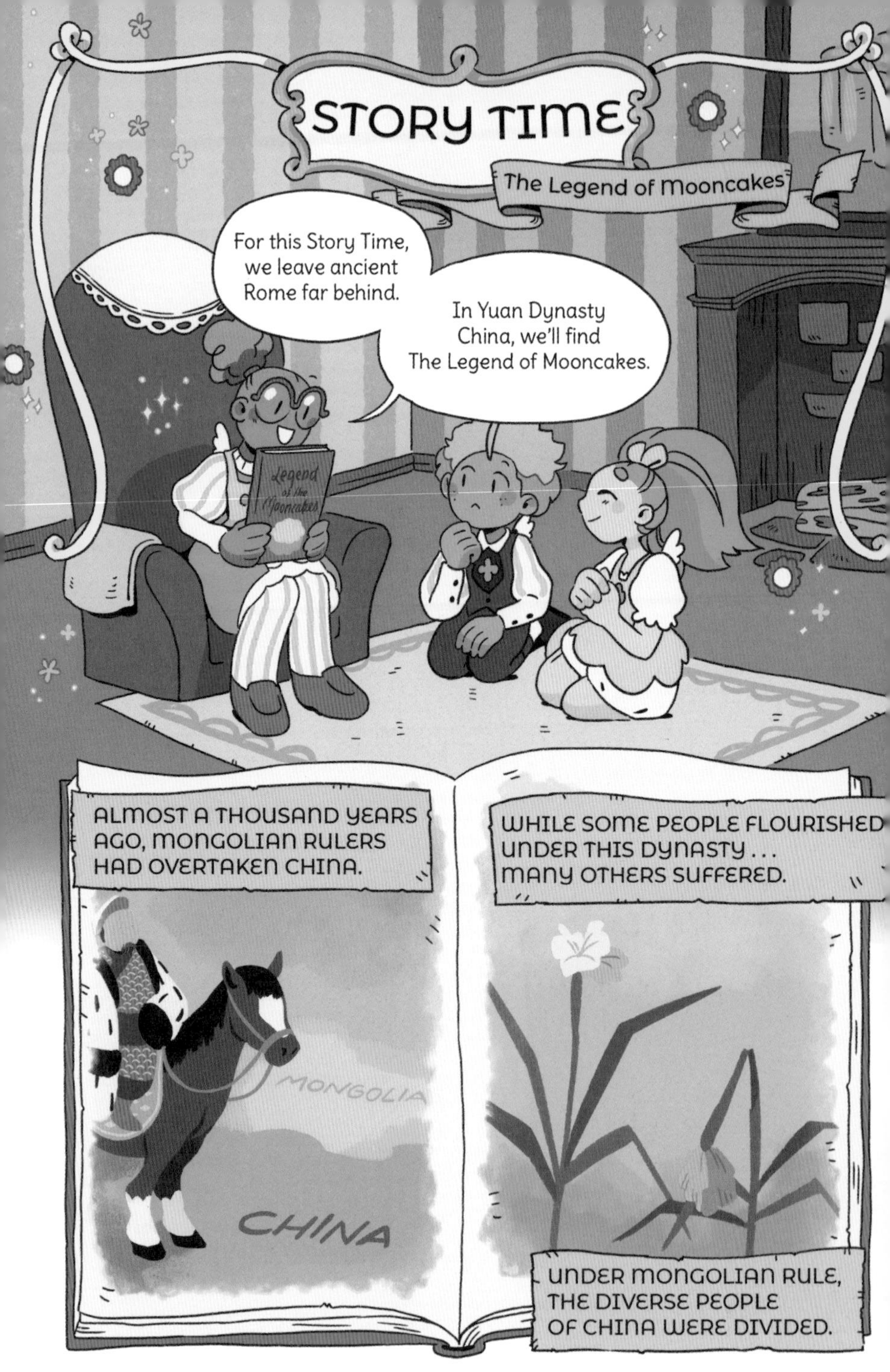
STORY TIME
The Legend of Mooncakes
For this Story Time, we leave ancient Rome far behind.
In Yuan Dynasty China, we'll find The Legend of Mooncakes.
Legend of the Mooncakes
ALMOST A THOUSAND YEARS AGO, MONGOLIAN RULERS HAD OVERTAKEN CHINA.
MONGOLIA
CHINA
WHILE SOME PEOPLE FLOURISHED UNDER THIS DYNASTY . . . MANY OTHERS SUFFERED.
UNDER MONGOLIAN RULE, THE DIVERSE PEOPLE OF CHINA WERE DIVIDED.

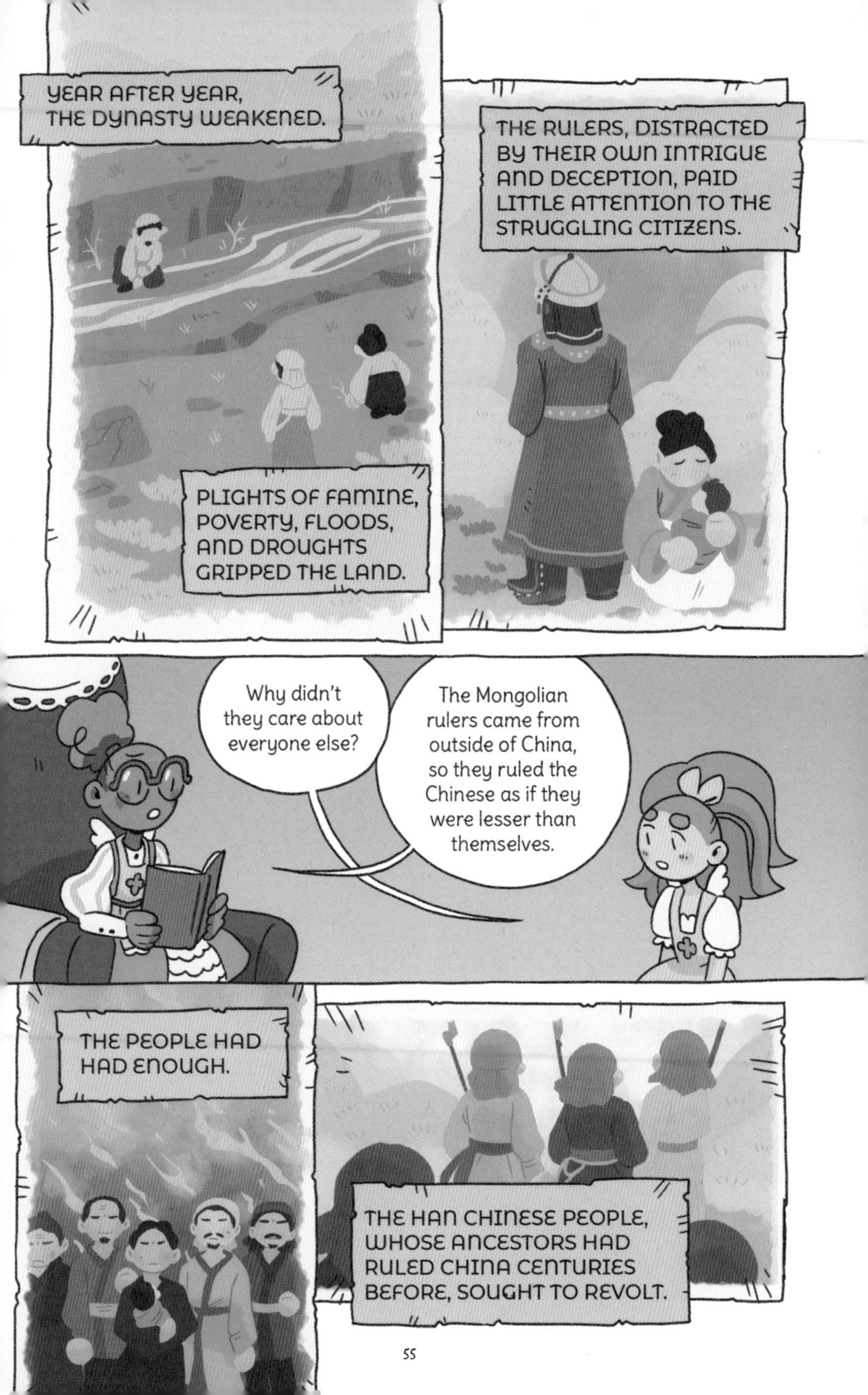
YEAR AFTER YEAR, THE DYNASTY WEAKENED.
PLIGHTS OF FAMINE, POVERTY, FLOODS, AND DROUGHTS GRIPPED THE LAND.
THE RULERS, DISTRACTED BY THEIR OWN INTRIGUE AND DECEPTION, PAID LITTLE ATTENTION TO THE STRUGGLING CITIZENS.
Why didn't they care about everyone else?
The Mongolian rulers came from outside of China, so they ruled the Chinese as if they were lesser than themselves.
THE PEOPLE HAD HAD ENOUGH.
THE HAN CHINESE PEOPLE, WHOSE ANCESTORS HAD RULED CHINA CENTURIES BEFORE, SOUGHT TO REVOLT.

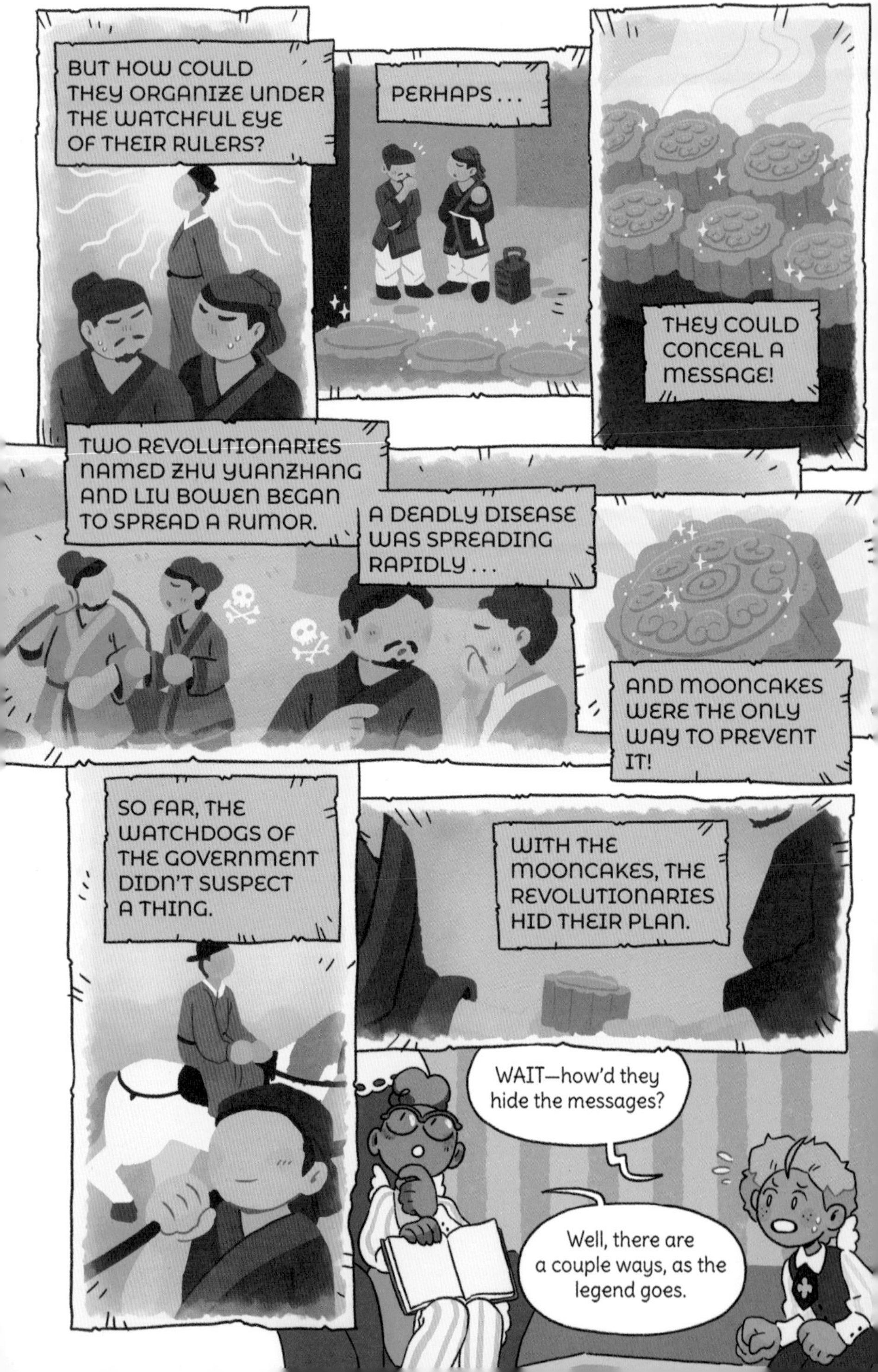
BUT HOW COULD THEY ORGANIZE UNDER THE WATCHFUL EYE OF THEIR RULERS?
PERHAPS . . .
THEY COULD CONCEAL A MESSAGE!
TWO REVOLUTIONARIES NAMED ZHU YUANZHANG AND LIU BOWEN BEGAN TO SPREAD A RUMOR.
A DEADLY DISEASE WAS SPREADING RAPIDLY . . .
AND MOONCAKES WERE THE ONLY WAY TO PREVENT IT!
SO FAR, THE WATCHDOGS OF THE GOVERNMENT DIDN'T SUSPECT A THING.
WITH THE MOONCAKES, THE REVOLUTIONARIES HID THEIR PLAN.
WAIT—how'd they hide the messages?
Well, there are a couple ways, as the legend goes.

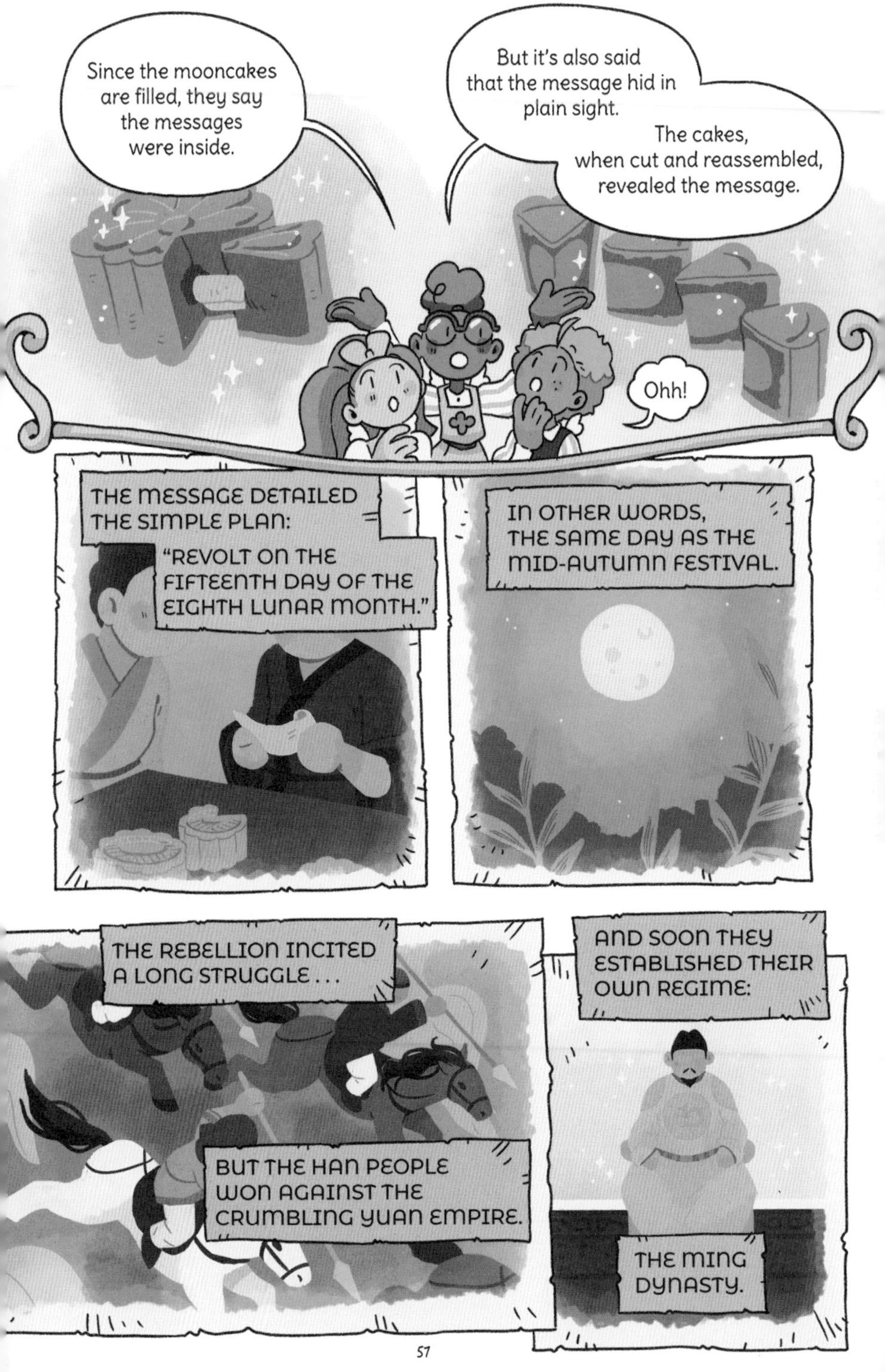

Since the mooncakes are filled, they say the messages were inside.
But it's also said that the message hid in plain sight.
The cakes, when cut and reassembled, revealed the message.
Ohh!
THE MESSAGE DETAILED THE SIMPLE PLAN:
"REVOLT ON THE FIFTEENTH DAY OF THE EIGHTH LUNAR MONTH."
IN OTHER WORDS, THE SAME DAY AS THE MID-AUTUMN FESTIVAL.
THE REBELLION INCITED A LONG STRUGGLE . . .
BUT THE HAN PEOPLE WON AGAINST THE CRUMBLING YUAN EMPIRE.
AND SOON THEY ESTABLISHED THEIR OWN REGIME:
THE MING DYNASTY.

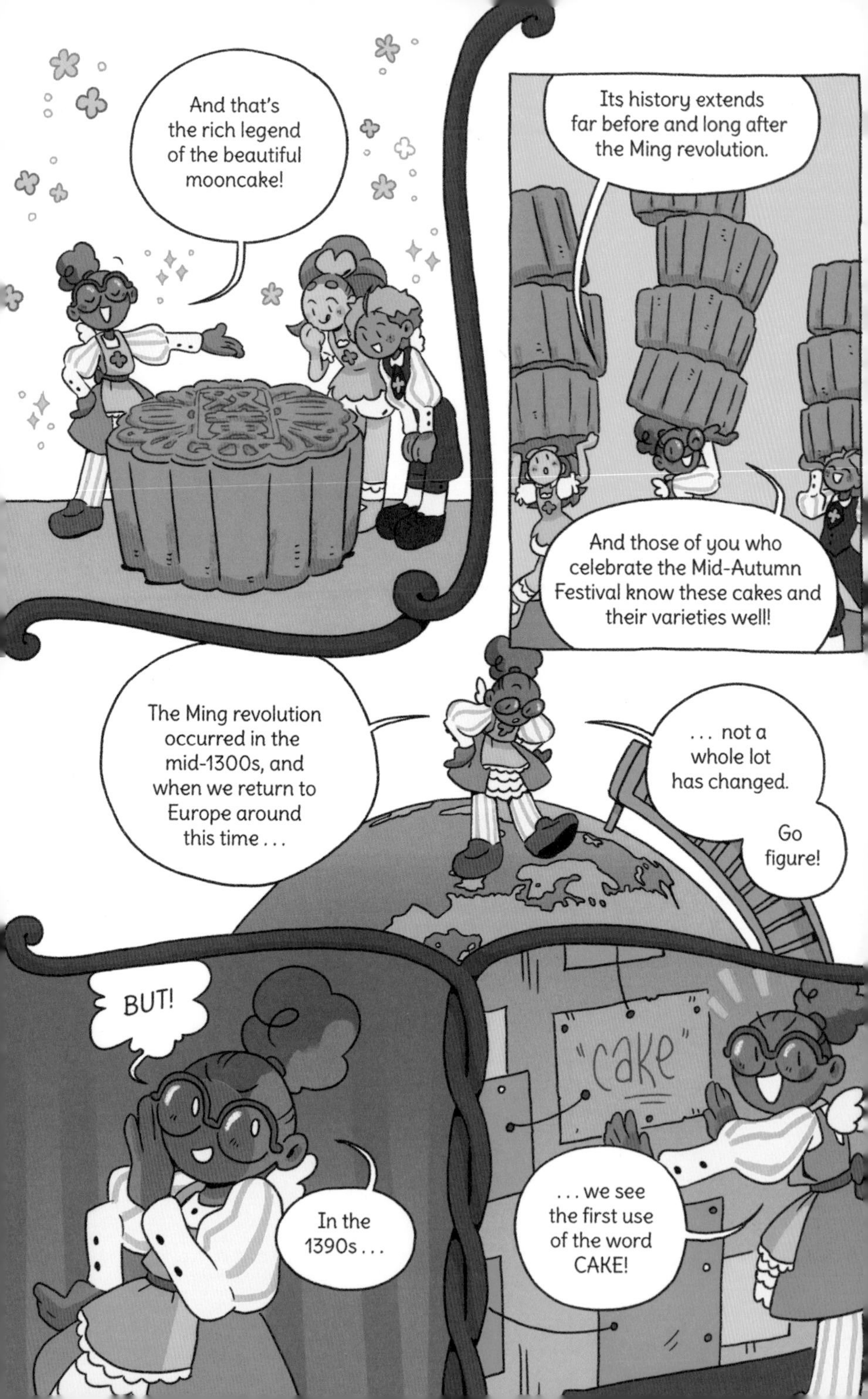
And that's the rich legend of the beautiful mooncake!
Its history extends far before and long after the Ming revolution.
And those of you who celebrate the Mid-Autumn Festival know these cakes and their varieties well!
The Ming revolution occurred in the mid-1300s, and when we return to Europe around this time . . .
. . . not a whole lot has changed.
Go figure!
BUT!
In the 1390s . . .
"CAKE"
. . . we see the first use of the word CAKE!

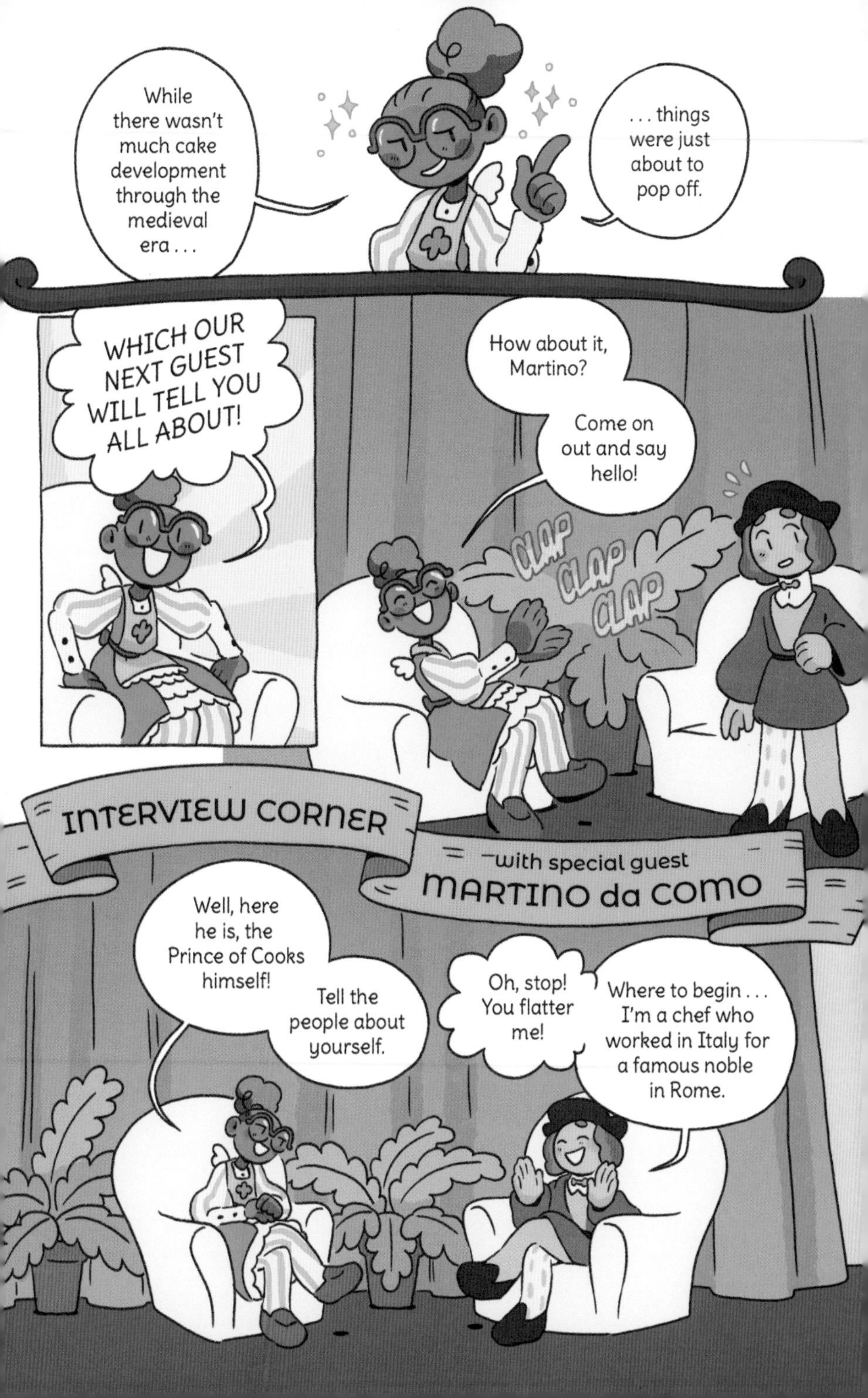
While there wasn't much cake development through the medieval era . . .
. . . things were just about to pop off.
WHICH OUR NEXT GUEST WILL TELL YOU ALL ABOUT!
How about it, Martino?
Come on out and say hello!
CLAP CLAP CLAP
INTERVIEW CORNER
with special guest MARTINO da COMO
Well, here he is, the Prince of Cooks himself!
Tell the people about yourself.
Oh, stop! You flatter me!
Where to begin . . . I'm a chef who worked in Italy for a famous noble in Rome.

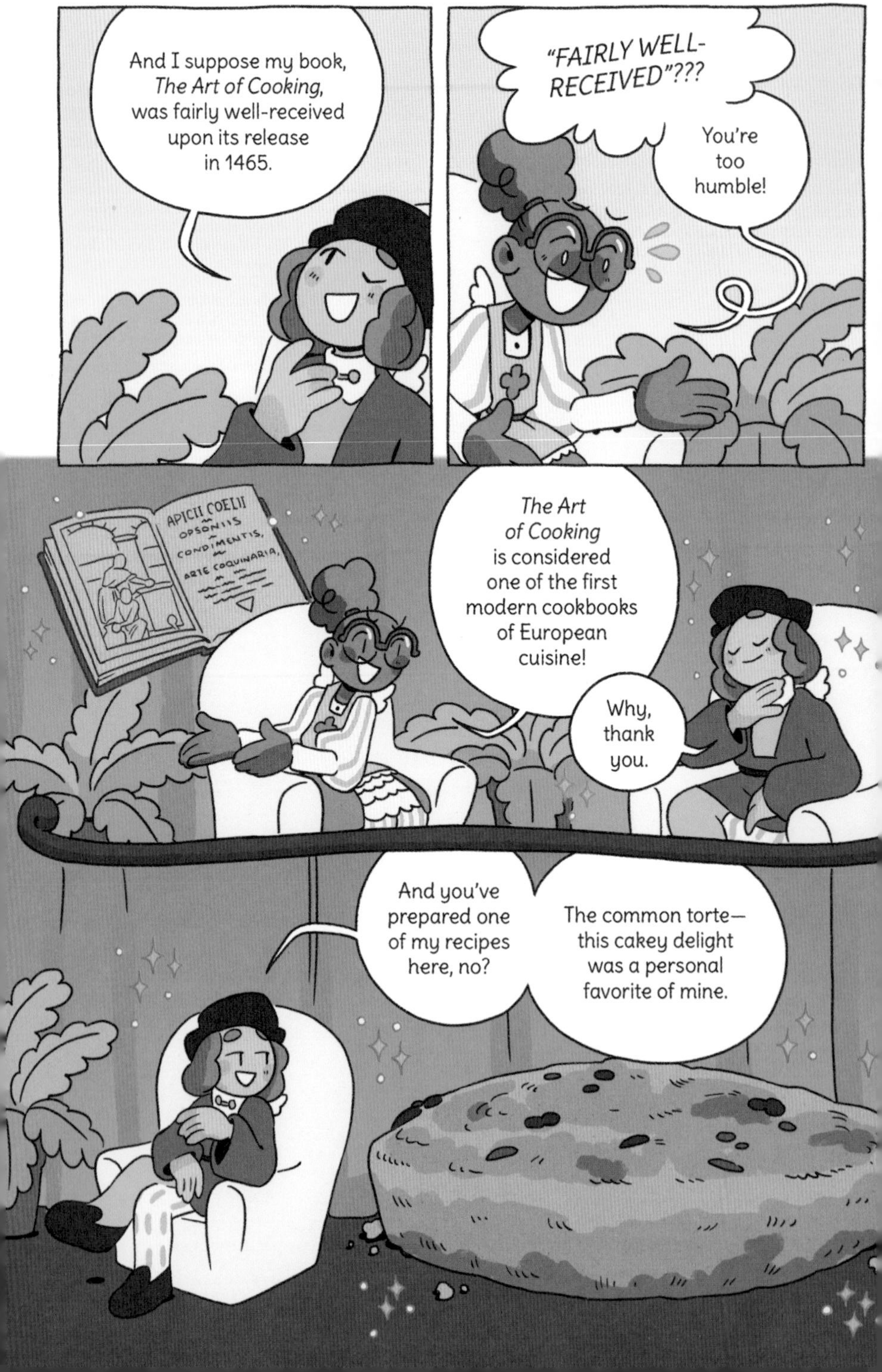
And I suppose my book, *The Art of Cooking*, was fairly well-received upon its release in 1465.
"FAIRLY WELL-RECEIVED"???
You're too humble!
APICII COELII
OPSONIIS
CONDIMENTIS,
ARTE COQUINARIA,
The Art of Cooking is considered one of the first modern cookbooks of European cuisine!
Why, thank you.
And you've prepared one of my recipes here, no?
The common torte—this cakey delight was a personal favorite of mine.

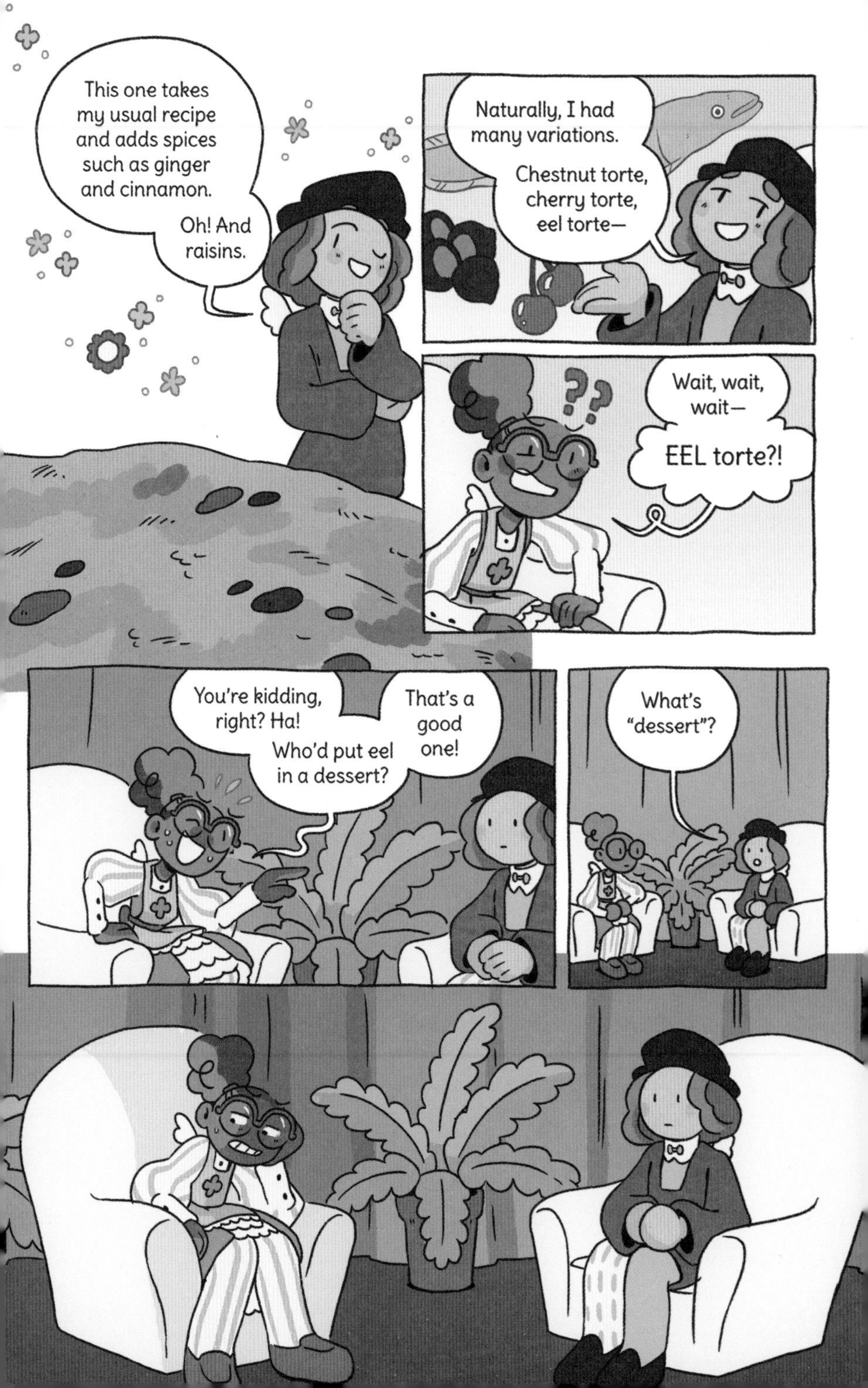
This one takes my usual recipe and adds spices such as ginger and cinnamon.
Oh! And raisins.
Naturally, I had many variations.
Chestnut torte, cherry torte, eel torte—
Wait, wait, wait—
EEL torte?!
You're kidding, right? Ha!
Who'd put eel in a dessert?
That's a good one!
What's "dessert"?

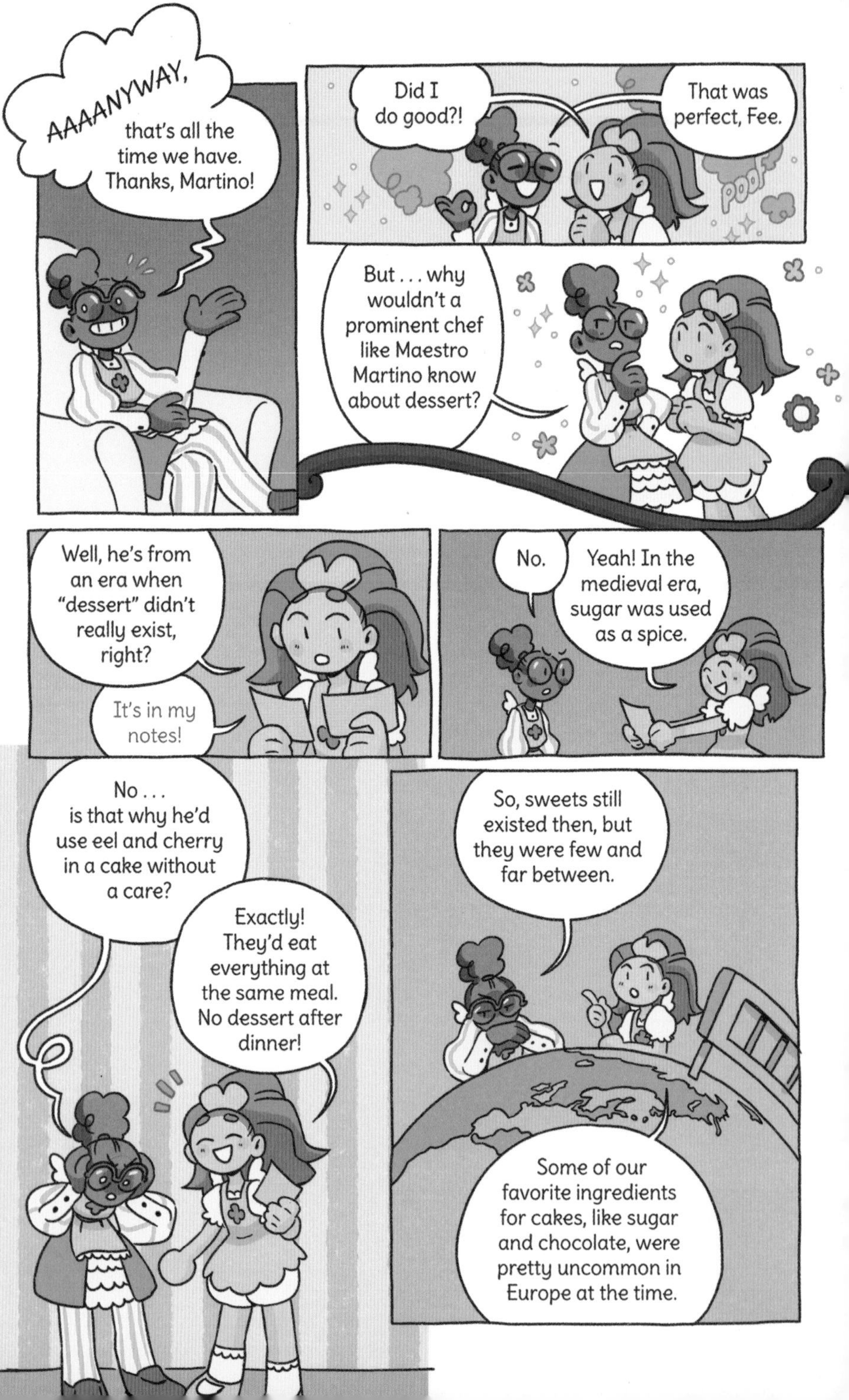
AAAANYWAY, that's all the time we have. Thanks, Martino!
Did I do good?!
That was perfect, Fee.
POOF
But . . . why wouldn't a prominent chef like Maestro Martino know about dessert?
Well, he's from an era when "dessert" didn't really exist, right?
It's in my notes!
No.
Yeah! In the medieval era, sugar was used as a spice.
No . . . is that why he'd use eel and cherry in a cake without a care?
Exactly! They'd eat everything at the same meal. No dessert after dinner!
So, sweets still existed then, but they were few and far between.
Some of our favorite ingredients for cakes, like sugar and chocolate, were pretty uncommon in Europe at the time.

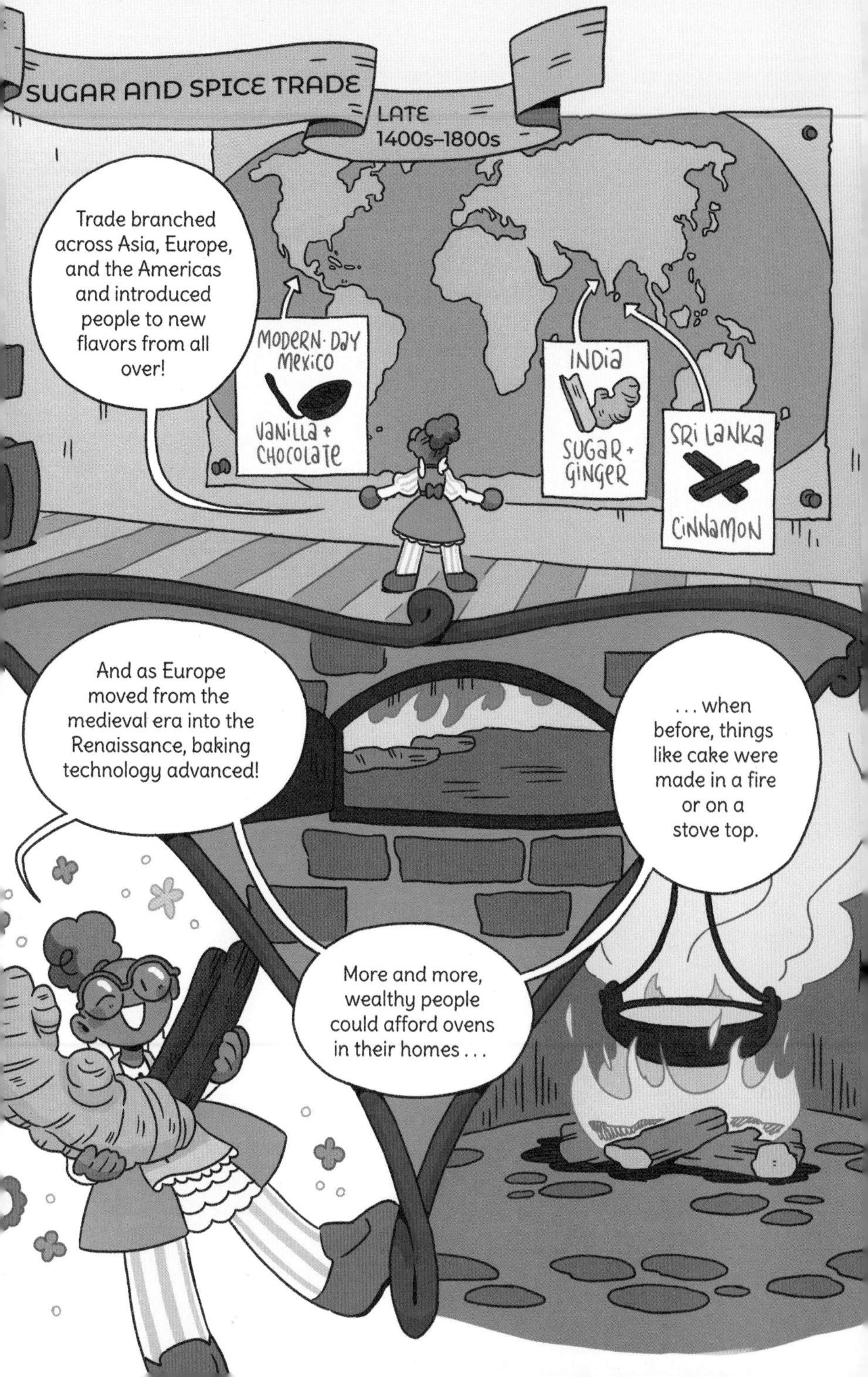
SUGAR AND SPICE TRADE
LATE 1400s–1800s
Trade branched across Asia, Europe, and the Americas and introduced people to new flavors from all over!
MODERN-DAY MEXICO
VANILLA + CHOCOLATE
INDIA
SUGAR + GINGER
SRI LANKA
CINNAMON
And as Europe moved from the medieval era into the Renaissance, baking technology advanced!
. . . when before, things like cake were made in a fire or on a stove top.
More and more, wealthy people could afford ovens in their homes . . .

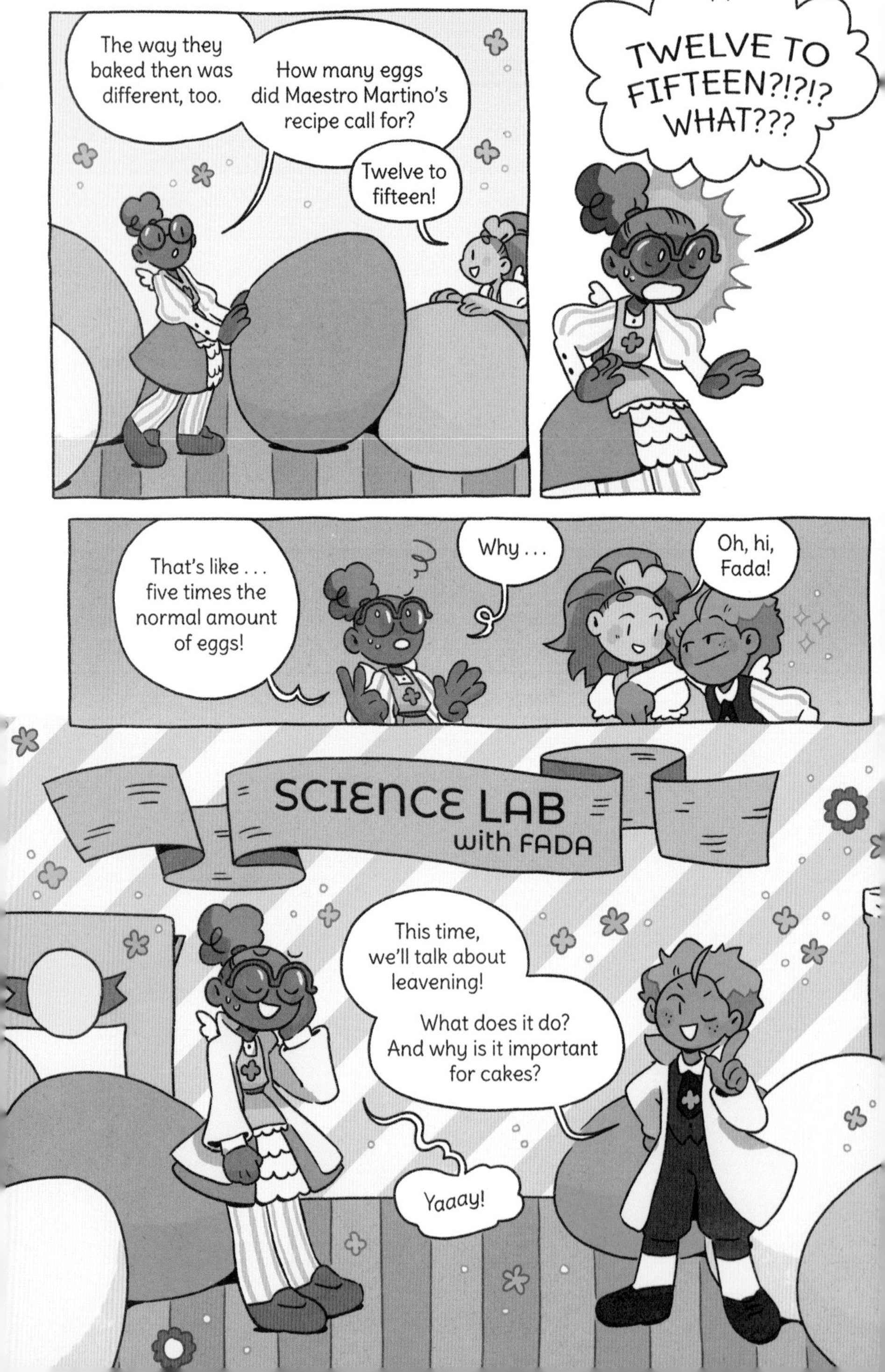
The way they baked then was different, too.
How many eggs did Maestro Martino's recipe call for?
Twelve to fifteen!
TWELVE TO FIFTEEN?!?!? WHAT???
That's like . . . five times the normal amount of eggs!
Why . . .
Oh, hi, Fada!
SCIENCE LAB with FADA
This time, we'll talk about leavening!
What does it do? And why is it important for cakes?
Yaaay!

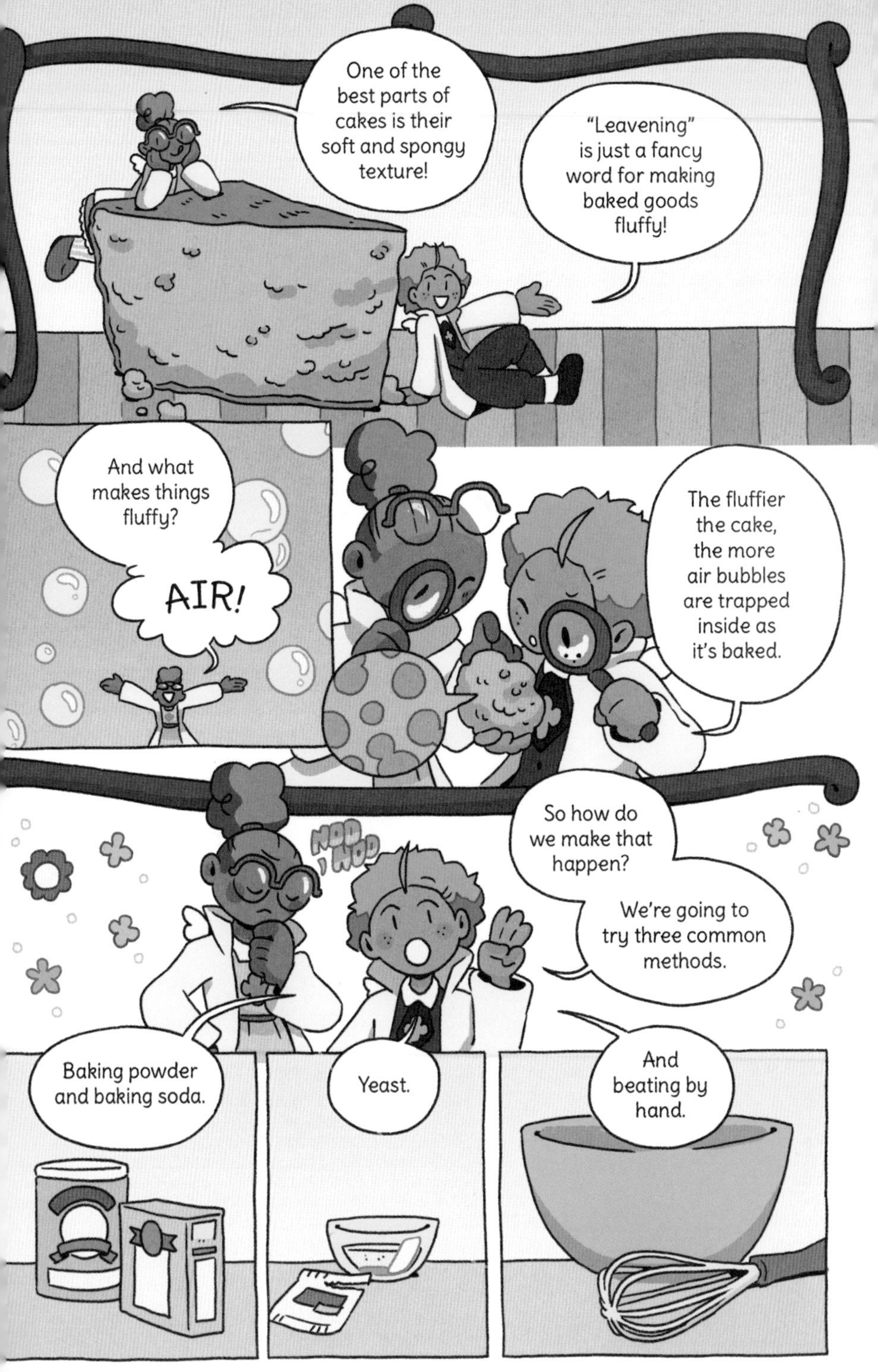

One of the best parts of cakes is their soft and spongy texture!
"Leavening" is just a fancy word for making baked goods fluffy!
And what makes things fluffy?
AIR!
The fluffier the cake, the more air bubbles are trapped inside as it's baked.
NOD NOD
So how do we make that happen?
We're going to try three common methods.
Baking powder and baking soda.
Yeast.
And beating by hand.

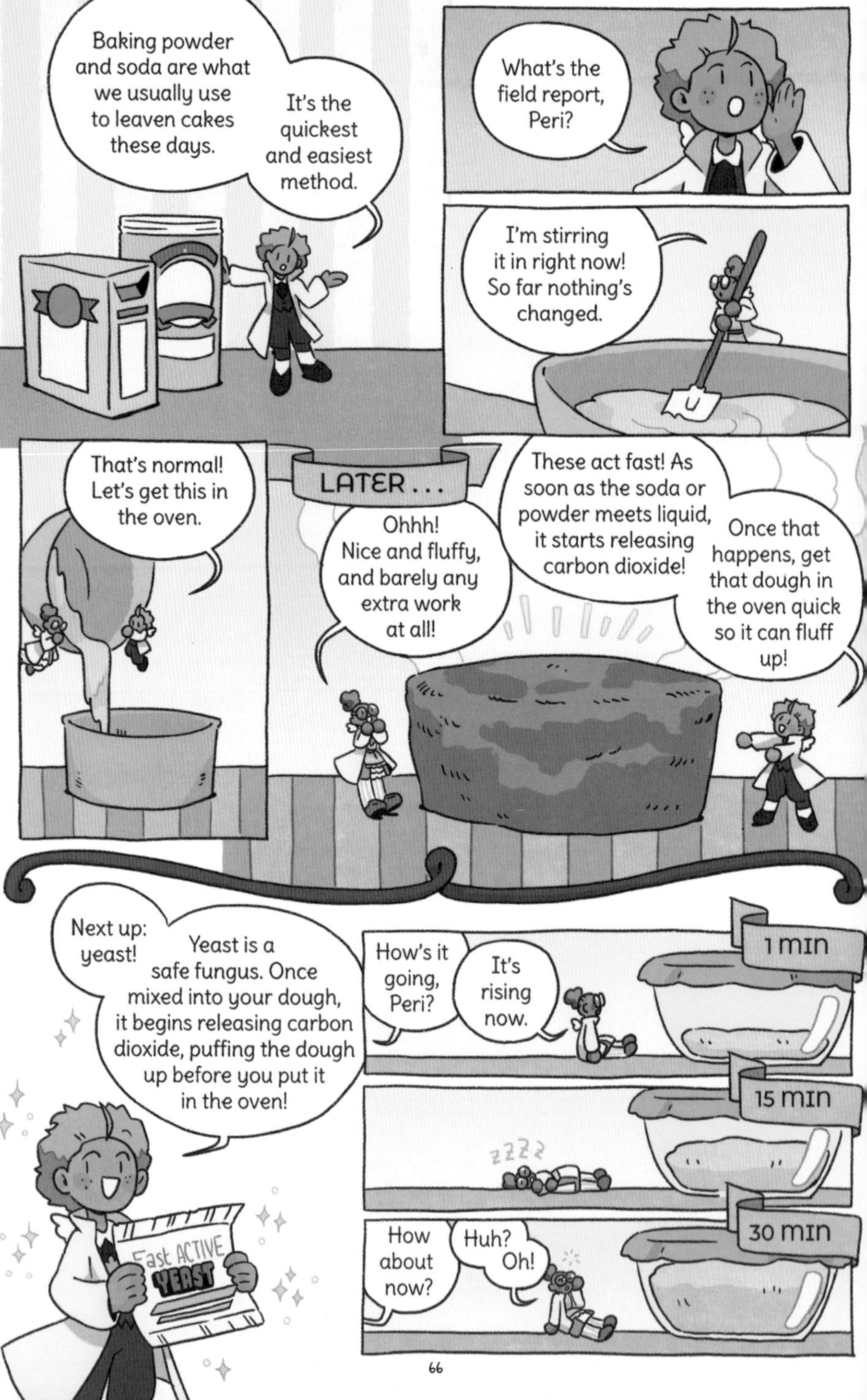
Baking powder and soda are what we usually use to leaven cakes these days.
It's the quickest and easiest method.
What's the field report, Peri?
I'm stirring it in right now! So far nothing's changed.
That's normal! Let's get this in the oven.
LATER . . .
Ohhh! Nice and fluffy, and barely any extra work at all!
These act fast! As soon as the soda or powder meets liquid, it starts releasing carbon dioxide!
Once that happens, get that dough in the oven quick so it can fluff up!
Next up: yeast!
Yeast is a safe fungus. Once mixed into your dough, it begins releasing carbon dioxide, puffing the dough up before you put it in the oven!
Fast ACTIVE YEAST
How's it going, Peri?
It's rising now.
1 MIN
15 MIN
ZZZZ
30 MIN
How about now?
Huh? Oh!

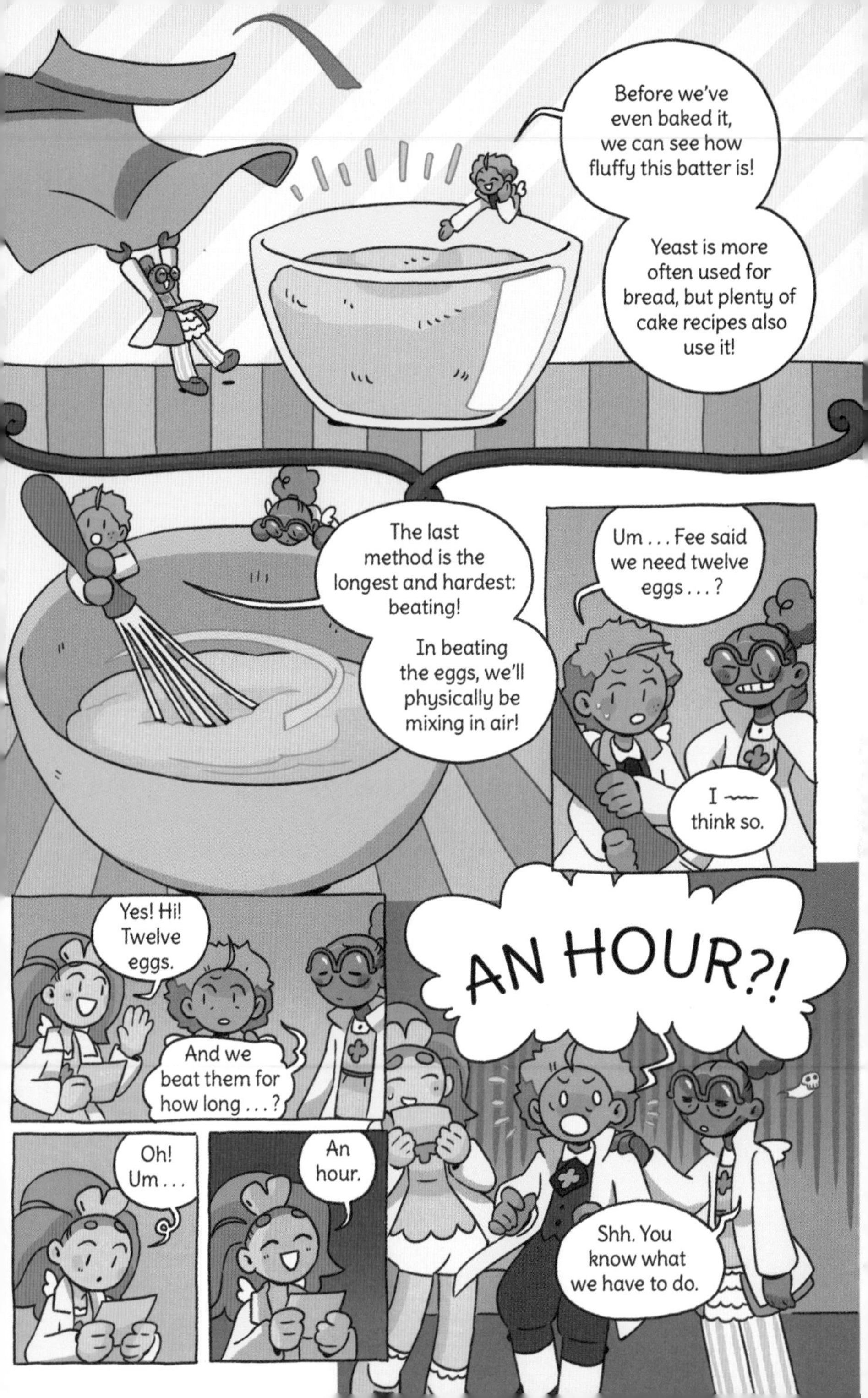
Before we've even baked it, we can see how fluffy this batter is!
Yeast is more often used for bread, but plenty of cake recipes also use it!
The last method is the longest and hardest: beating!
In beating the eggs, we'll physically be mixing in air!
Um . . . Fee said we need twelve eggs . . . ?
I — think so.
Yes! Hi! Twelve eggs.
And we beat them for how long . . . ?
Oh! Um . . .
An hour.
AN HOUR?!
Shh. You know what we have to do.

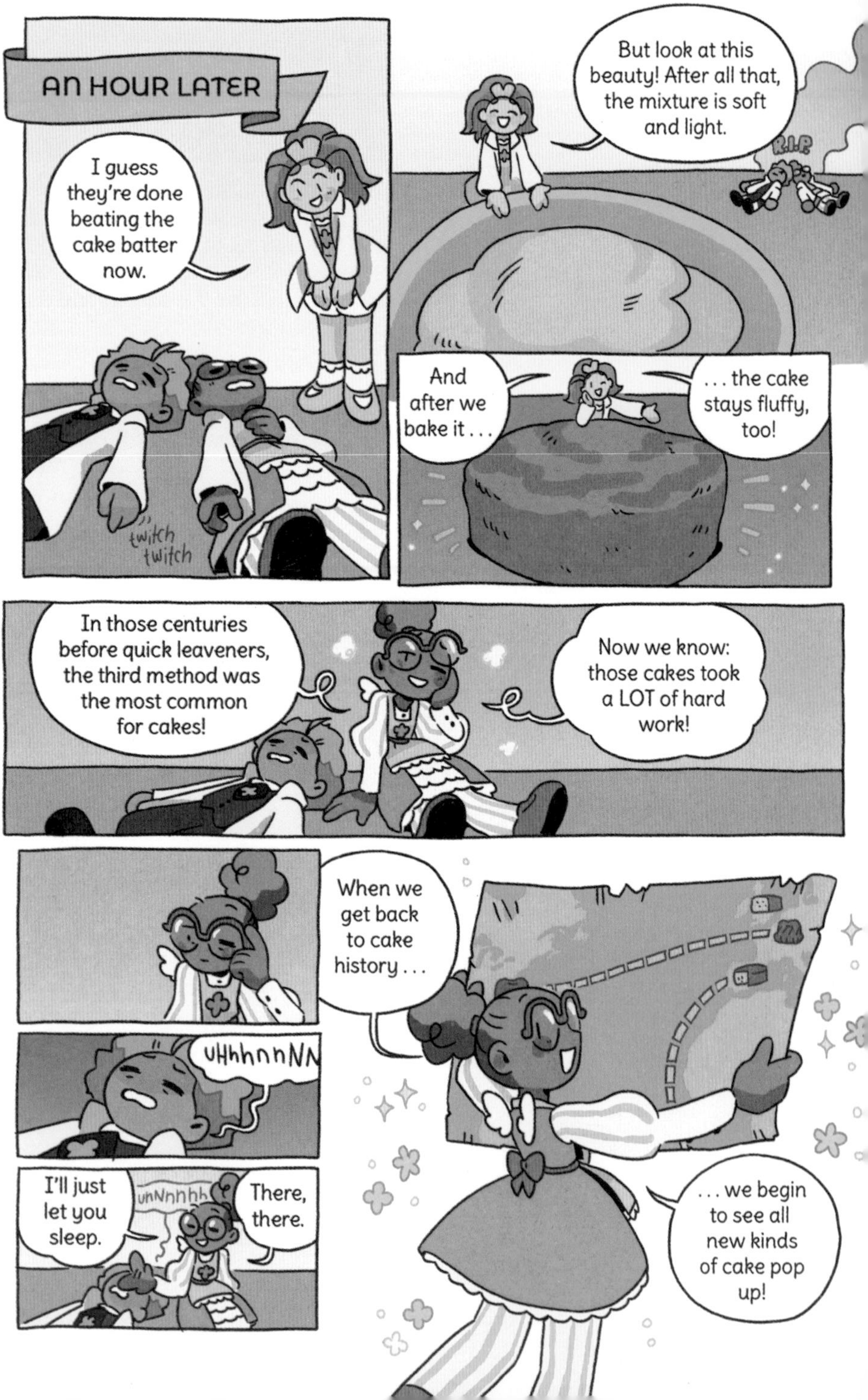
AN HOUR LATER
I guess they're done beating the cake batter now.
twitch twitch
But look at this beauty! After all that, the mixture is soft and light.
R.I.P.
And after we bake it . . .
. . . the cake stays fluffy, too!
In those centuries before quick leaveners, the third method was the most common for cakes!
Now we know: those cakes took a LOT of hard work!
When we get back to cake history . . .
UHhhnnNN
I'll just let you sleep.
uhNnnhh
There, there.
. . . we begin to see all new kinds of cake pop up!

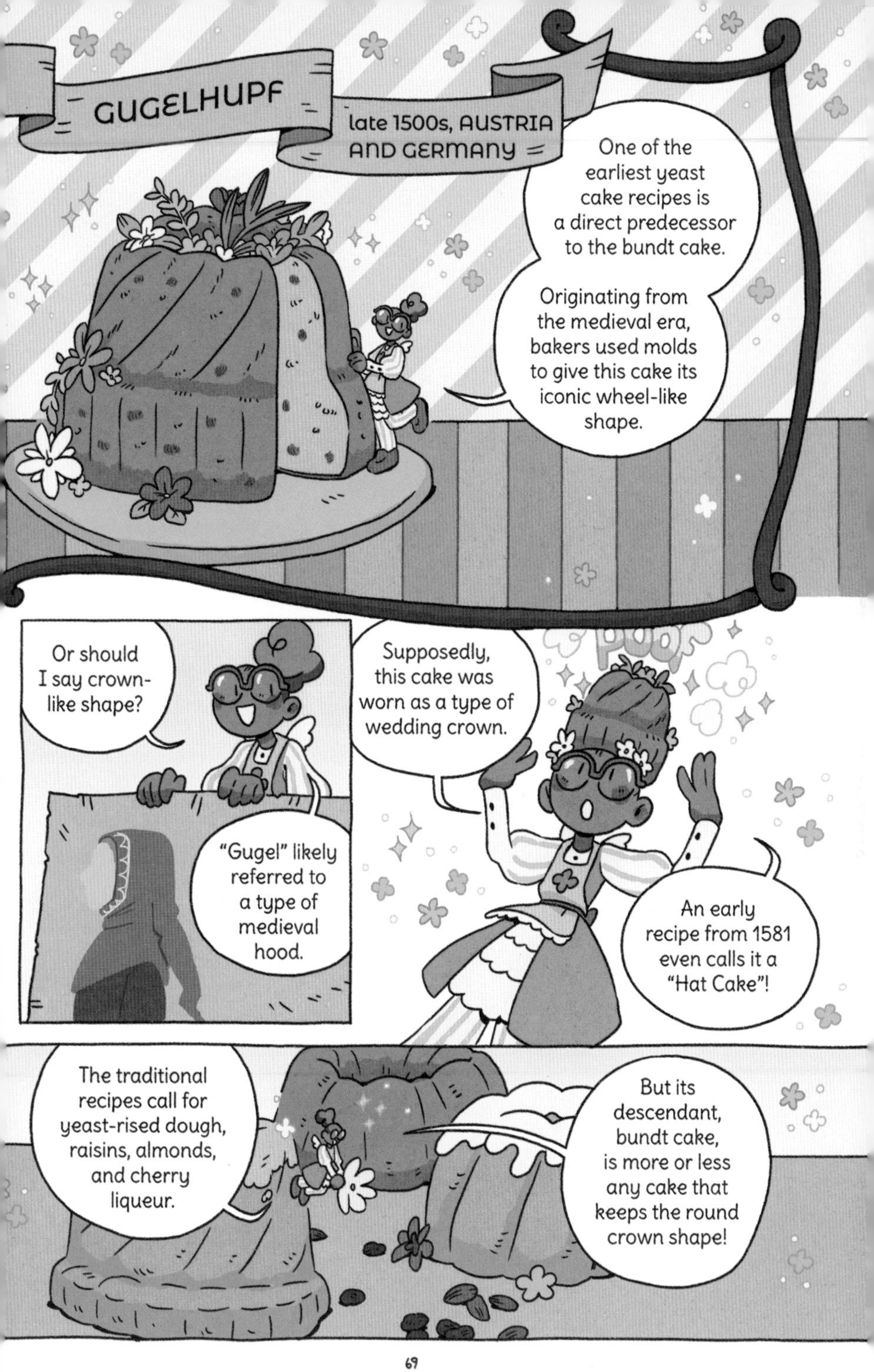
GUGELHUPF
late 1500s, AUSTRIA AND GERMANY
One of the earliest yeast cake recipes is a direct predecessor to the bundt cake.
Originating from the medieval era, bakers used molds to give this cake its iconic wheel-like shape.
Or should I say crown-like shape?
"Gugel" likely referred to a type of medieval hood.
Supposedly, this cake was worn as a type of wedding crown.
An early recipe from 1581 even calls it a "Hat Cake"!
The traditional recipes call for yeast-rised dough, raisins, almonds, and cherry liqueur.
But its descendant, bundt cake, is more or less any cake that keeps the round crown shape!

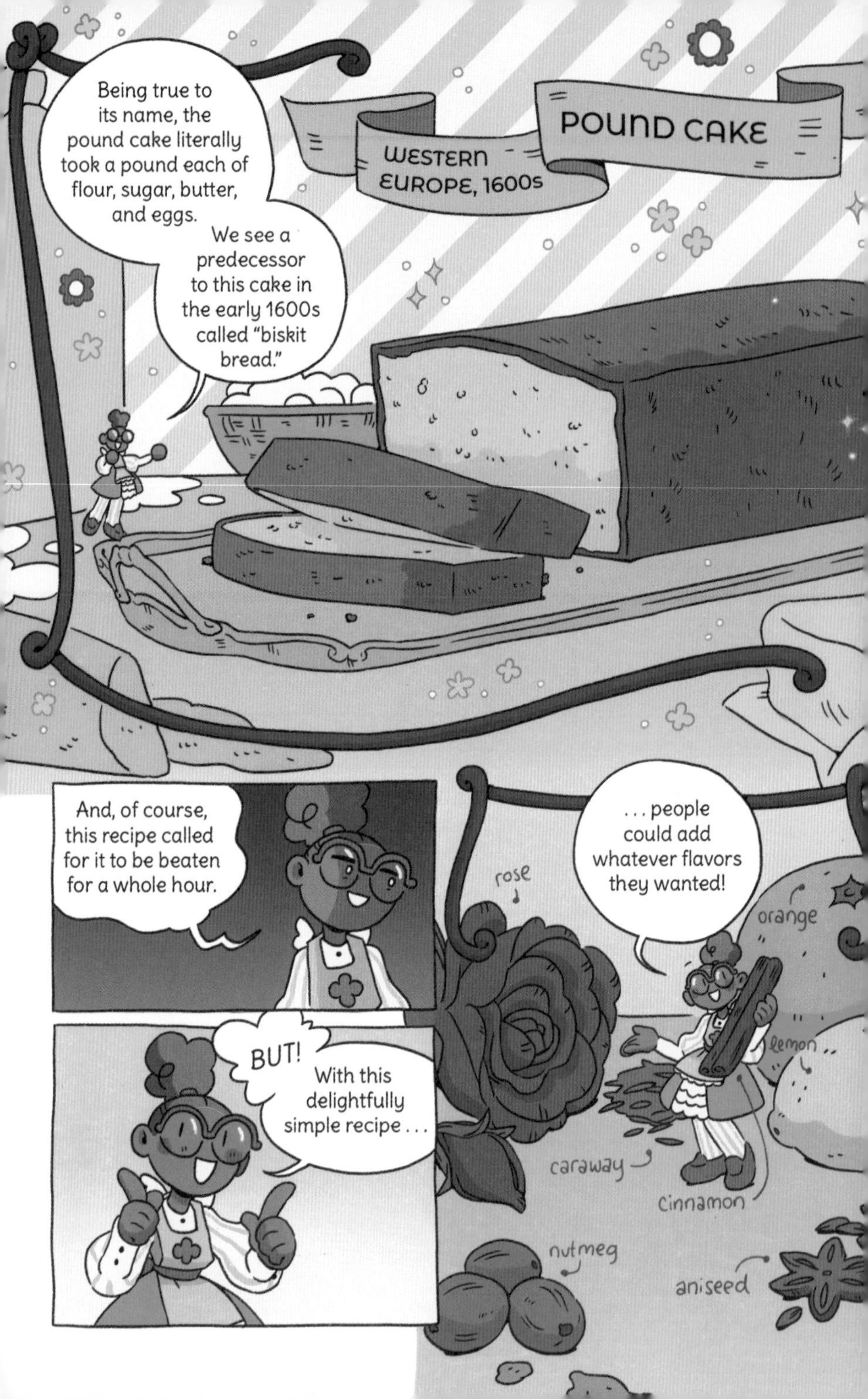
POUND CAKE
WESTERN EUROPE, 1600s
Being true to its name, the pound cake literally took a pound each of flour, sugar, butter, and eggs.
We see a predecessor to this cake in the early 1600s called "biskit bread."
And, of course, this recipe called for it to be beaten for a whole hour.
BUT!
With this delightfully simple recipe . . .
. . . people could add whatever flavors they wanted!
rose
orange
lemon
caraway
cinnamon
nutmeg
aniseed

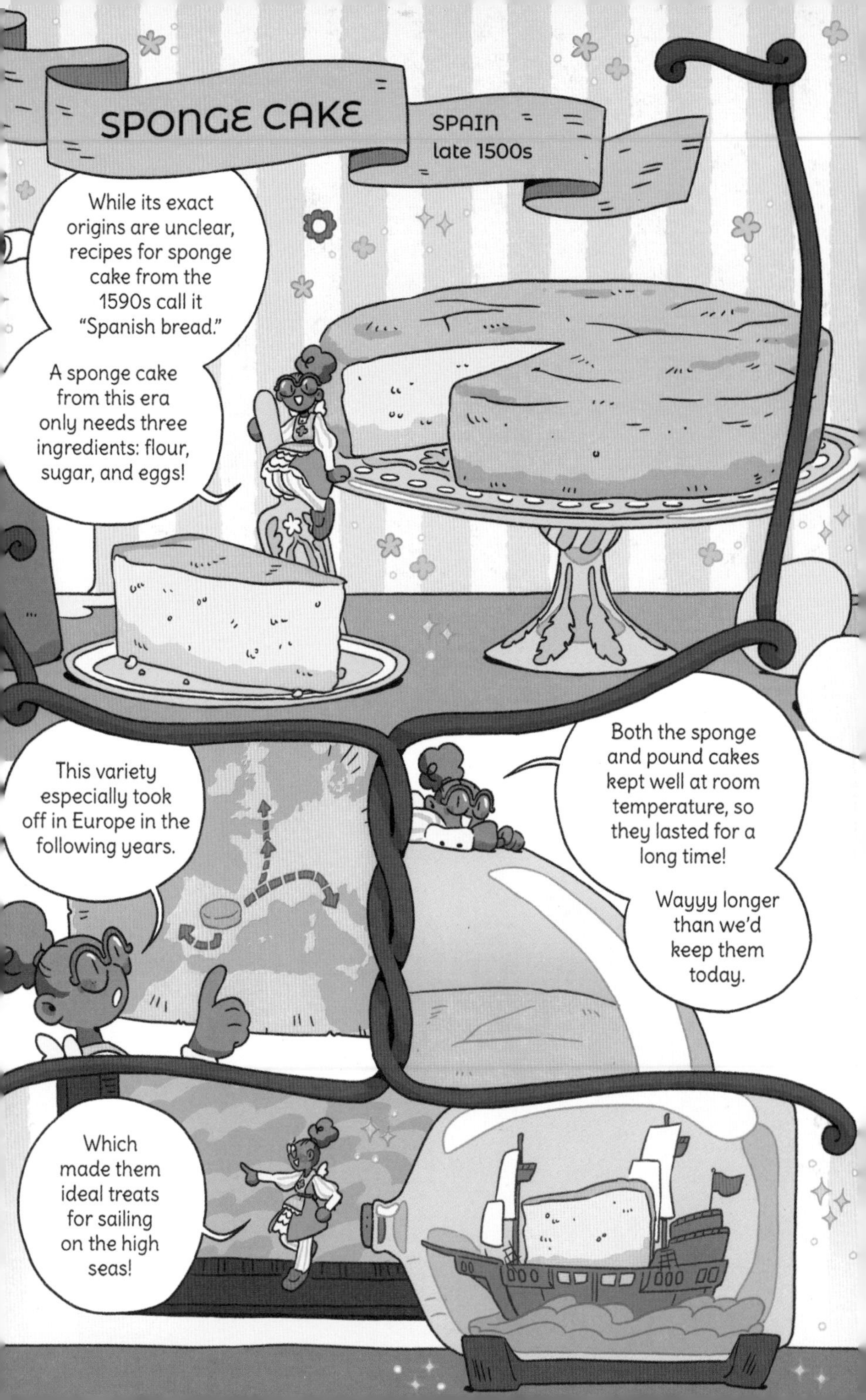
SPONGE CAKE
SPAIN late 1500s
While its exact origins are unclear, recipes for sponge cake from the 1590s call it "Spanish bread."
A sponge cake from this era only needs three ingredients: flour, sugar, and eggs!
This variety especially took off in Europe in the following years.
Both the sponge and pound cakes kept well at room temperature, so they lasted for a long time!
Wayyy longer than we'd keep them today.
Which made them ideal treats for sailing on the high seas!

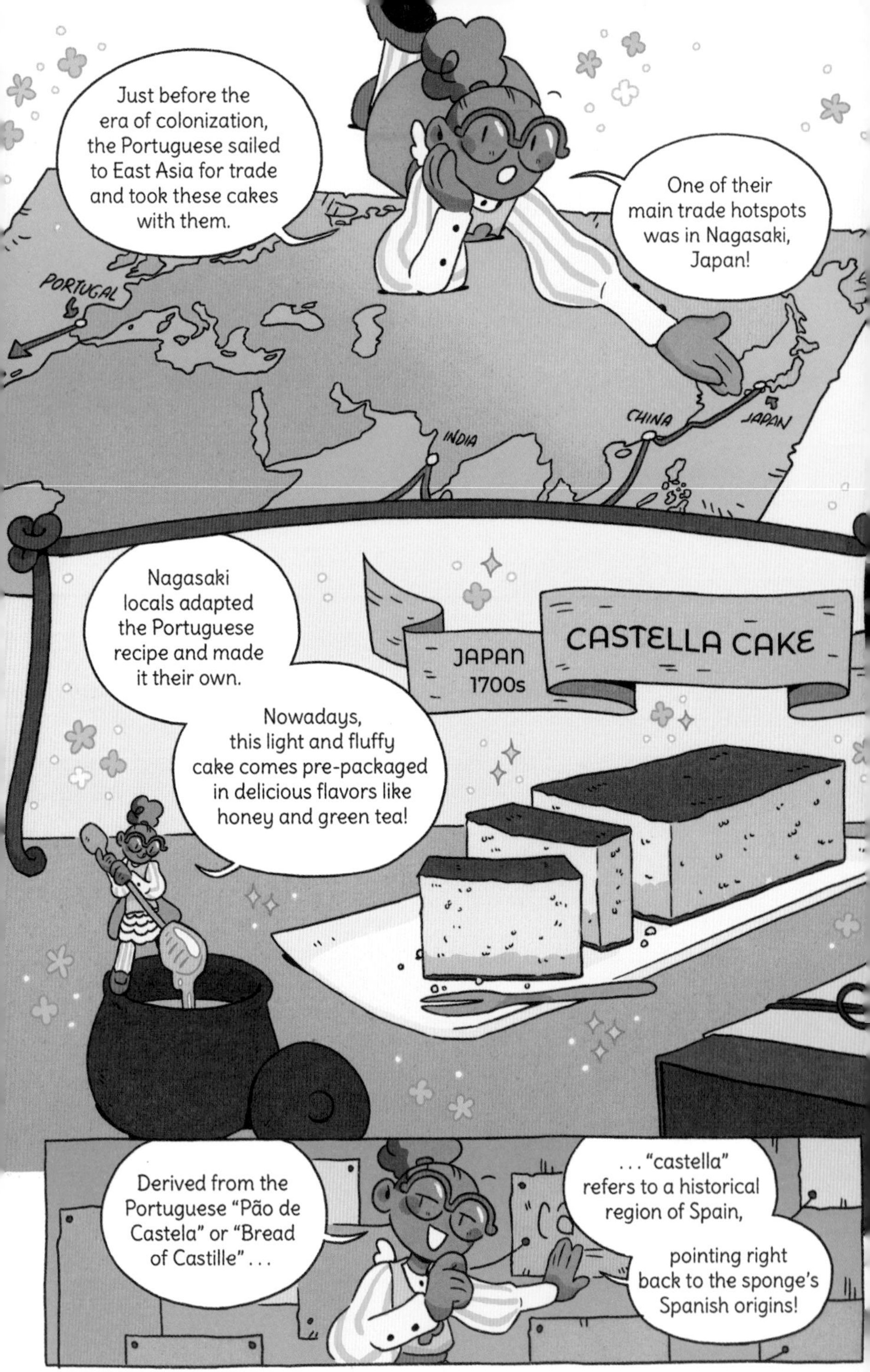
Just before the era of colonization, the Portuguese sailed to East Asia for trade and took these cakes with them.
One of their main trade hotspots was in Nagasaki, Japan!
PORTUGAL
INDIA
CHINA
JAPAN
Nagasaki locals adapted the Portuguese recipe and made it their own.
JAPAN 1700s
CASTELLA CAKE
Nowadays, this light and fluffy cake comes pre-packaged in delicious flavors like honey and green tea!
Derived from the Portuguese "Pão de Castela" or "Bread of Castille" . . .
. . . "castella" refers to a historical region of Spain,
pointing right back to the sponge's Spanish origins!

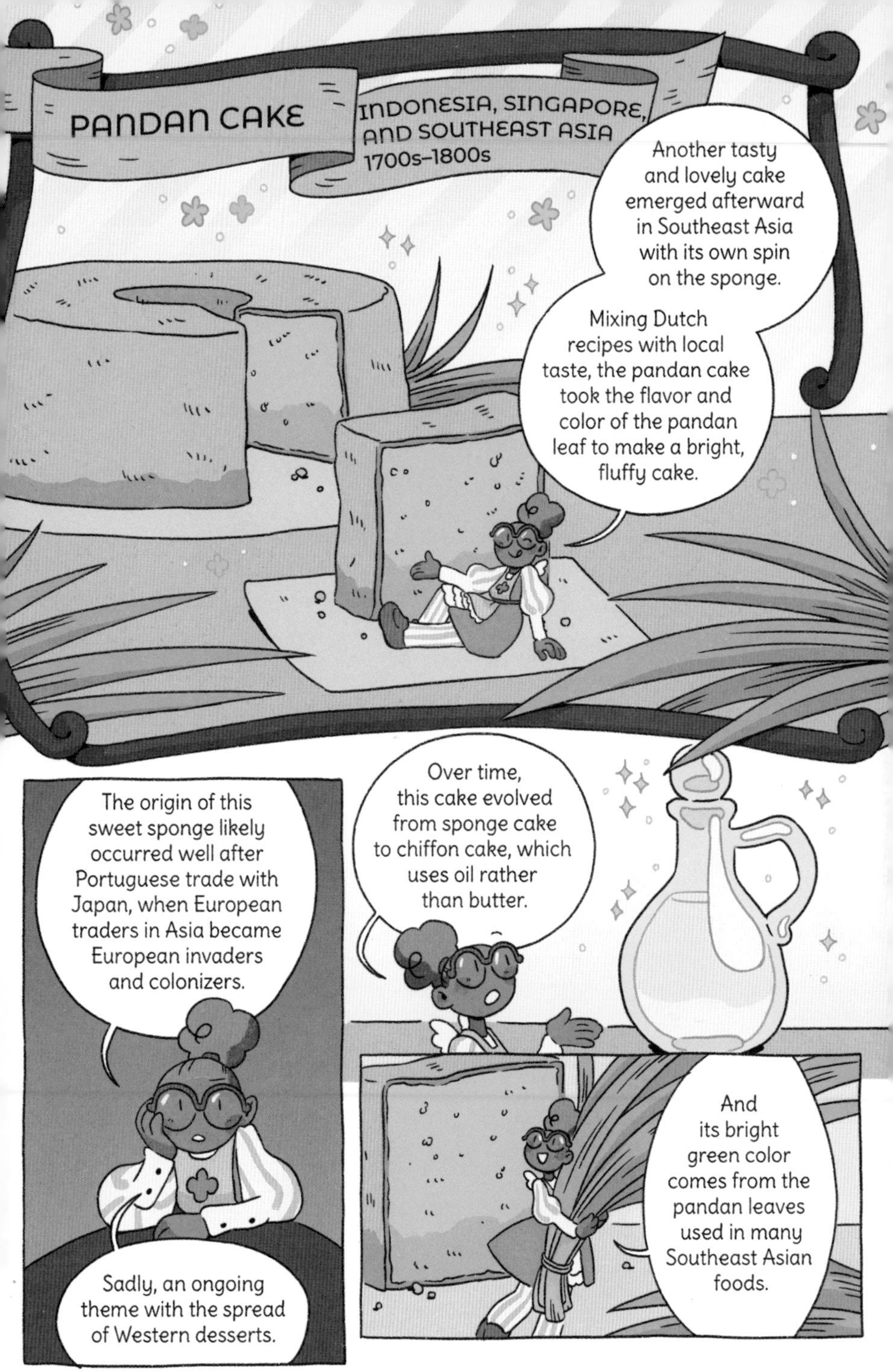
PANDAN CAKE
INDONESIA, SINGAPORE, AND SOUTHEAST ASIA 1700s–1800s
Another tasty and lovely cake emerged afterward in Southeast Asia with its own spin on the sponge.
Mixing Dutch recipes with local taste, the pandan cake took the flavor and color of the pandan leaf to make a bright, fluffy cake.
The origin of this sweet sponge likely occurred well after Portuguese trade with Japan, when European traders in Asia became European invaders and colonizers.
Sadly, an ongoing theme with the spread of Western desserts.
Over time, this cake evolved from sponge cake to chiffon cake, which uses oil rather than butter.
And its bright green color comes from the pandan leaves used in many Southeast Asian foods.

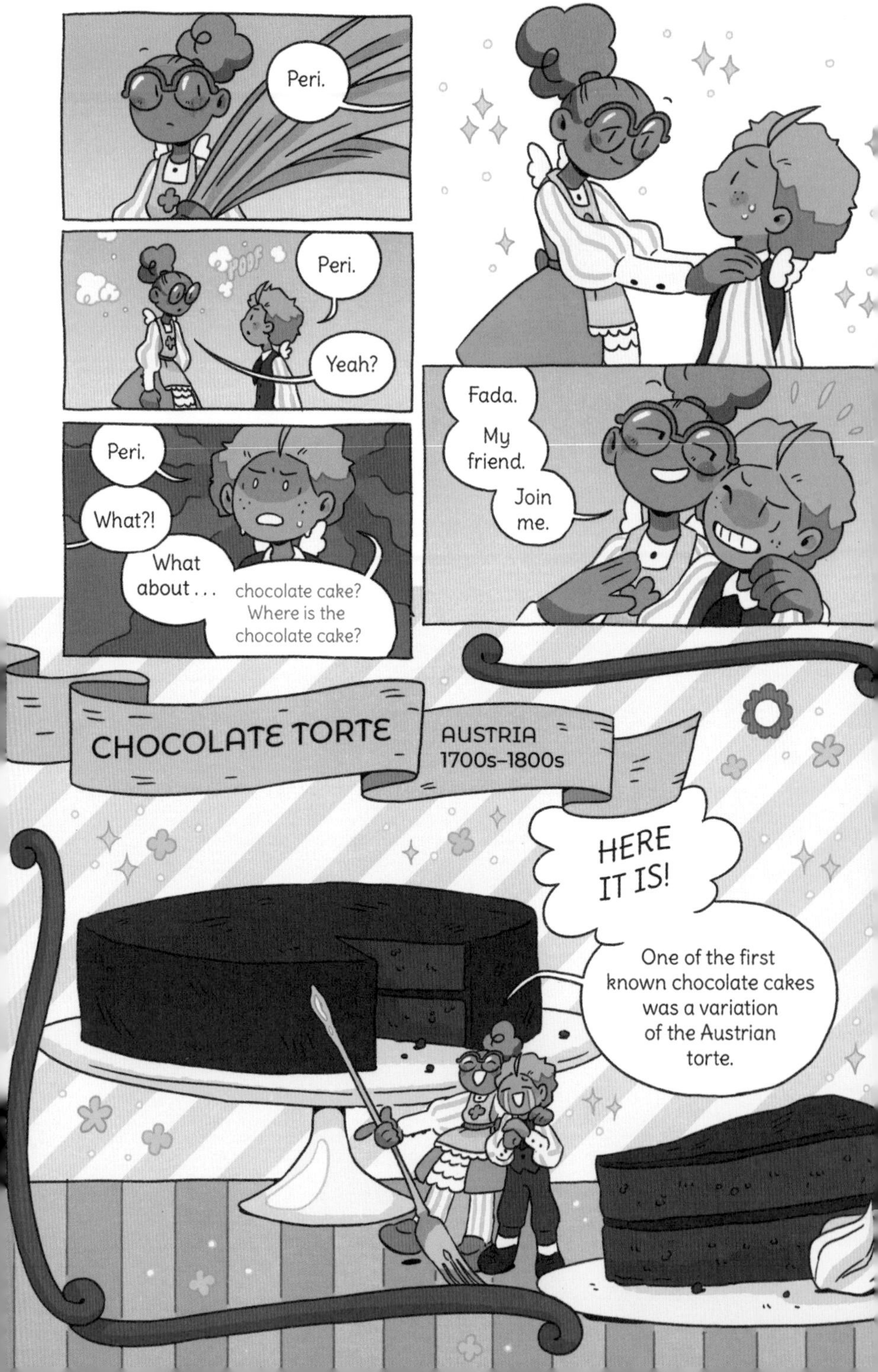
Peri.
POOF
Peri.
Yeah?
Peri.
What?!
What about . . .
chocolate cake? Where is the chocolate cake?
Fada.
My friend.
Join me.
CHOCOLATE TORTE
AUSTRIA 1700s–1800s
HERE IT IS!
One of the first known chocolate cakes was a variation of the Austrian torte.

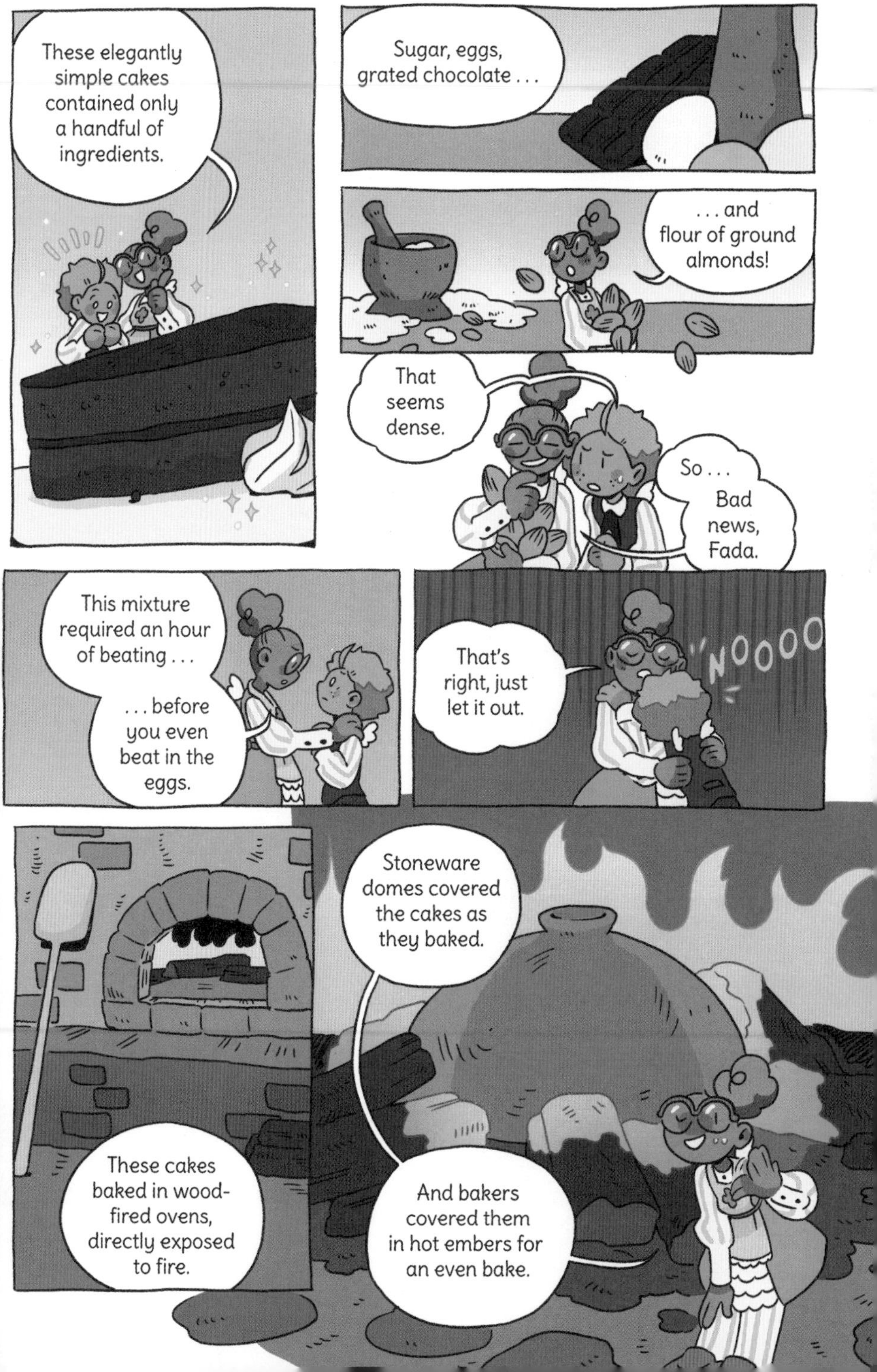
These elegantly simple cakes contained only a handful of ingredients.
Sugar, eggs, grated chocolate . . .
. . . and flour of ground almonds!
That seems dense.
So . . .
Bad news, Fada.
This mixture required an hour of beating . . .
. . . before you even beat in the eggs.
That's right, just let it out.
NOOOO
These cakes baked in wood-fired ovens, directly exposed to fire.
Stoneware domes covered the cakes as they baked.
And bakers covered them in hot embers for an even bake.

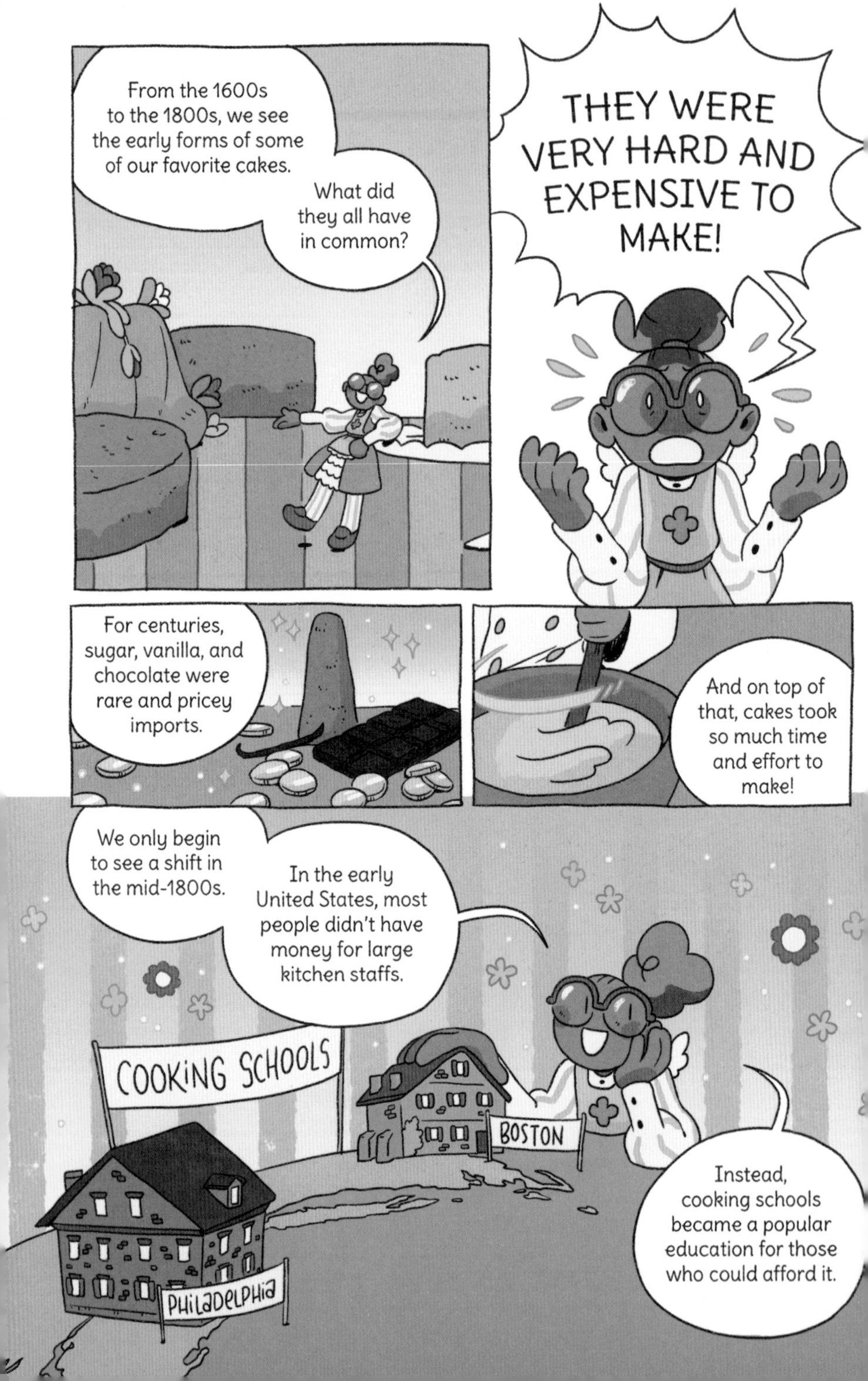
From the 1600s to the 1800s, we see the early forms of some of our favorite cakes.
What did they all have in common?
THEY WERE VERY HARD AND EXPENSIVE TO MAKE!
For centuries, sugar, vanilla, and chocolate were rare and pricey imports.
And on top of that, cakes took so much time and effort to make!
We only begin to see a shift in the mid-1800s.
In the early United States, most people didn't have money for large kitchen staffs.
COOKING SCHOOLS
BOSTON
PHILADELPHIA
Instead, cooking schools became a popular education for those who could afford it.

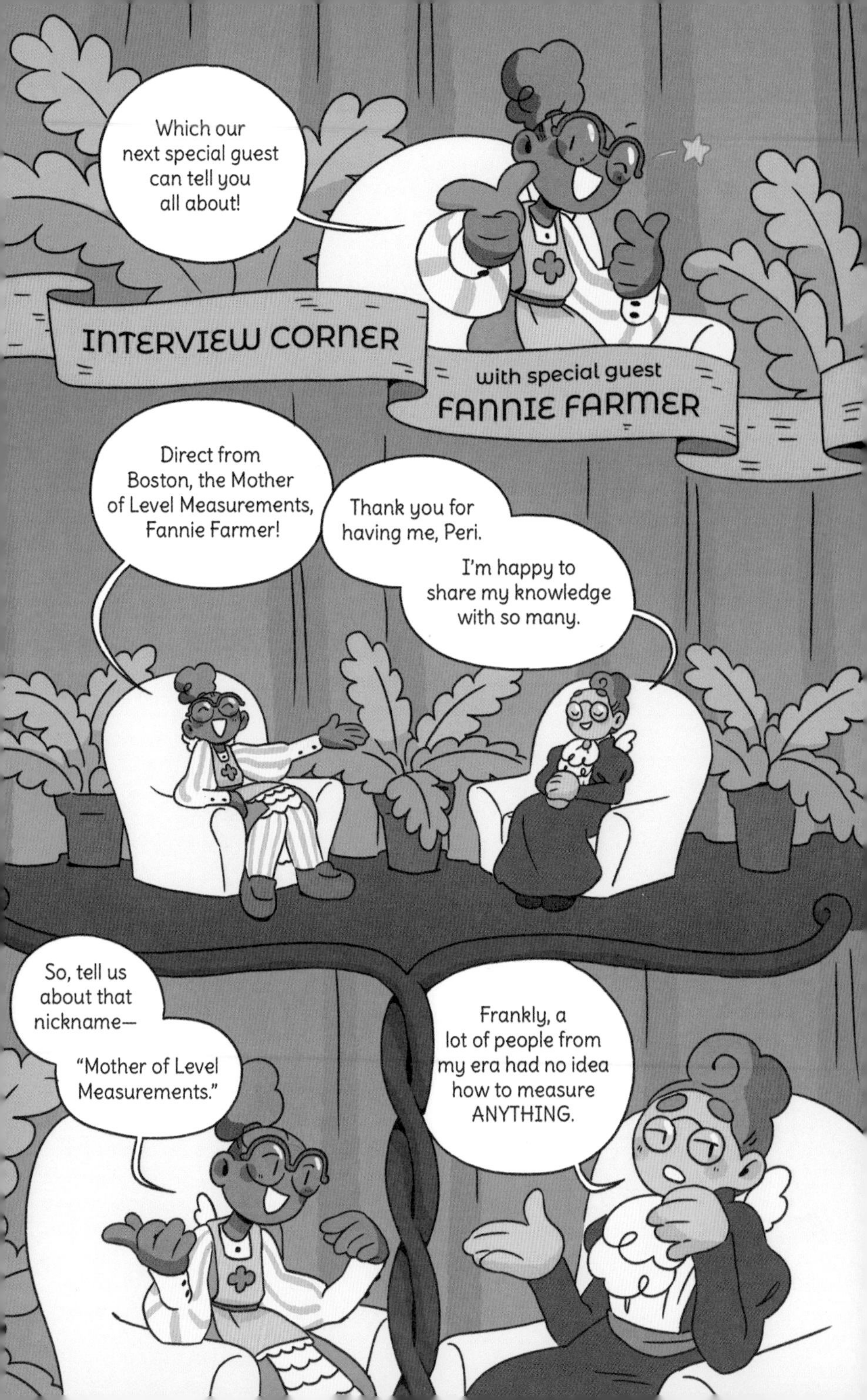
Which our next special guest can tell you all about!
INTERVIEW CORNER
with special guest FANNIE FARMER
Direct from Boston, the Mother of Level Measurements, Fannie Farmer!
Thank you for having me, Peri.
I'm happy to share my knowledge with so many.
So, tell us about that nickname—
"Mother of Level Measurements."
Frankly, a lot of people from my era had no idea how to measure ANYTHING.

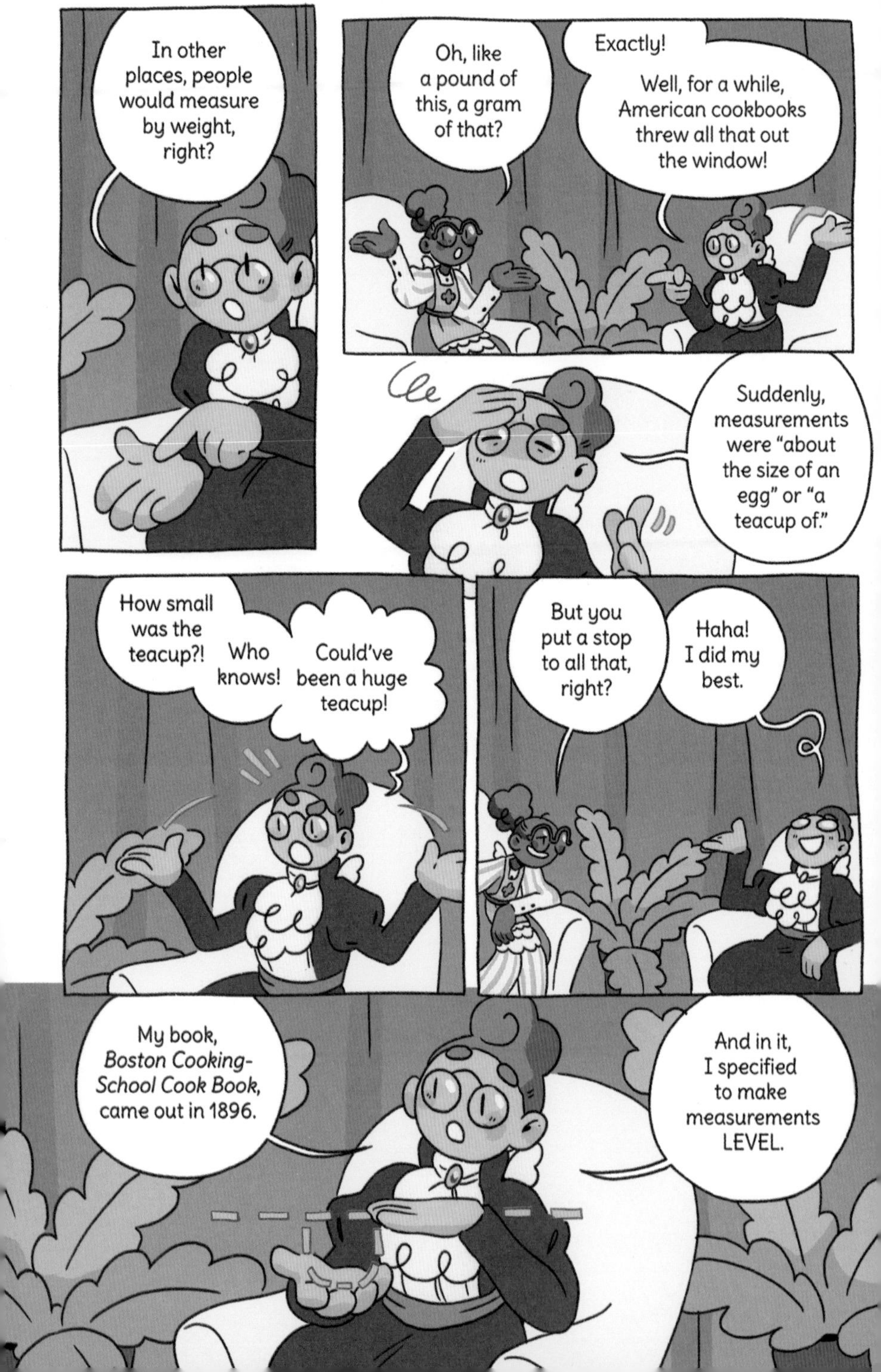
In other places, people would measure by weight, right?
Oh, like a pound of this, a gram of that?
Exactly!
Well, for a while, American cookbooks threw all that out the window!
Suddenly, measurements were "about the size of an egg" or "a teacup of."
How small was the teacup?!
Who knows!
Could've been a huge teacup!
But you put a stop to all that, right?
Haha! I did my best.
My book, *Boston Cooking-School Cook Book*, came out in 1896.
And in it, I specified to make measurements LEVEL.

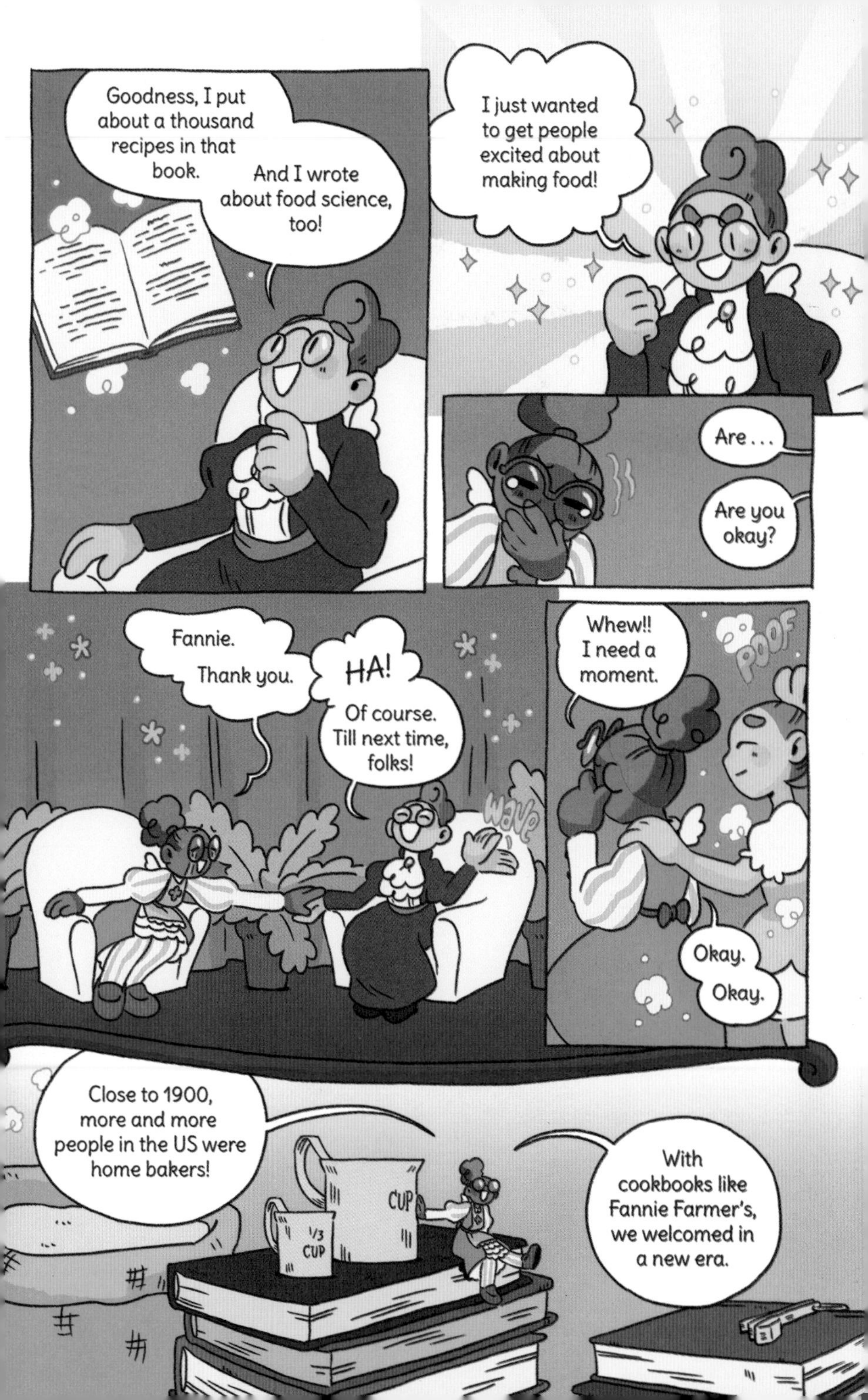
Goodness, I put about a thousand recipes in that book.
And I wrote about food science, too!
I just wanted to get people excited about making food!
Are . . .
Are you okay?
Fannie.
Thank you.
HA!
Of course. Till next time, folks!
WAVE
Whew!! I need a moment.
POOF
Okay.
Okay.
Close to 1900, more and more people in the US were home bakers!
1/3 CUP
CUP
With cookbooks like Fannie Farmer's, we welcomed in a new era.

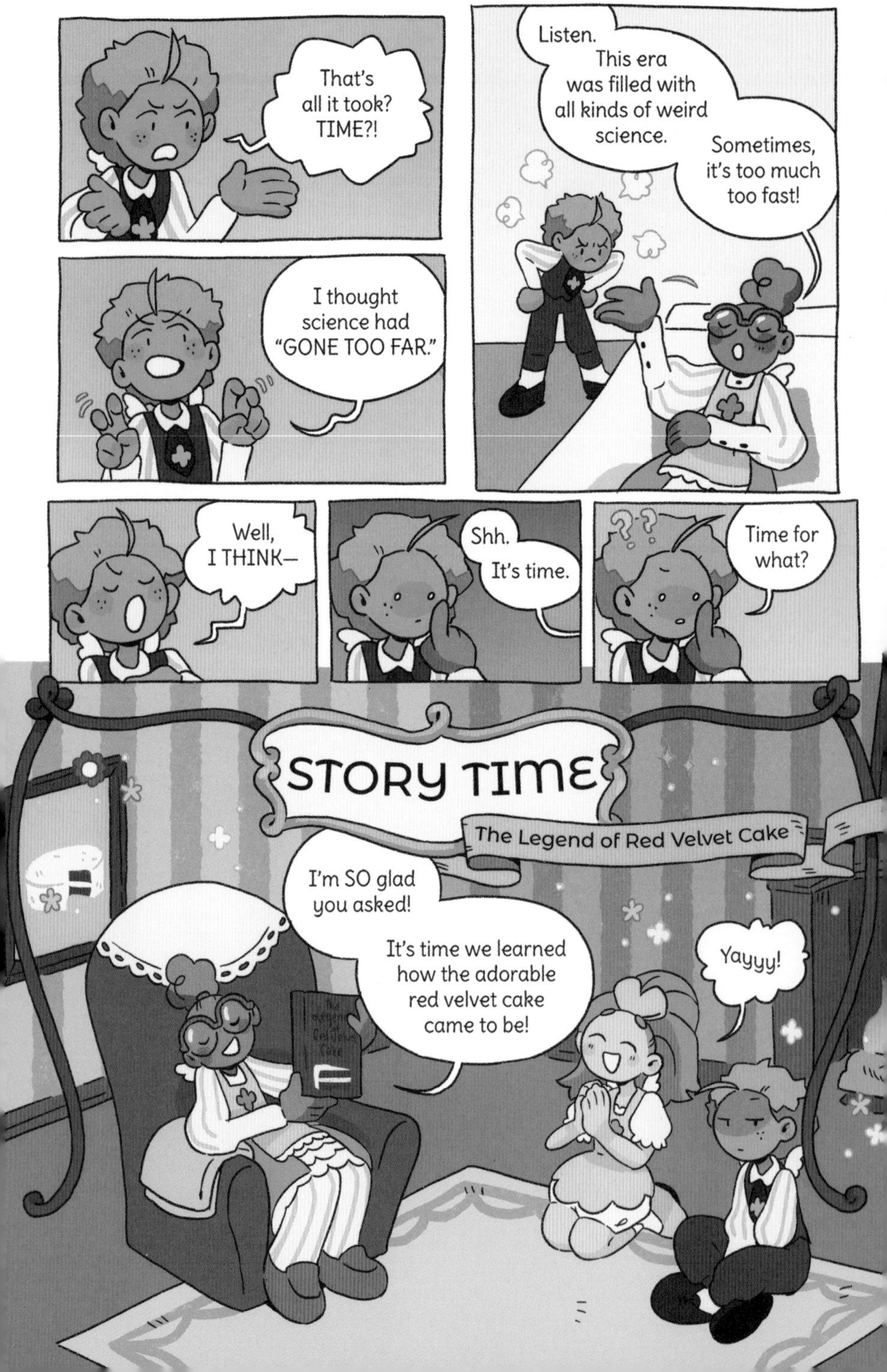

That's all it took? TIME?!
Listen.
This era was filled with all kinds of weird science.
Sometimes, it's too much too fast!
I thought science had "GONE TOO FAR."
Well, I THINK—
Shh.
It's time.
Time for what?
STORY TIME
The Legend of Red Velvet Cake
I'm SO glad you asked!
It's time we learned how the adorable red velvet cake came to be!
Yayyy!

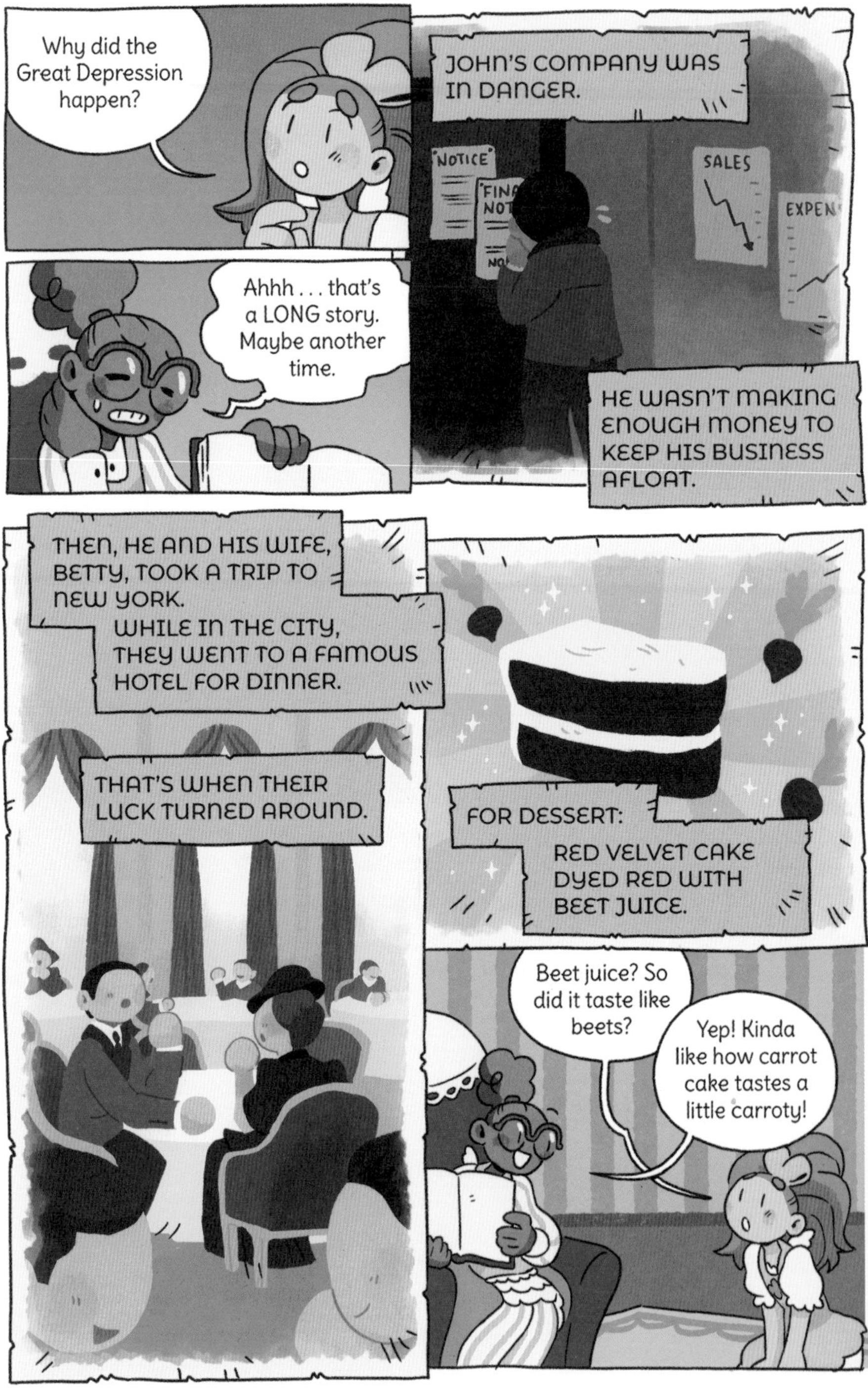
Why did the Great Depression happen?
JOHN'S COMPANY WAS IN DANGER.
NOTICE
SALES
Ahhh . . . that's a LONG story. Maybe another time.
HE WASN'T MAKING ENOUGH MONEY TO KEEP HIS BUSINESS AFLOAT.
THEN, HE AND HIS WIFE, BETTY, TOOK A TRIP TO NEW YORK.
WHILE IN THE CITY, THEY WENT TO A FAMOUS HOTEL FOR DINNER.
THAT'S WHEN THEIR LUCK TURNED AROUND.
FOR DESSERT:
RED VELVET CAKE DYED RED WITH BEET JUICE.
Beet juice? So did it taste like beets?
Yep! Kinda like how carrot cake tastes a little carroty!

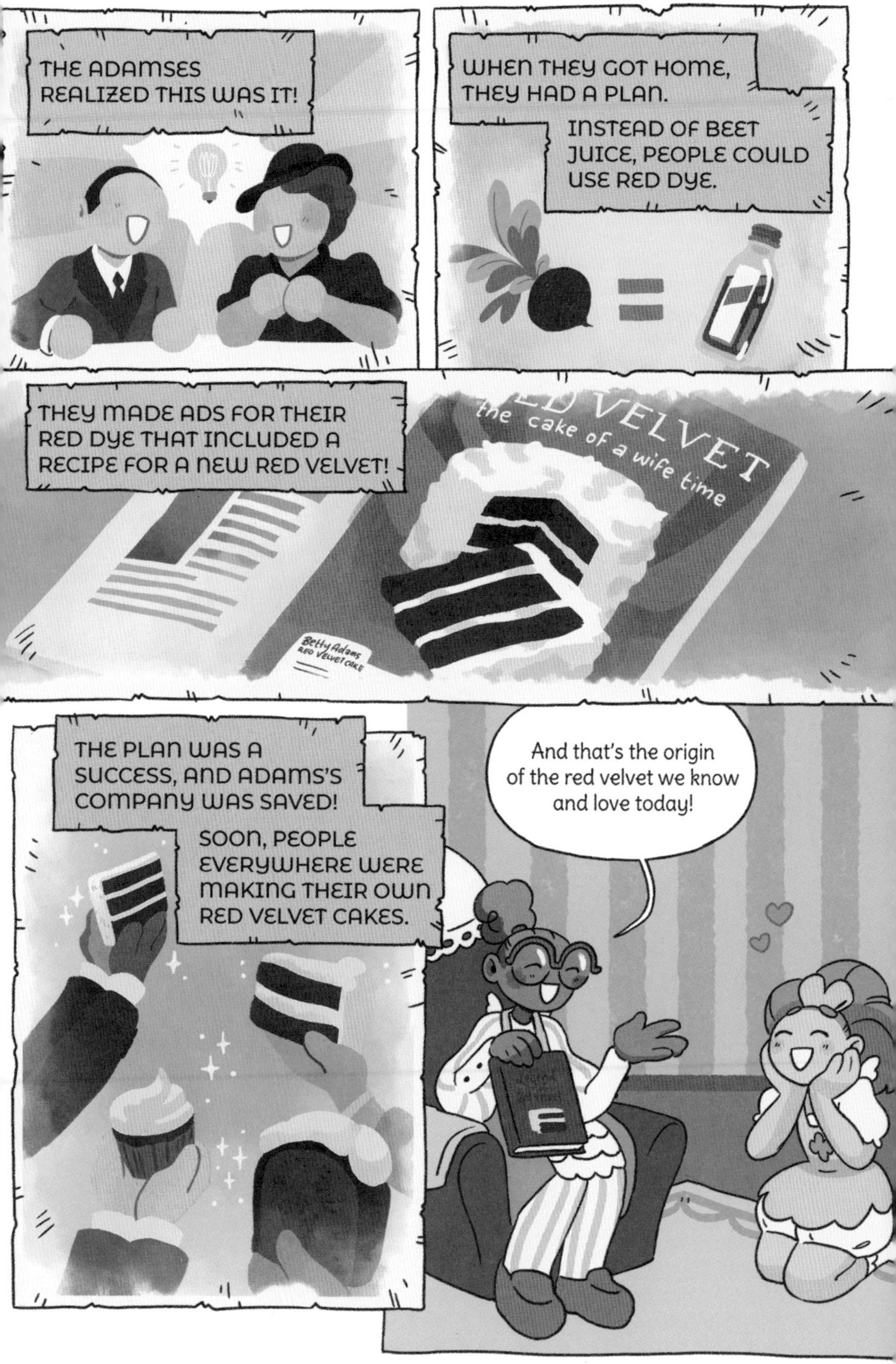
THE ADAMSES REALIZED THIS WAS IT!
WHEN THEY GOT HOME, THEY HAD A PLAN.
INSTEAD OF BEET JUICE, PEOPLE COULD USE RED DYE.
THEY MADE ADS FOR THEIR RED DYE THAT INCLUDED A RECIPE FOR A NEW RED VELVET!
the cake of a wife time
Betty Adams RED VELVET CAKE
THE PLAN WAS A SUCCESS, AND ADAMS'S COMPANY WAS SAVED!
SOON, PEOPLE EVERYWHERE WERE MAKING THEIR OWN RED VELVET CAKES.
And that's the origin of the red velvet we know and love today!

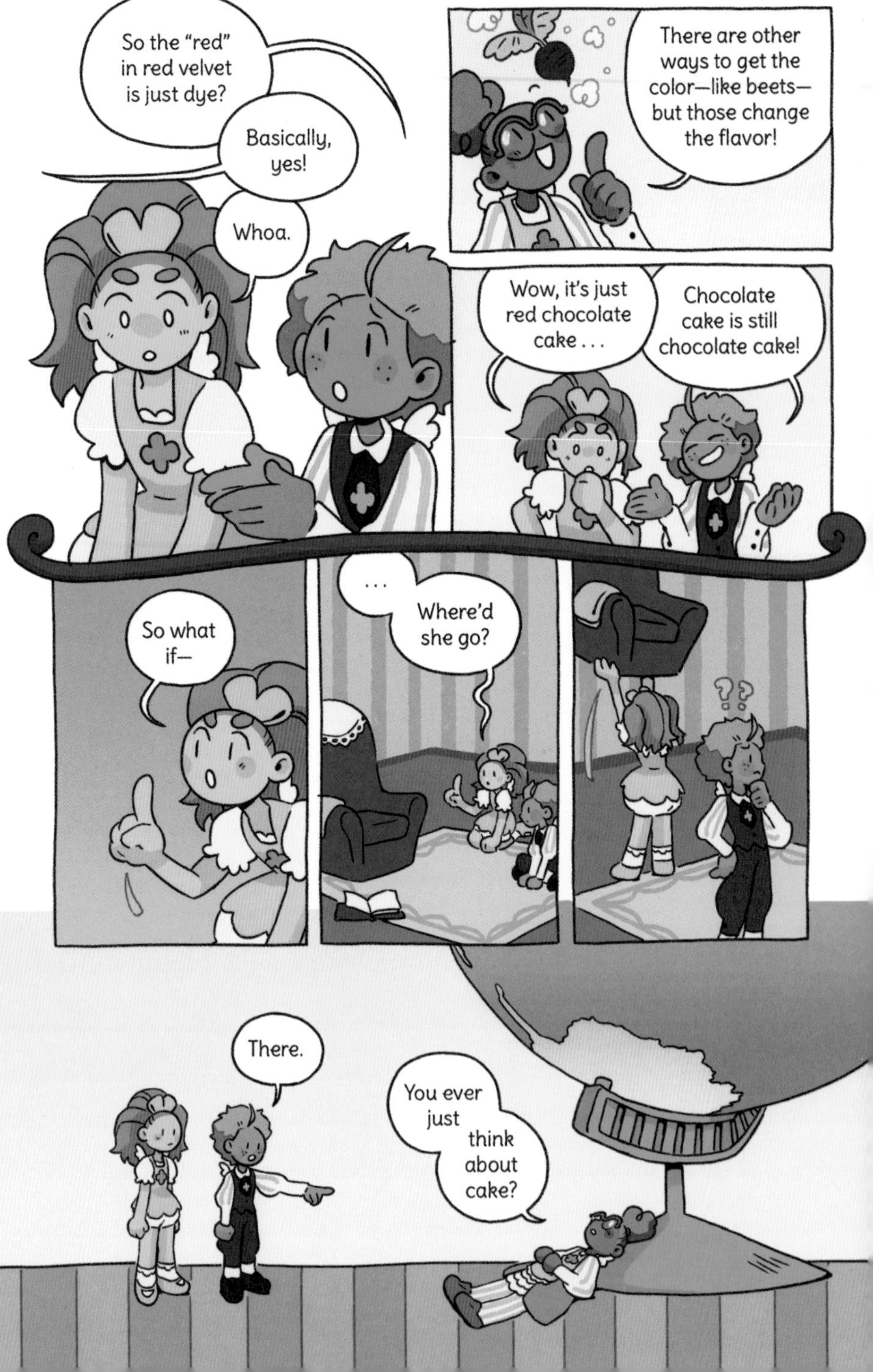
So the "red" in red velvet is just dye?
Basically, yes!
Whoa.
There are other ways to get the color—like beets—but those change the flavor!
Wow, it's just red chocolate cake . . .
Chocolate cake is still chocolate cake!
So what if—
. . .
Where'd she go?
There.
You ever just think about cake?

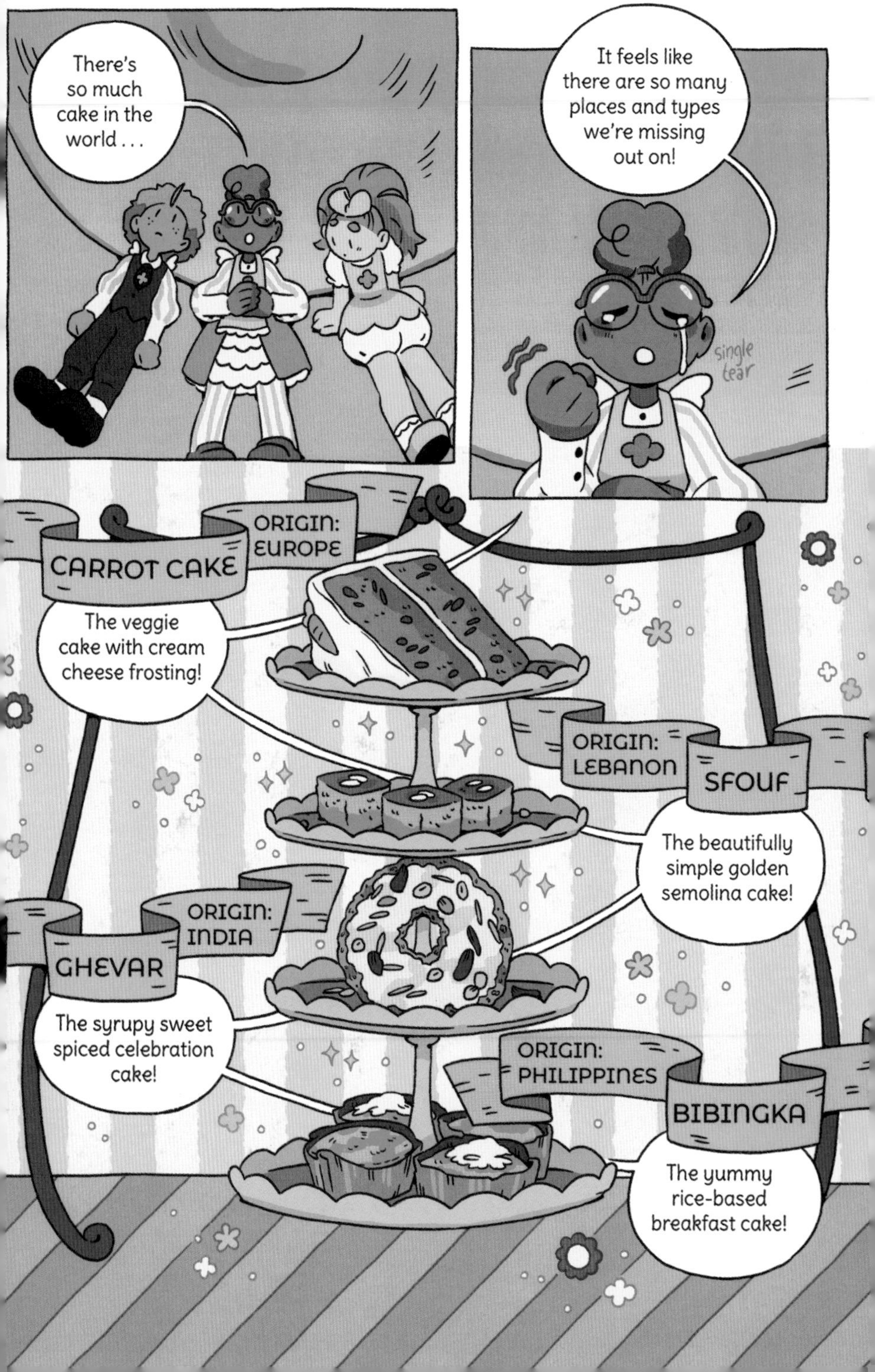

There's so much cake in the world . . .
It feels like there are so many places and types we're missing out on!
single tear
CARROT CAKE
ORIGIN: EUROPE
The veggie cake with cream cheese frosting!
SFOUF
ORIGIN: LEBANON
The beautifully simple golden semolina cake!
GHEVAR
ORIGIN: INDIA
The syrupy sweet spiced celebration cake!
BIBINGKA
ORIGIN: PHILIPPINES
The yummy rice-based breakfast cake!

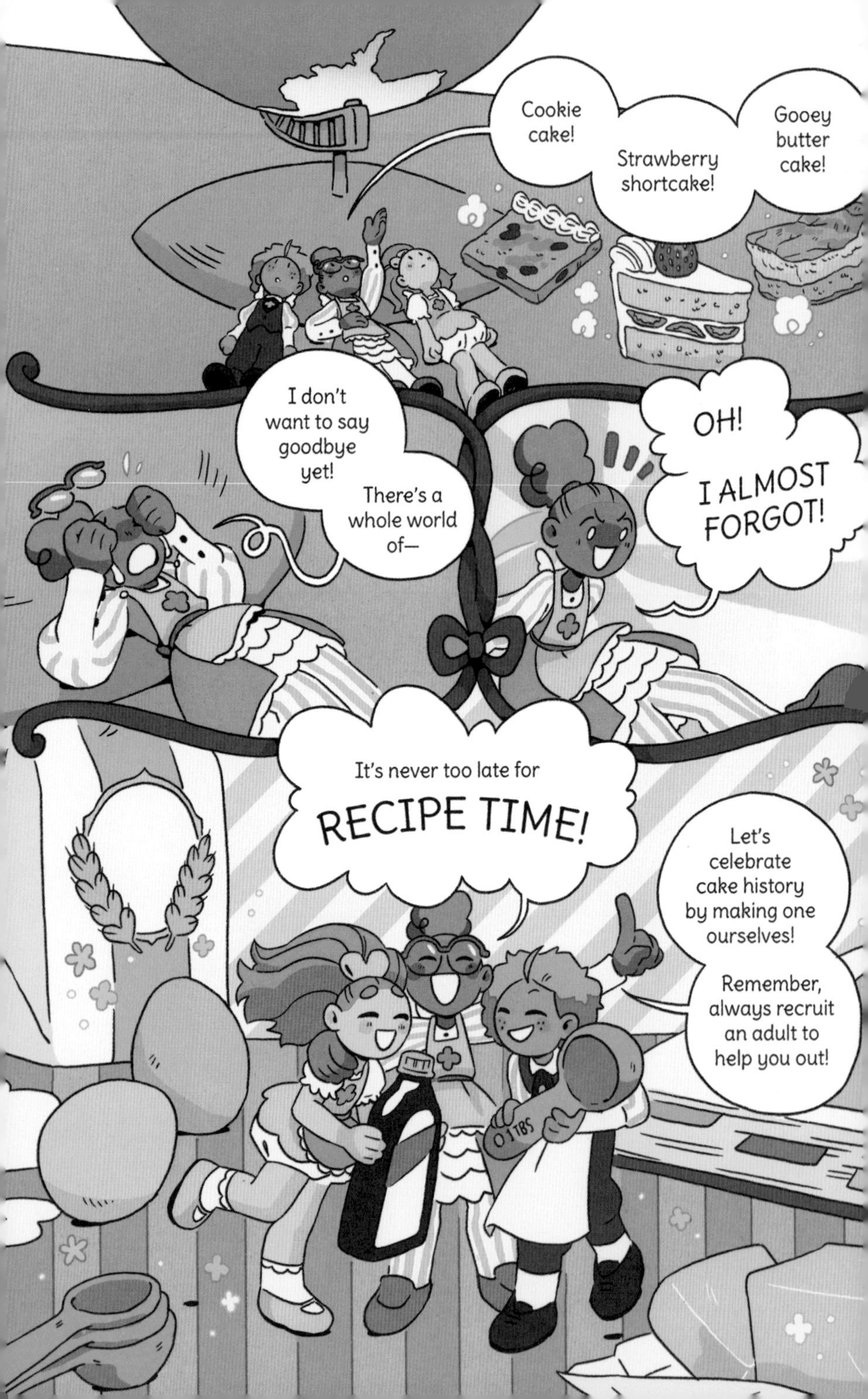
Cookie cake!
Strawberry shortcake!
Gooey butter cake!
I don't want to say goodbye yet!
There's a whole world of—
OH!
I ALMOST FORGOT!
It's never too late for
RECIPE TIME!
Let's celebrate cake history by making one ourselves!
Remember, always recruit an adult to help you out!
1 TBS

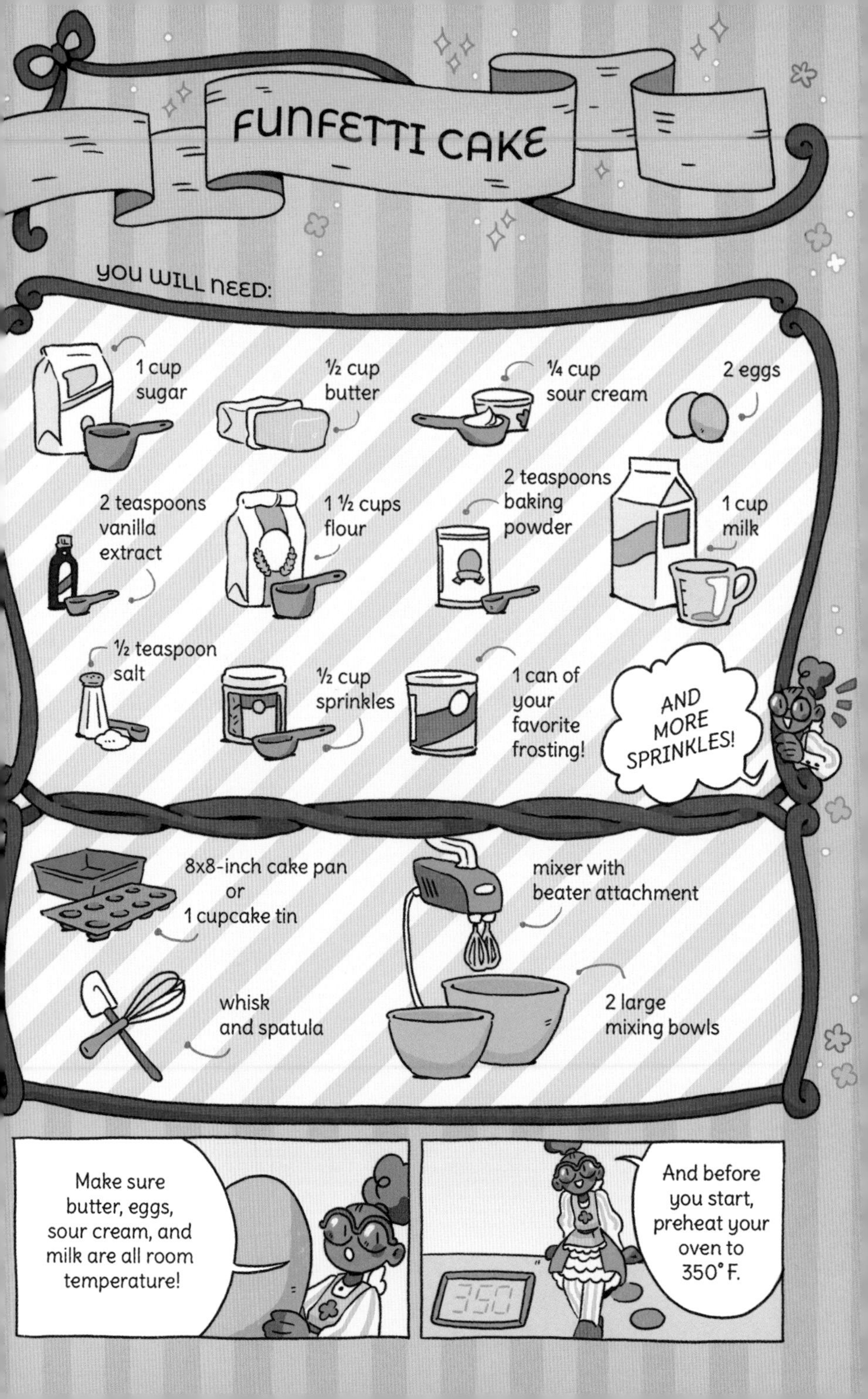
FUNFETTI CAKE
YOU WILL NEED:
1 cup sugar
½ cup butter
¼ cup sour cream
2 eggs
2 teaspoons vanilla extract
1 ½ cups flour
2 teaspoons baking powder
1 cup milk
½ teaspoon salt
½ cup sprinkles
1 can of your favorite frosting!
AND MORE SPRINKLES!
8x8-inch cake pan or 1 cupcake tin
mixer with beater attachment
whisk and spatula
2 large mixing bowls
Make sure butter, eggs, sour cream, and milk are all room temperature!
350
And before you start, preheat your oven to 350° F.

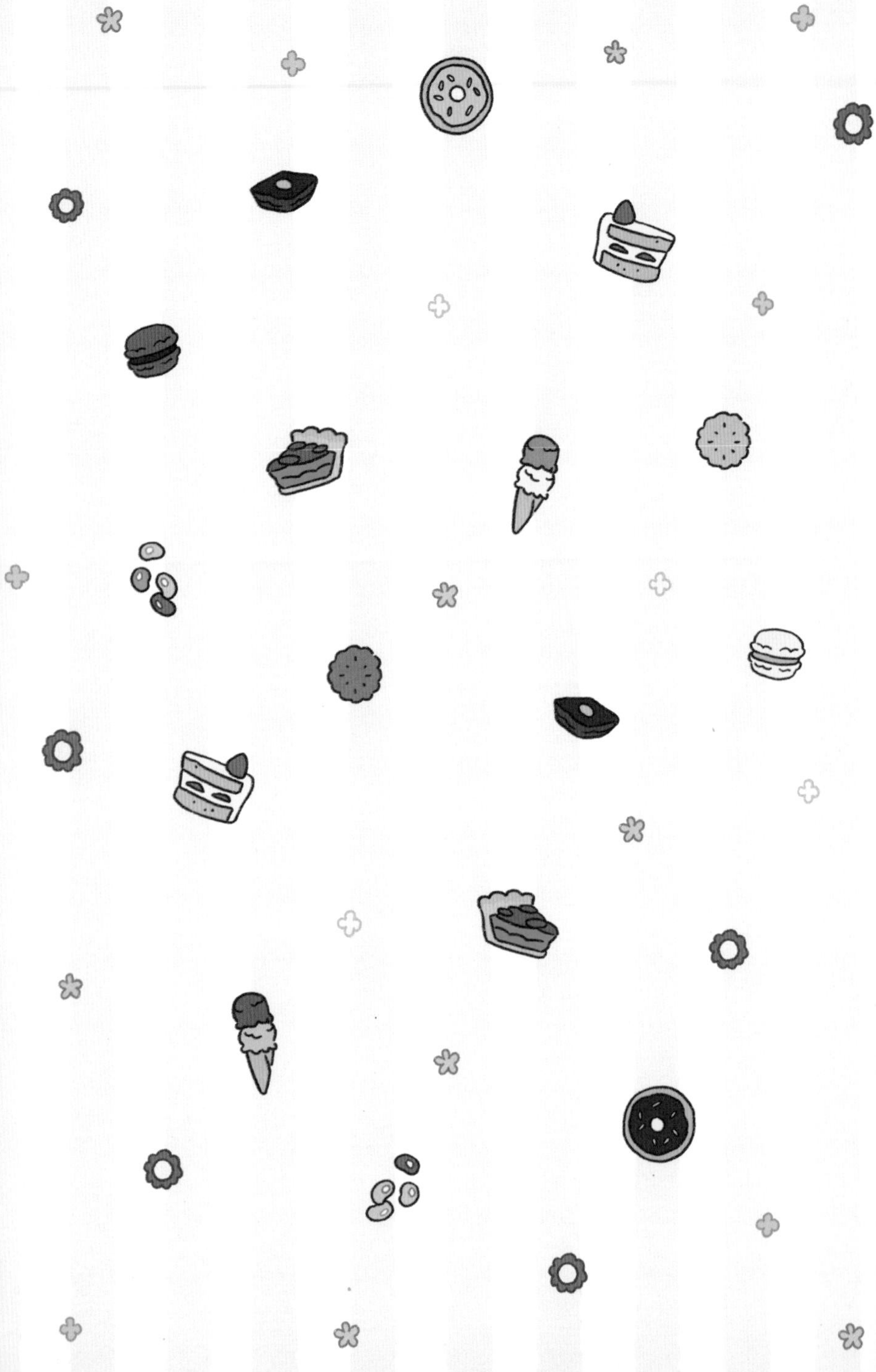

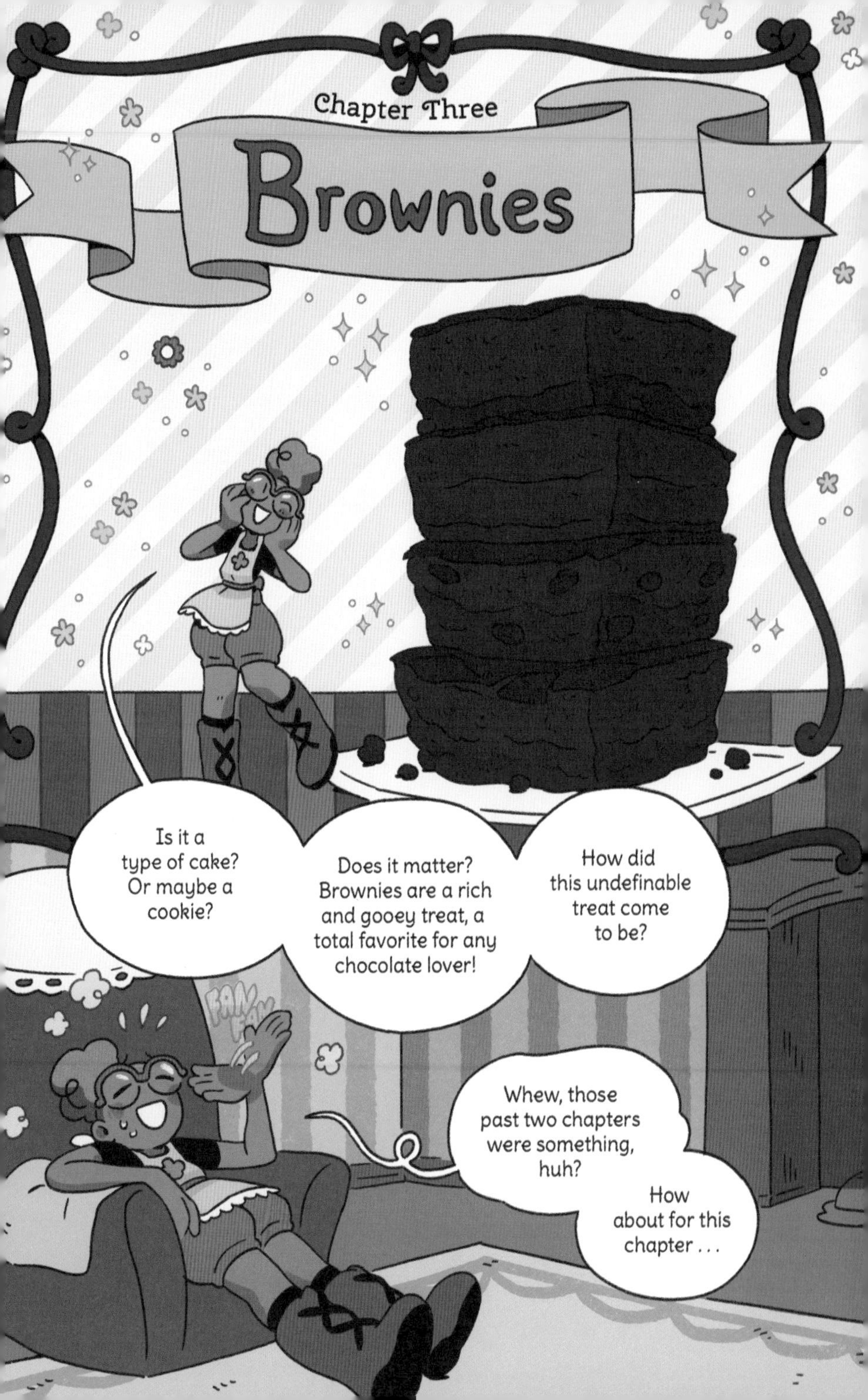
Chapter Three
Brownies
Is it a type of cake? Or maybe a cookie?
Does it matter? Brownies are a rich and gooey treat, a total favorite for any chocolate lover!
How did this undefinable treat come to be?
Whew, those past two chapters were something, huh?
How about for this chapter . . .

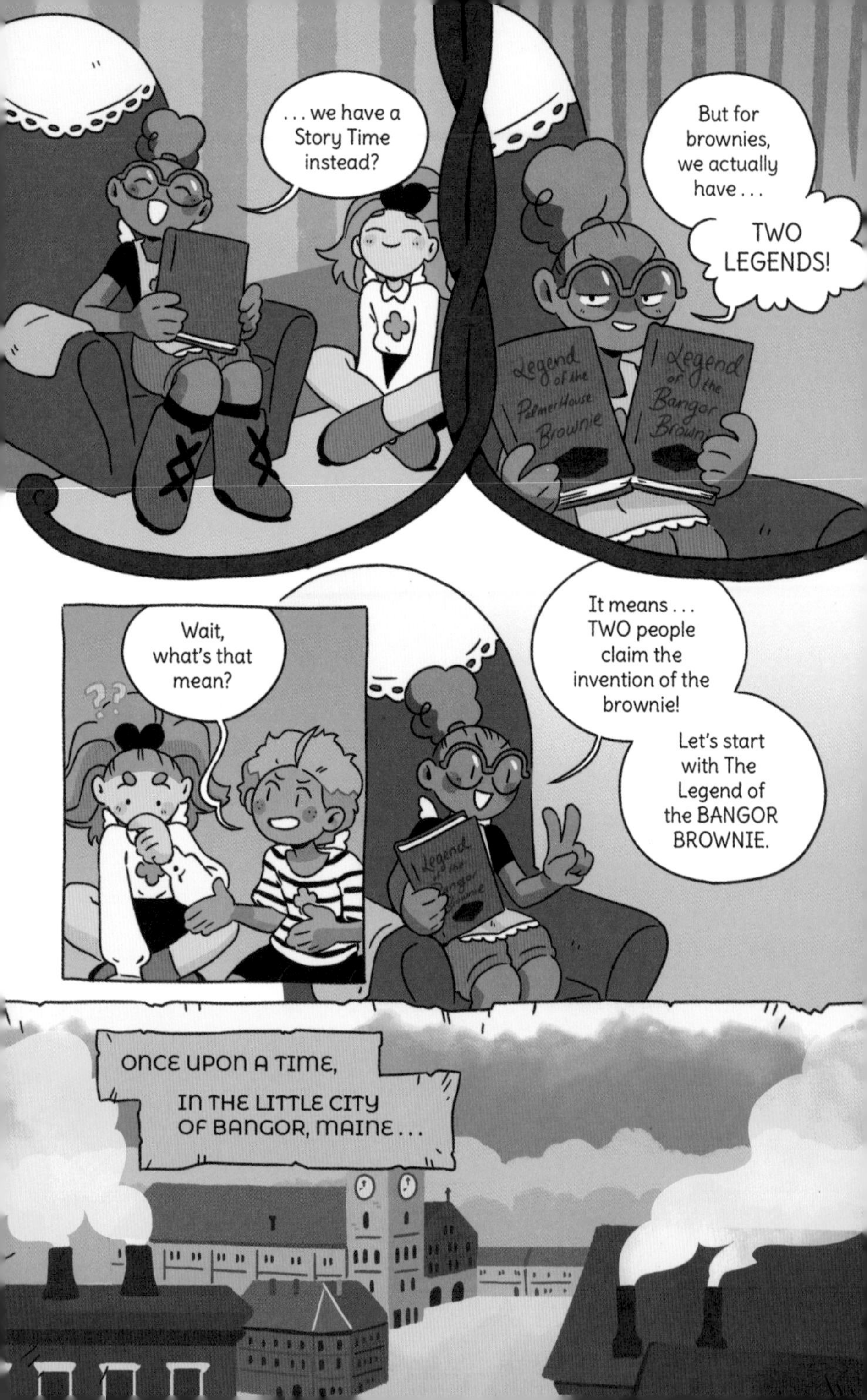

. . . we have a Story Time instead?
But for brownies, we actually have . . .
TWO LEGENDS!
Legend of the Palmer House Brownie
Legend of the Bangor Brownie
Wait, what's that mean?
??
It means . . . TWO people claim the invention of the brownie!
Let's start with The Legend of the BANGOR BROWNIE.
Legend of the Bangor Brownie
ONCE UPON A TIME,
IN THE LITTLE CITY OF BANGOR, MAINE . . .

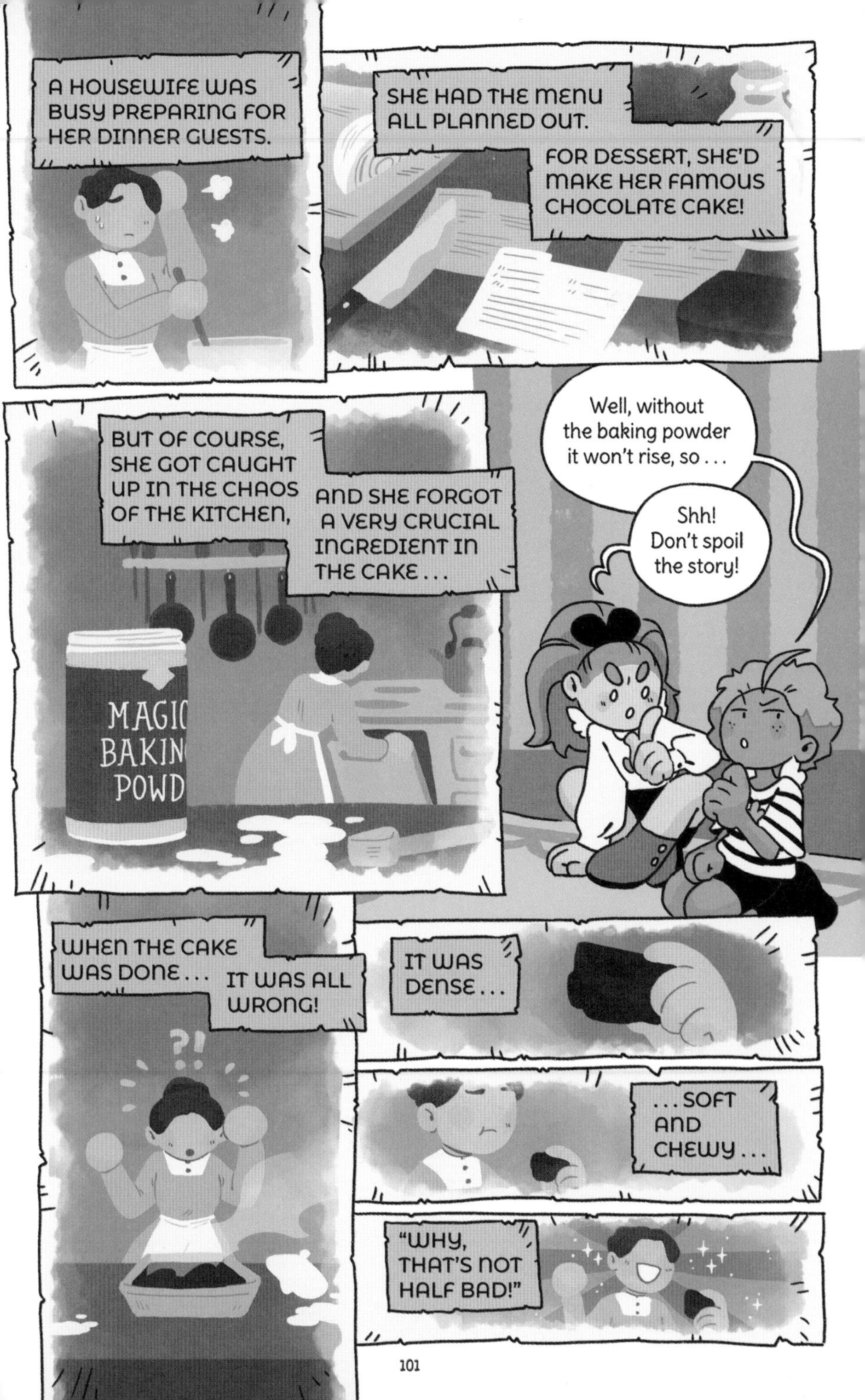
A HOUSEWIFE WAS BUSY PREPARING FOR HER DINNER GUESTS.
SHE HAD THE MENU ALL PLANNED OUT.
FOR DESSERT, SHE'D MAKE HER FAMOUS CHOCOLATE CAKE!
BUT OF COURSE, SHE GOT CAUGHT UP IN THE CHAOS OF THE KITCHEN,
AND SHE FORGOT A VERY CRUCIAL INGREDIENT IN THE CAKE . . .
MAGIC BAKING POWD
Well, without the baking powder it won't rise, so . . .
Shh! Don't spoil the story!
WHEN THE CAKE WAS DONE . . .
IT WAS ALL WRONG!
?!
IT WAS DENSE . . .
. . . SOFT AND CHEWY . . .
"WHY, THAT'S NOT HALF BAD!"

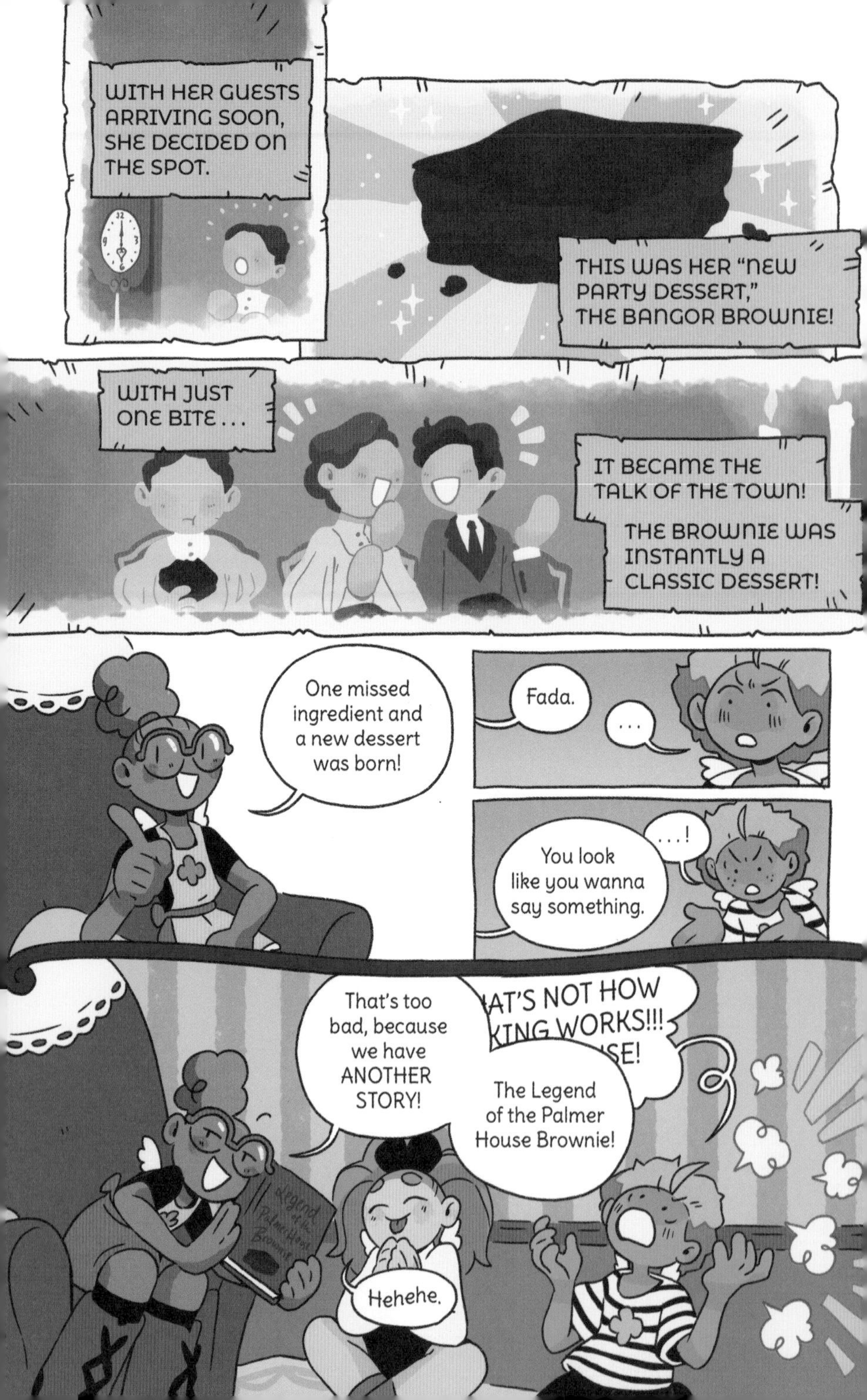
WITH HER GUESTS ARRIVING SOON, SHE DECIDED ON THE SPOT.
THIS WAS HER "NEW PARTY DESSERT," THE BANGOR BROWNIE!
WITH JUST ONE BITE . . .
IT BECAME THE TALK OF THE TOWN!
THE BROWNIE WAS INSTANTLY A CLASSIC DESSERT!
One missed ingredient and a new dessert was born!
Fada.
. . .
. . . !
You look like you wanna say something.
That's too bad, because we have ANOTHER STORY!
AT'S NOT HOW
KING WORKS!!!
SE!
The Legend of the Palmer House Brownie!
Hehehe.

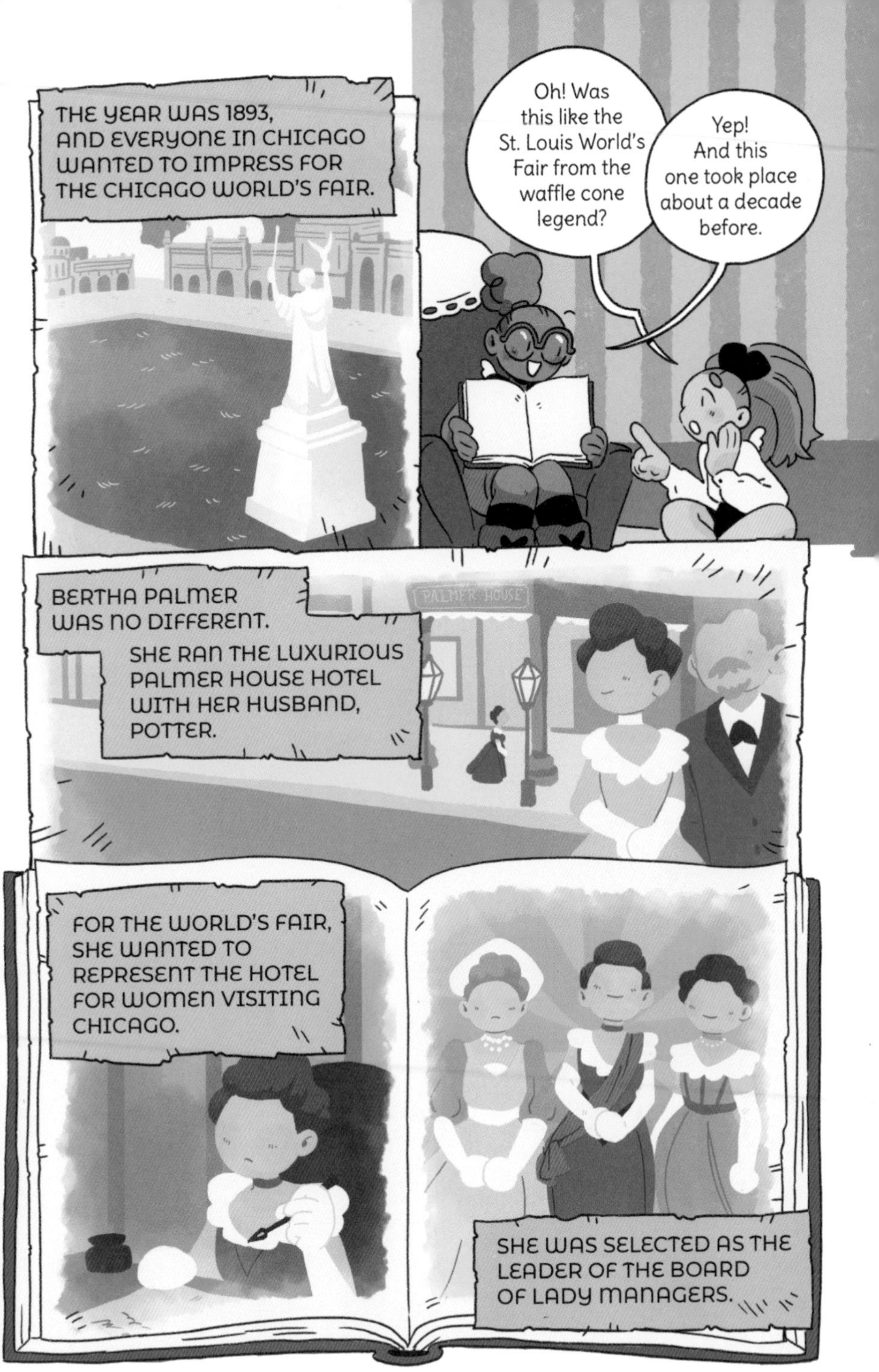
THE YEAR WAS 1893, AND EVERYONE IN CHICAGO WANTED TO IMPRESS FOR THE CHICAGO WORLD'S FAIR.
Oh! Was this like the St. Louis World's Fair from the waffle cone legend?
Yep! And this one took place about a decade before.
BERTHA PALMER WAS NO DIFFERENT.
SHE RAN THE LUXURIOUS PALMER HOUSE HOTEL WITH HER HUSBAND, POTTER.
PALMER HOUSE
FOR THE WORLD'S FAIR, SHE WANTED TO REPRESENT THE HOTEL FOR WOMEN VISITING CHICAGO.
SHE WAS SELECTED AS THE LEADER OF THE BOARD OF LADY MANAGERS.

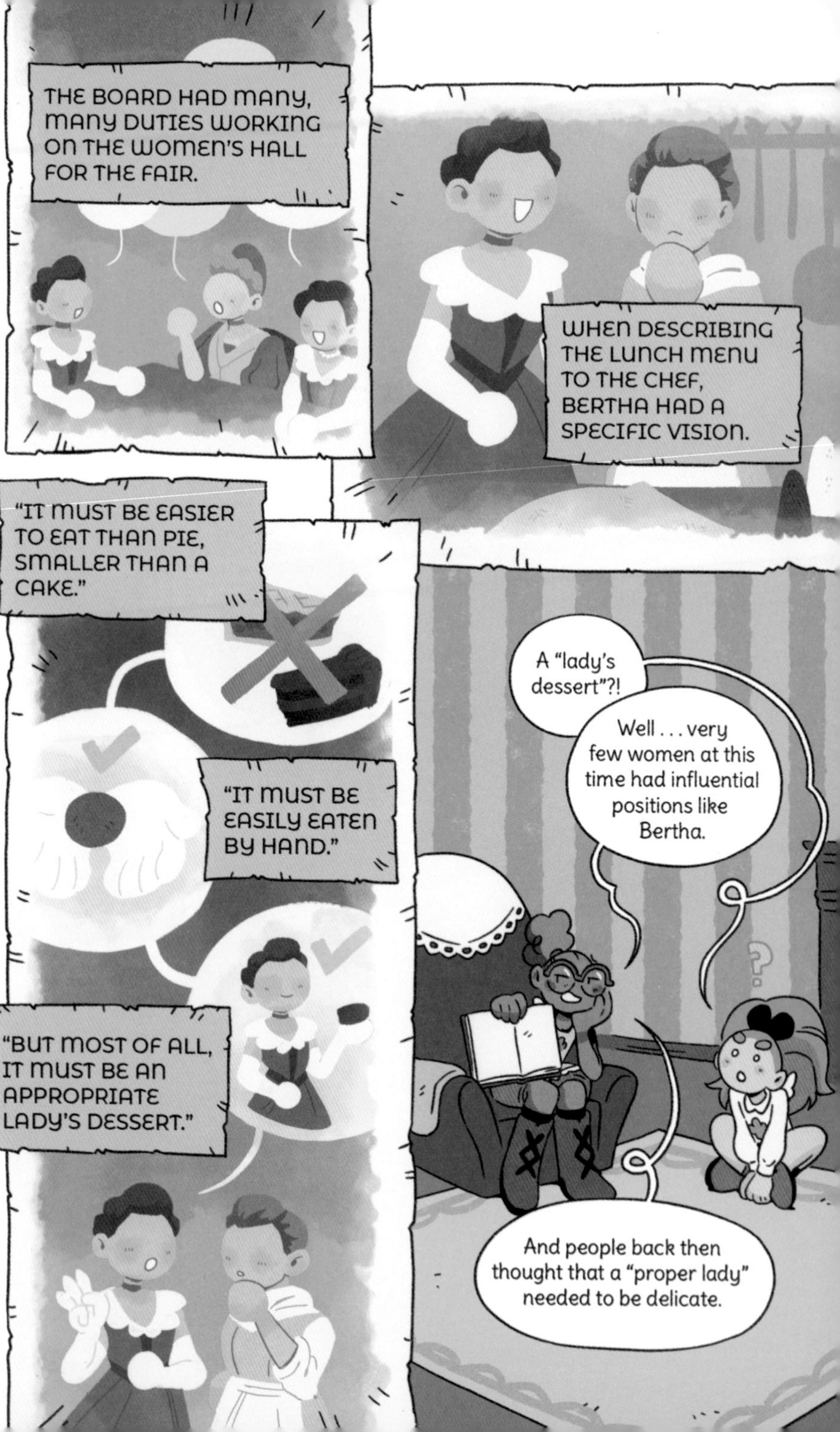
THE BOARD HAD MANY, MANY DUTIES WORKING ON THE WOMEN'S HALL FOR THE FAIR.
WHEN DESCRIBING THE LUNCH MENU TO THE CHEF, BERTHA HAD A SPECIFIC VISION.
"IT MUST BE EASIER TO EAT THAN PIE, SMALLER THAN A CAKE."
"IT MUST BE EASILY EATEN BY HAND."
"BUT MOST OF ALL, IT MUST BE AN APPROPRIATE LADY'S DESSERT."
A "lady's dessert"?!
Well . . . very few women at this time had influential positions like Bertha.
And people back then thought that a "proper lady" needed to be delicate.

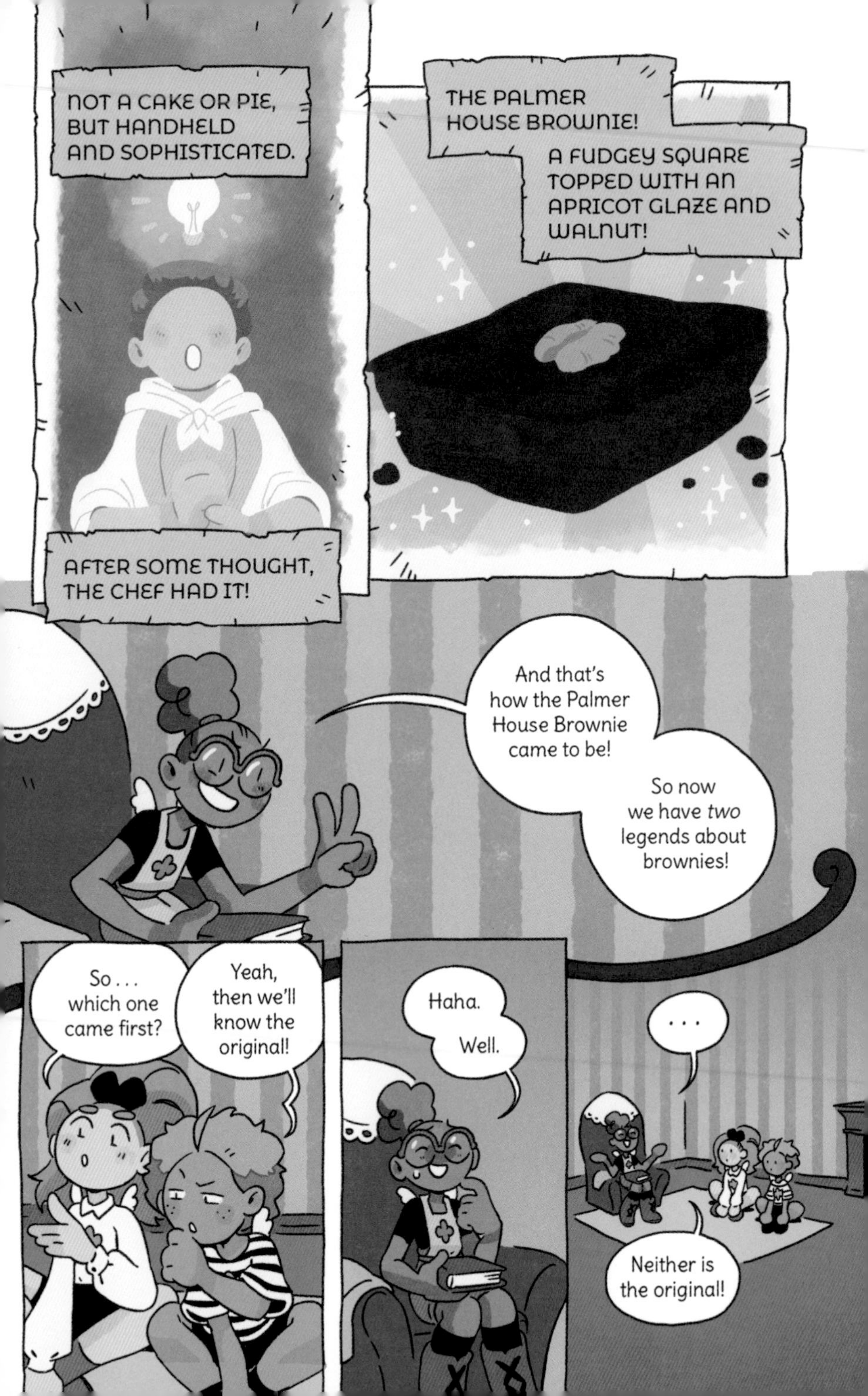
NOT A CAKE OR PIE, BUT HANDHELD AND SOPHISTICATED.
AFTER SOME THOUGHT, THE CHEF HAD IT!
THE PALMER HOUSE BROWNIE!
A FUDGEY SQUARE TOPPED WITH AN APRICOT GLAZE AND WALNUT!
And that's how the Palmer House Brownie came to be!
So now we have *two* legends about brownies!
So . . . which one came first?
Yeah, then we'll know the original!
Haha.
Well.
. . .
Neither is the original!

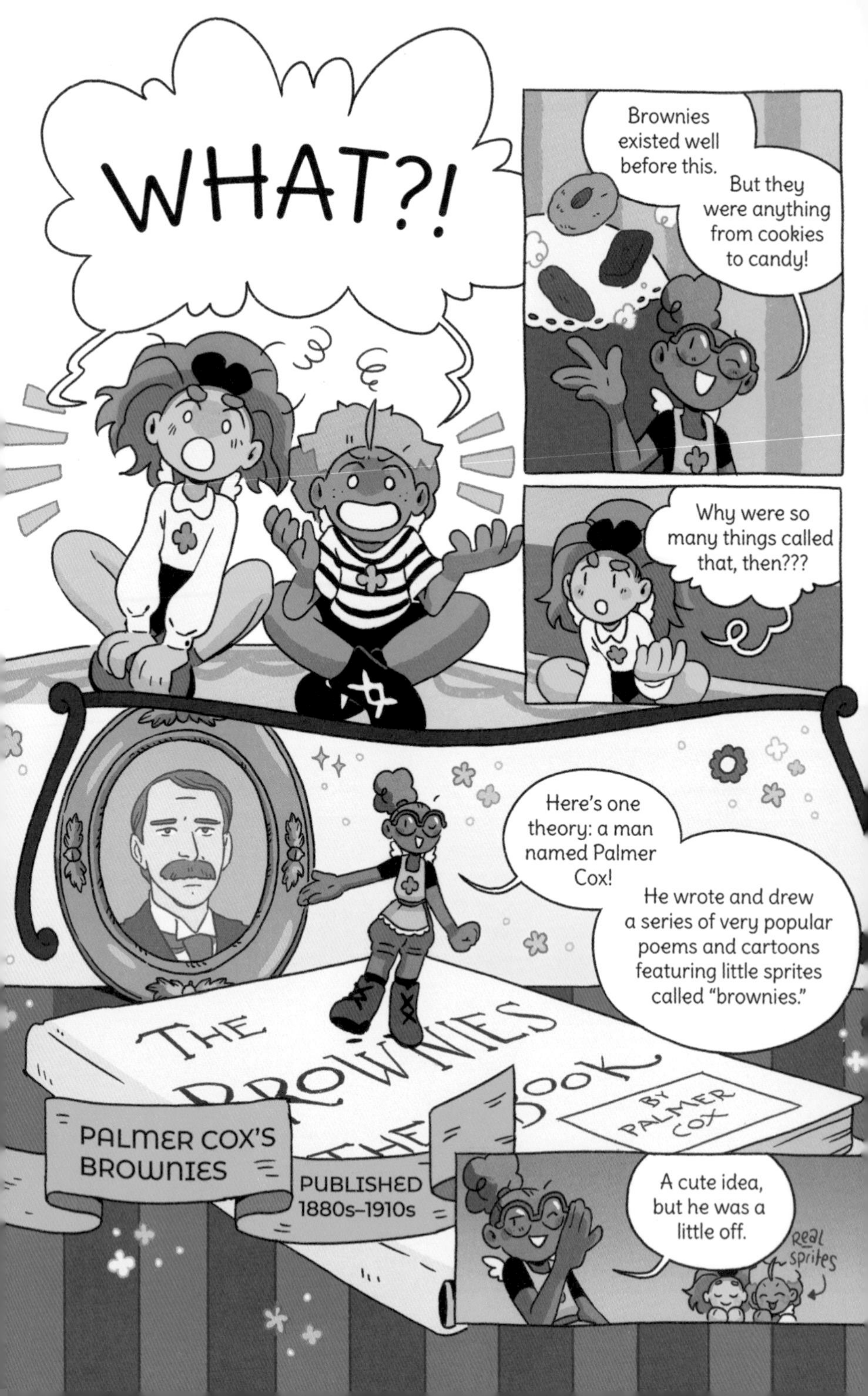
WHAT?!
Brownies existed well before this.
But they were anything from cookies to candy!
Why were so many things called that, then???
Here's one theory: a man named Palmer Cox!
He wrote and drew a series of very popular poems and cartoons featuring little sprites called "brownies."
THE BROWNIES THE BOOK
BY PALMER COX
PALMER COX'S BROWNIES
PUBLISHED 1880s–1910s
A cute idea, but he was a little off.
Real sprites

The Abridged
Atlas of Donut History

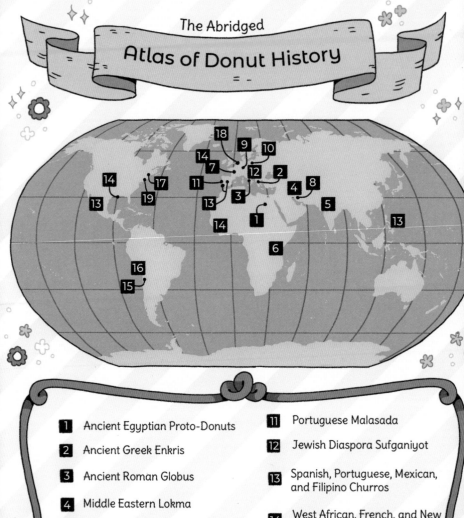

1   Ancient Egyptian Proto-Donuts

2   Ancient Greek Enkris

3   Ancient Roman Globus

4   Middle Eastern Lokma

5   Indian Gulab Jamun

6   African Great Lakes Mandazi

7   French Nun's Farts

8   Islamic World Jalebi

9   German Fastnachts

10   Polish Pączki

11   Portuguese Malasada

12   Jewish Diaspora Sufganiyot

13   Spanish, Portuguese, Mexican, and Filipino Churros

14   West African, French, and New Orleans Calas and Beignets

15   Chilean Calzones Rotos

16   Chilean and Peruvian Picarones

17   Captain Hanson Gregory

18   Dutch Olie Koeken

19   Adolph Levitt's Donut Machine

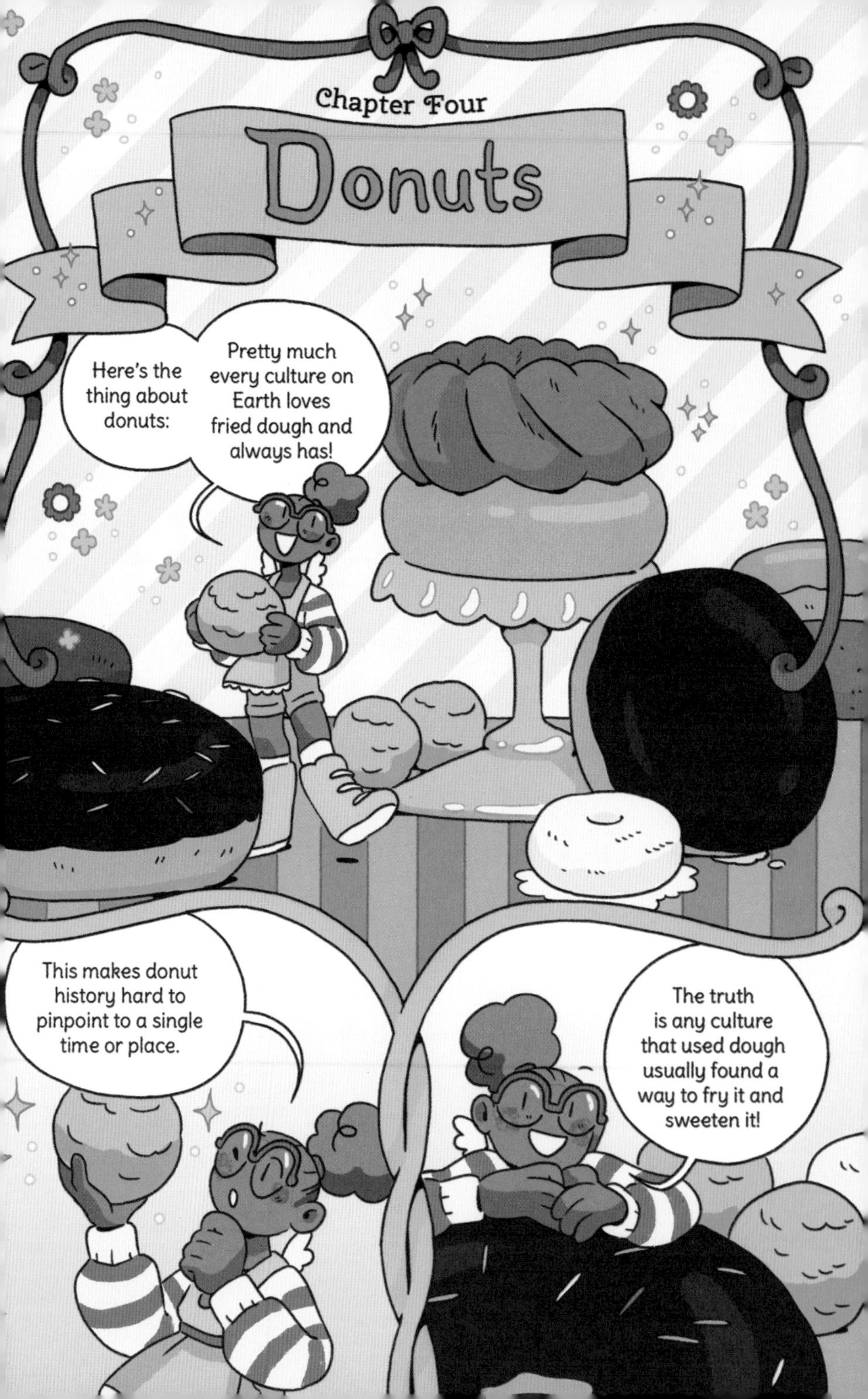
Chapter Four
Donuts
Here's the thing about donuts:
Pretty much every culture on Earth loves fried dough and always has!
This makes donut history hard to pinpoint to a single time or place.
The truth is any culture that used dough usually found a way to fry it and sweeten it!

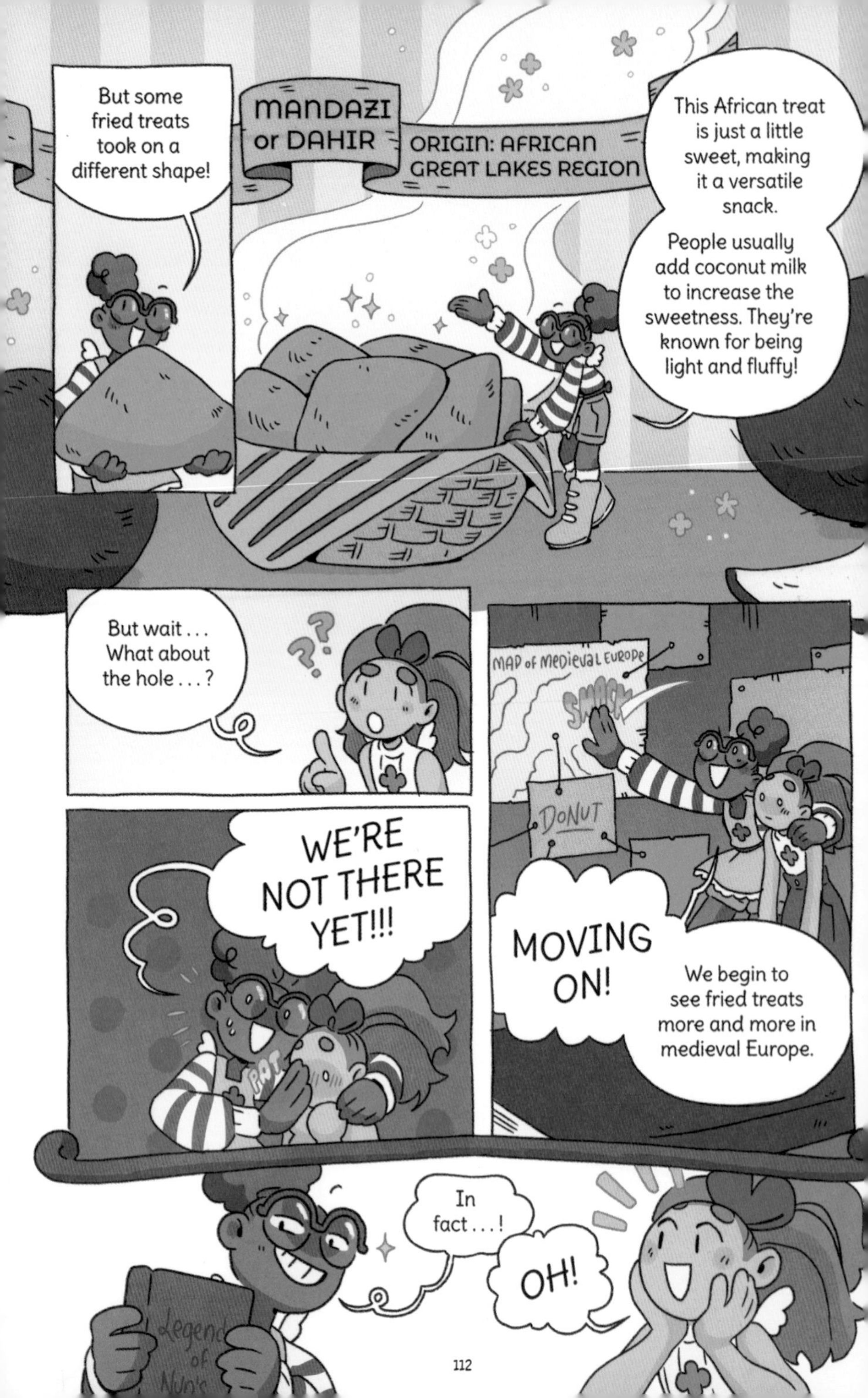
But some fried treats took on a different shape!
MANDAZI or DAHIR
ORIGIN: AFRICAN GREAT LAKES REGION
This African treat is just a little sweet, making it a versatile snack.
People usually add coconut milk to increase the sweetness. They're known for being light and fluffy!
But wait . . . What about the hole . . . ?
MAP of MEDIEVAL EUROPE
SMACK
DONUT
WE'RE NOT THERE YET!!!
PAT
MOVING ON!
We begin to see fried treats more and more in medieval Europe.
In fact . . . !
OH!

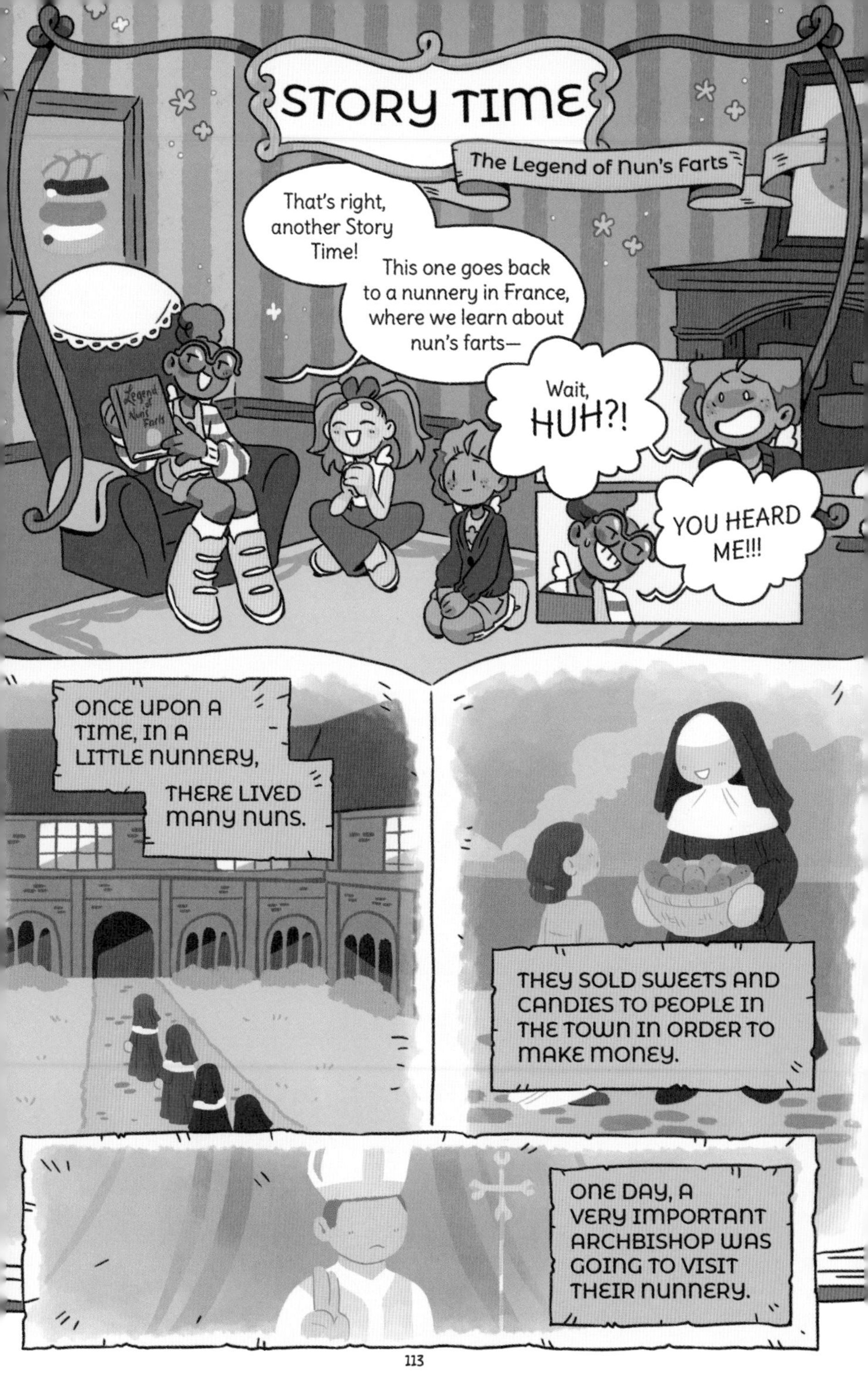
STORY TIME
The Legend of Nun's Farts
That's right, another Story Time!
This one goes back to a nunnery in France, where we learn about nun's farts—
Wait, HUH?!
YOU HEARD ME!!!
Legend of Nun's Farts
ONCE UPON A TIME, IN A LITTLE NUNNERY,
THERE LIVED MANY NUNS.
THEY SOLD SWEETS AND CANDIES TO PEOPLE IN THE TOWN IN ORDER TO MAKE MONEY.
ONE DAY, A VERY IMPORTANT ARCHBISHOP WAS GOING TO VISIT THEIR NUNNERY.

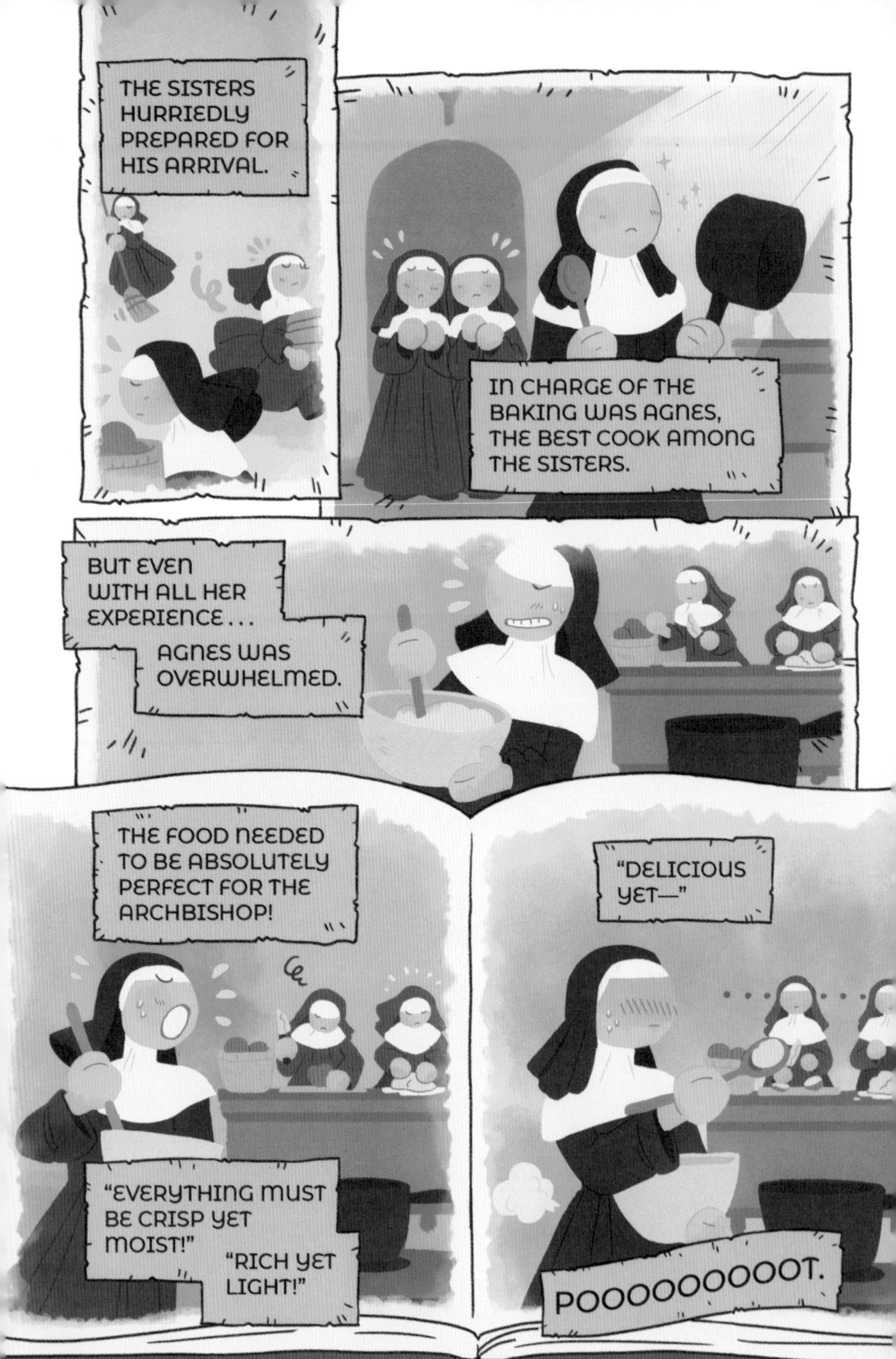
THE SISTERS HURRIEDLY PREPARED FOR HIS ARRIVAL.
IN CHARGE OF THE BAKING WAS AGNES, THE BEST COOK AMONG THE SISTERS.
BUT EVEN WITH ALL HER EXPERIENCE . . .
AGNES WAS OVERWHELMED.
THE FOOD NEEDED TO BE ABSOLUTELY PERFECT FOR THE ARCHBISHOP!
"EVERYTHING MUST BE CRISP YET MOIST!"
"RICH YET LIGHT!"
"DELICIOUS YET—"
POOOOOOOOOT.

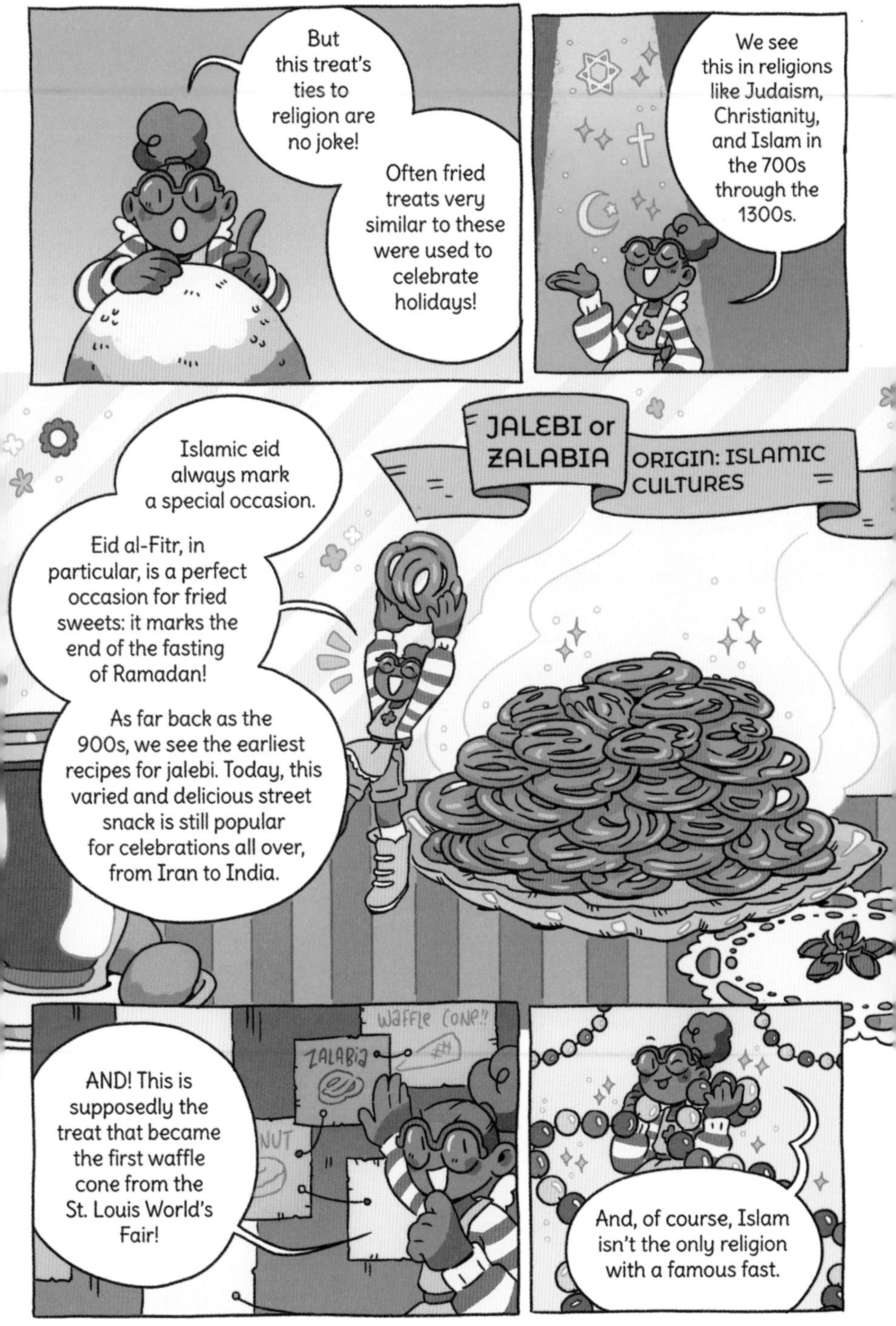
But this treat's ties to religion are no joke!
Often fried treats very similar to these were used to celebrate holidays!
We see this in religions like Judaism, Christianity, and Islam in the 700s through the 1300s.
JALEBI or ZALABIA
ORIGIN: ISLAMIC CULTURES
Islamic eid always mark a special occasion.
Eid al-Fitr, in particular, is a perfect occasion for fried sweets: it marks the end of the fasting of Ramadan!
As far back as the 900s, we see the earliest recipes for jalebi. Today, this varied and delicious street snack is still popular for celebrations all over, from Iran to India.
WAFFLE CONE!!
ZALABIA
AND! This is supposedly the treat that became the first waffle cone from the St. Louis World's Fair!
And, of course, Islam isn't the only religion with a famous fast.

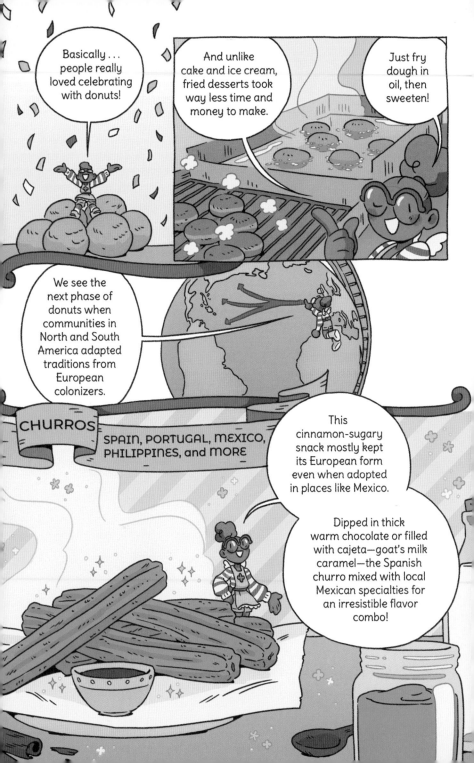

The Abridged
Atlas of Pie History

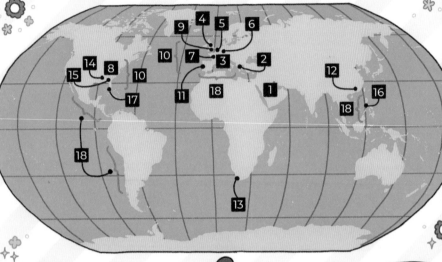

1. Arabic Peninsula Pastry Dough

2. Greek Phyllo Dough

3. European Coffyns

4. Tartys in Applys and *Forme of Cury*

5. Dutch Appeltaarten

6. German Apfeltorte and Apfelstrudel

7. French Tarte Tatin

8. American Blackberry and Blueberry Pie

9. Hannah Glasse's *The Art of Cookery Made Plain and Easy*

10. Areas of Pumpkin and Sweet Potato Pie Traditions

11. Portuguese Pastel de Nata

12. Chinese Egg Tart

13. South African Melktert

14. American Buttermilk Pie

15. American Pecan Pie

16. Filipino Buko Pie

17. American Key Lime Pie

18. Areas of Empanada Traditions

Chapter Five
Pie

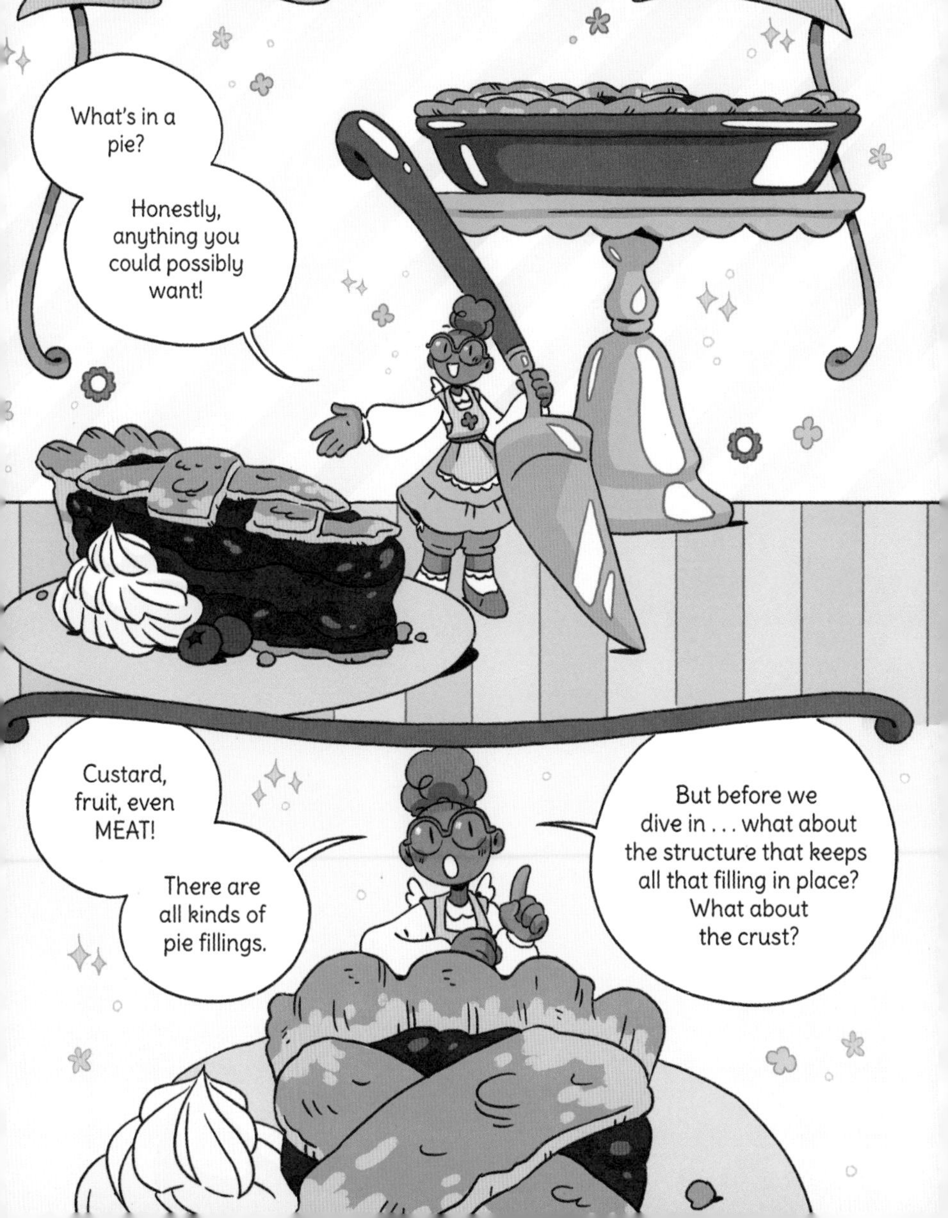
What's in a pie?
Honestly, anything you could possibly want!
Custard, fruit, even MEAT!
There are all kinds of pie fillings.
But before we dive in . . . what about the structure that keeps all that filling in place? What about the crust?

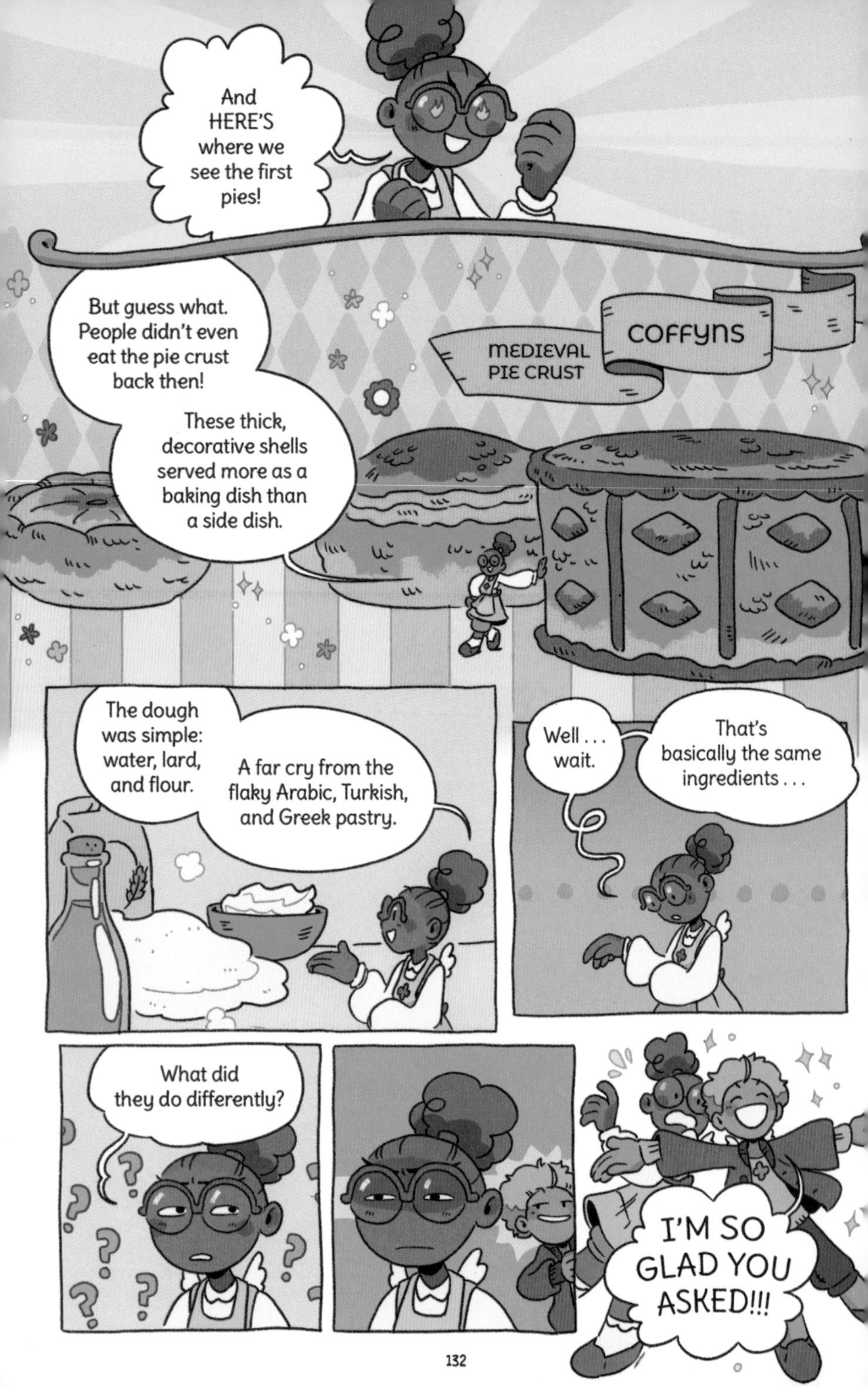
And HERE'S where we see the first pies!
But guess what. People didn't even eat the pie crust back then!
MEDIEVAL PIE CRUST
COFFYNS
These thick, decorative shells served more as a baking dish than a side dish.
The dough was simple: water, lard, and flour.
A far cry from the flaky Arabic, Turkish, and Greek pastry.
Well . . . wait.
That's basically the same ingredients . . .
What did they do differently?
I'M SO GLAD YOU ASKED!!!

135

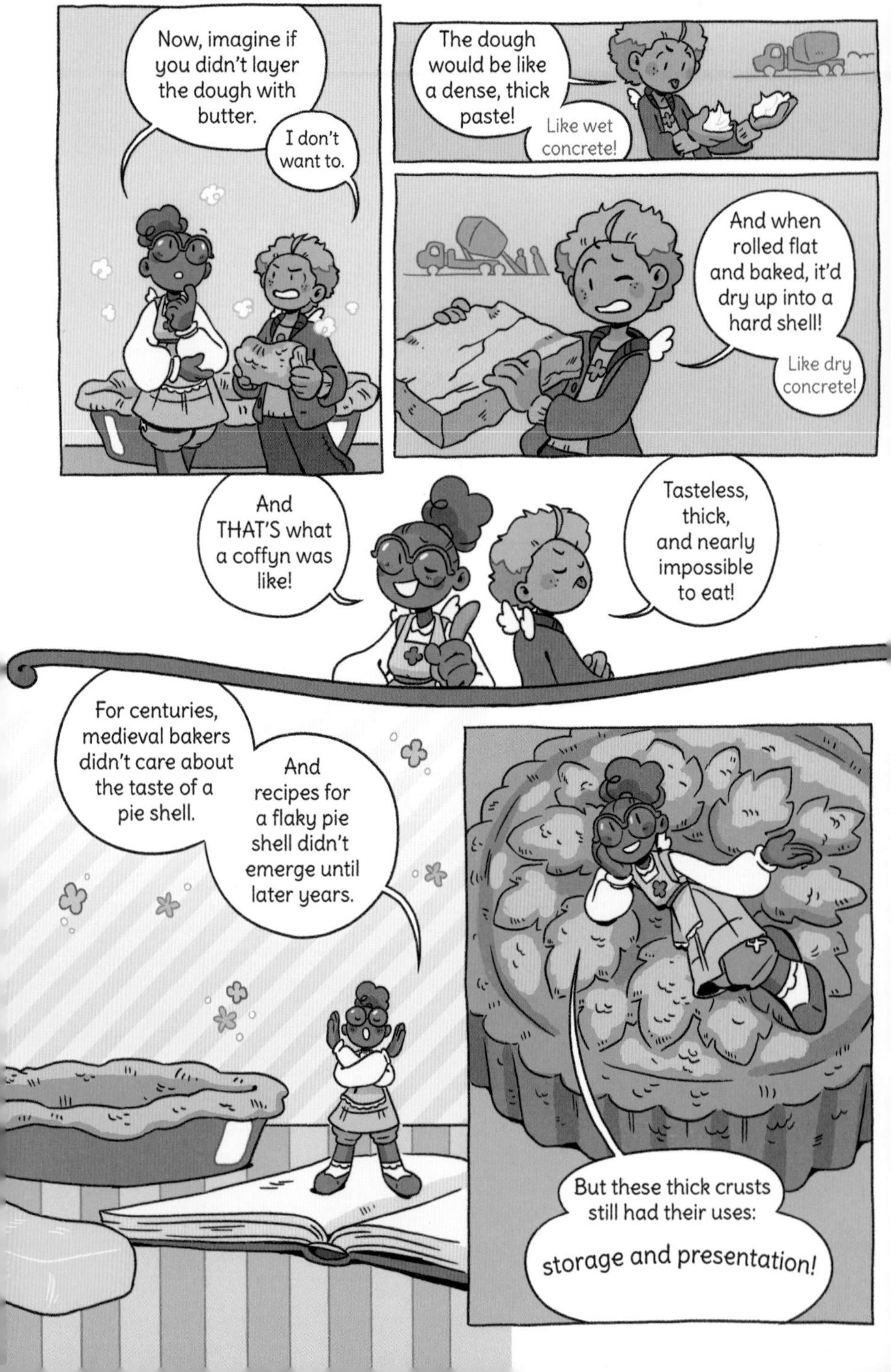
Now, imagine if you didn't layer the dough with butter.
I don't want to.
The dough would be like a dense, thick paste!
Like wet concrete!
And when rolled flat and baked, it'd dry up into a hard shell!
Like dry concrete!
And THAT'S what a coffyn was like!
Tasteless, thick, and nearly impossible to eat!
For centuries, medieval bakers didn't care about the taste of a pie shell.
And recipes for a flaky pie shell didn't emerge until later years.
But these thick crusts still had their uses:
storage and presentation!

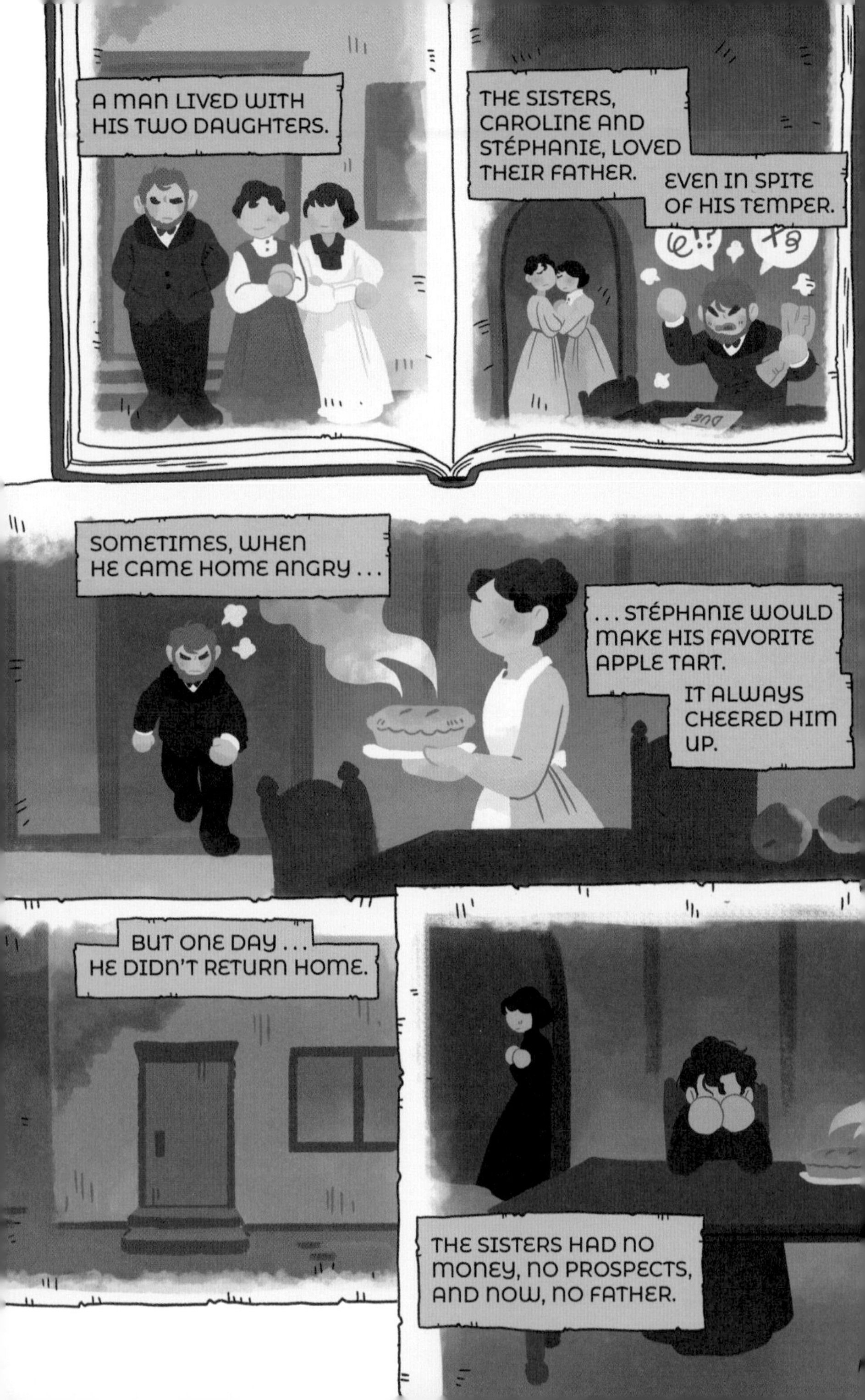
A MAN LIVED WITH HIS TWO DAUGHTERS.
THE SISTERS, CAROLINE AND STÉPHANIE, LOVED THEIR FATHER.
EVEN IN SPITE OF HIS TEMPER.
SOMETIMES, WHEN HE CAME HOME ANGRY . . .
. . . STÉPHANIE WOULD MAKE HIS FAVORITE APPLE TART.
IT ALWAYS CHEERED HIM UP.
BUT ONE DAY . . . HE DIDN'T RETURN HOME.
THE SISTERS HAD NO MONEY, NO PROSPECTS, AND NOW, NO FATHER.

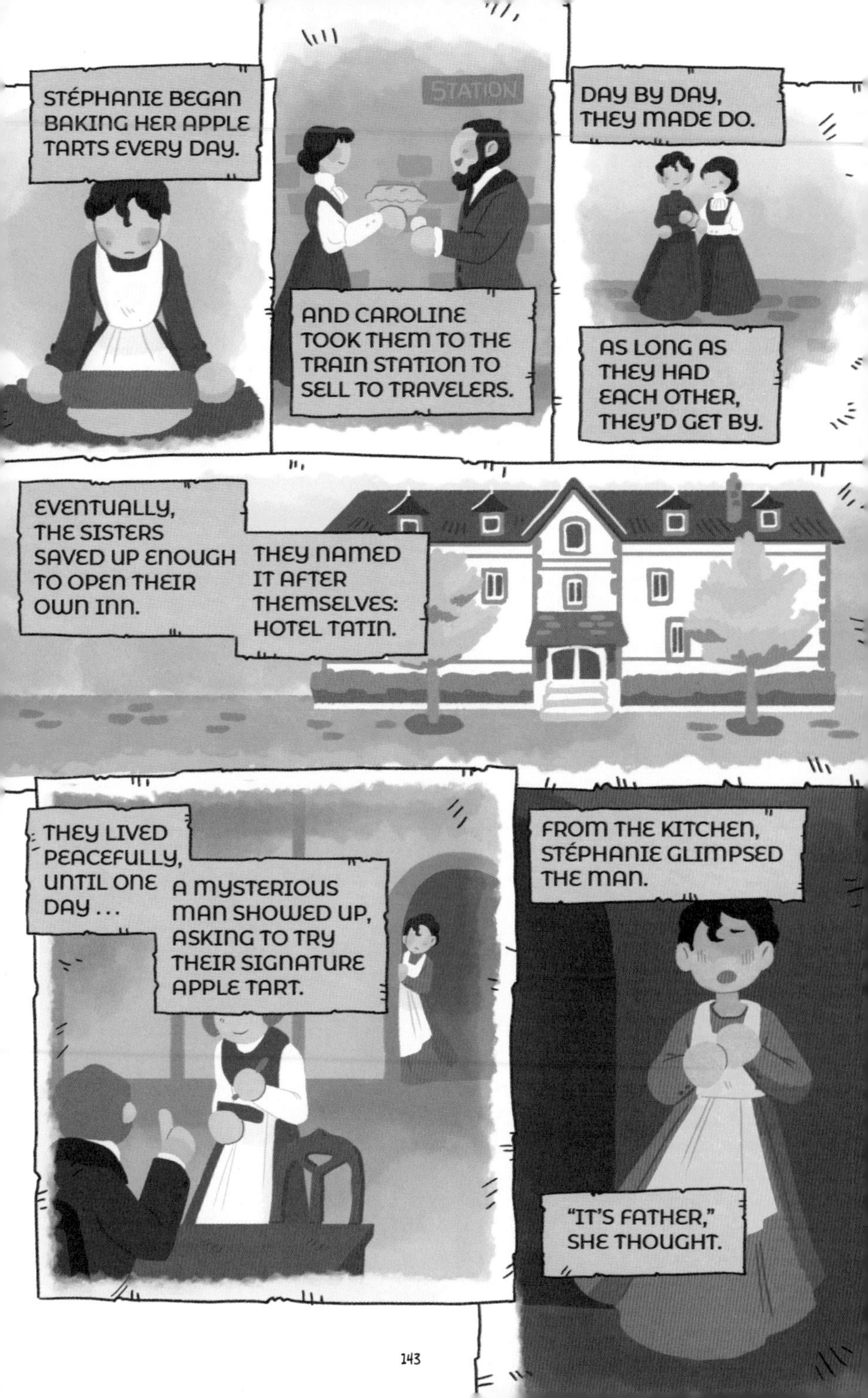
STÉPHANIE BEGAN BAKING HER APPLE TARTS EVERY DAY.
STATION
AND CAROLINE TOOK THEM TO THE TRAIN STATION TO SELL TO TRAVELERS.
DAY BY DAY, THEY MADE DO.
AS LONG AS THEY HAD EACH OTHER, THEY'D GET BY.
EVENTUALLY, THE SISTERS SAVED UP ENOUGH TO OPEN THEIR OWN INN.
THEY NAMED IT AFTER THEMSELVES: HOTEL TATIN.
THEY LIVED PEACEFULLY, UNTIL ONE DAY . . .
A MYSTERIOUS MAN SHOWED UP, ASKING TO TRY THEIR SIGNATURE APPLE TART.
FROM THE KITCHEN, STÉPHANIE GLIMPSED THE MAN.
"IT'S FATHER," SHE THOUGHT.

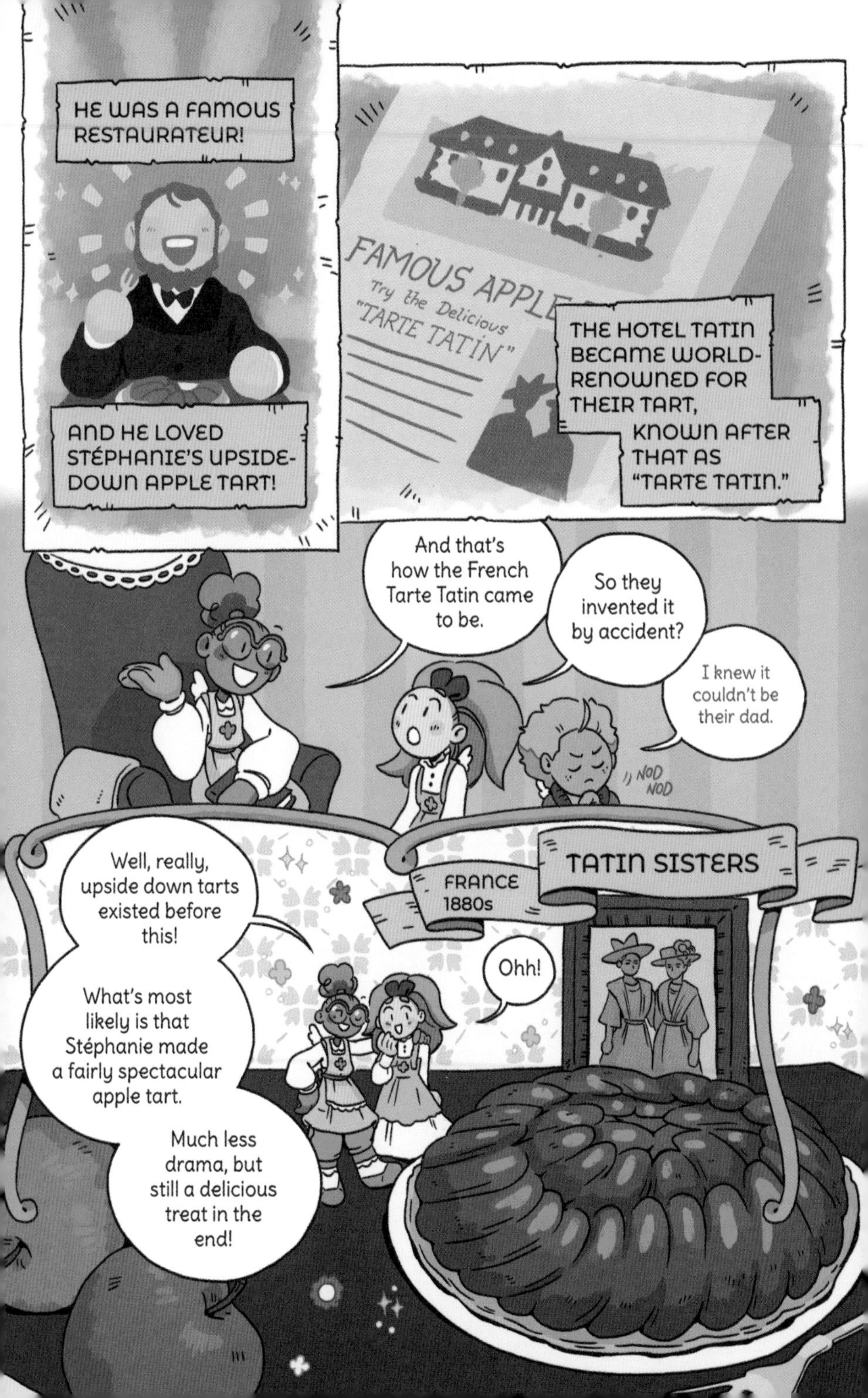
HE WAS A FAMOUS RESTAURATEUR!
AND HE LOVED STÉPHANIE'S UPSIDE-DOWN APPLE TART!
FAMOUS APPLE
Try the Delicious "TARTE TATIN"
THE HOTEL TATIN BECAME WORLD-RENOWNED FOR THEIR TART,
KNOWN AFTER THAT AS "TARTE TATIN."
And that's how the French Tarte Tatin came to be.
So they invented it by accident?
I knew it couldn't be their dad.
NOD NOD
TATIN SISTERS
FRANCE 1880s
Well, really, upside down tarts existed before this!
What's most likely is that Stéphanie made a fairly spectacular apple tart.
Much less drama, but still a delicious treat in the end!
Ohh!

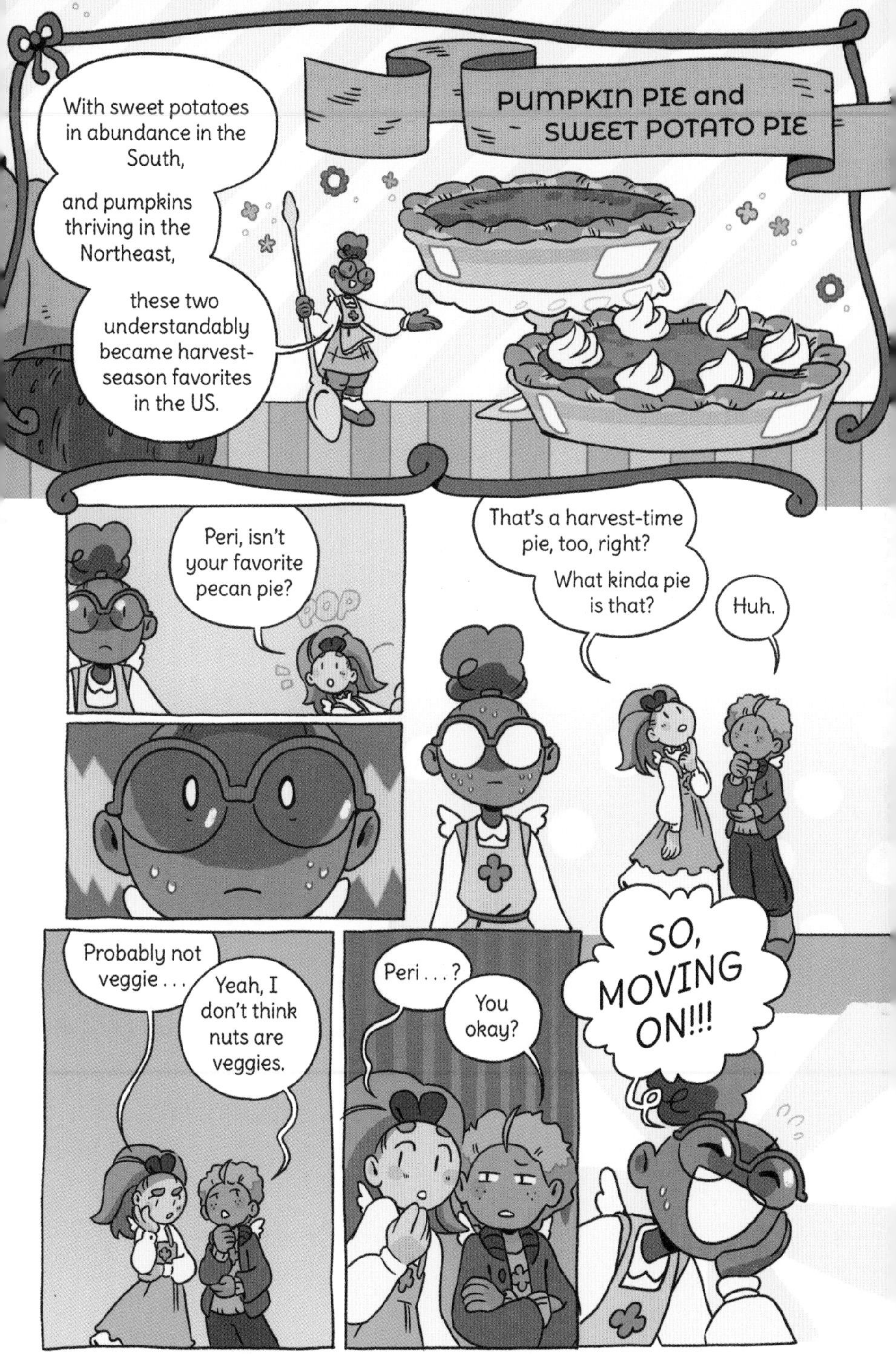
PUMPKIN PIE and SWEET POTATO PIE
With sweet potatoes in abundance in the South,
and pumpkins thriving in the Northeast,
these two understandably became harvest-season favorites in the US.
Peri, isn't your favorite pecan pie?
POP
That's a harvest-time pie, too, right?
What kinda pie is that?
Huh.
Probably not veggie . . .
Yeah, I don't think nuts are veggies.
Peri . . . ?
You okay?
SO, MOVING ON!!!

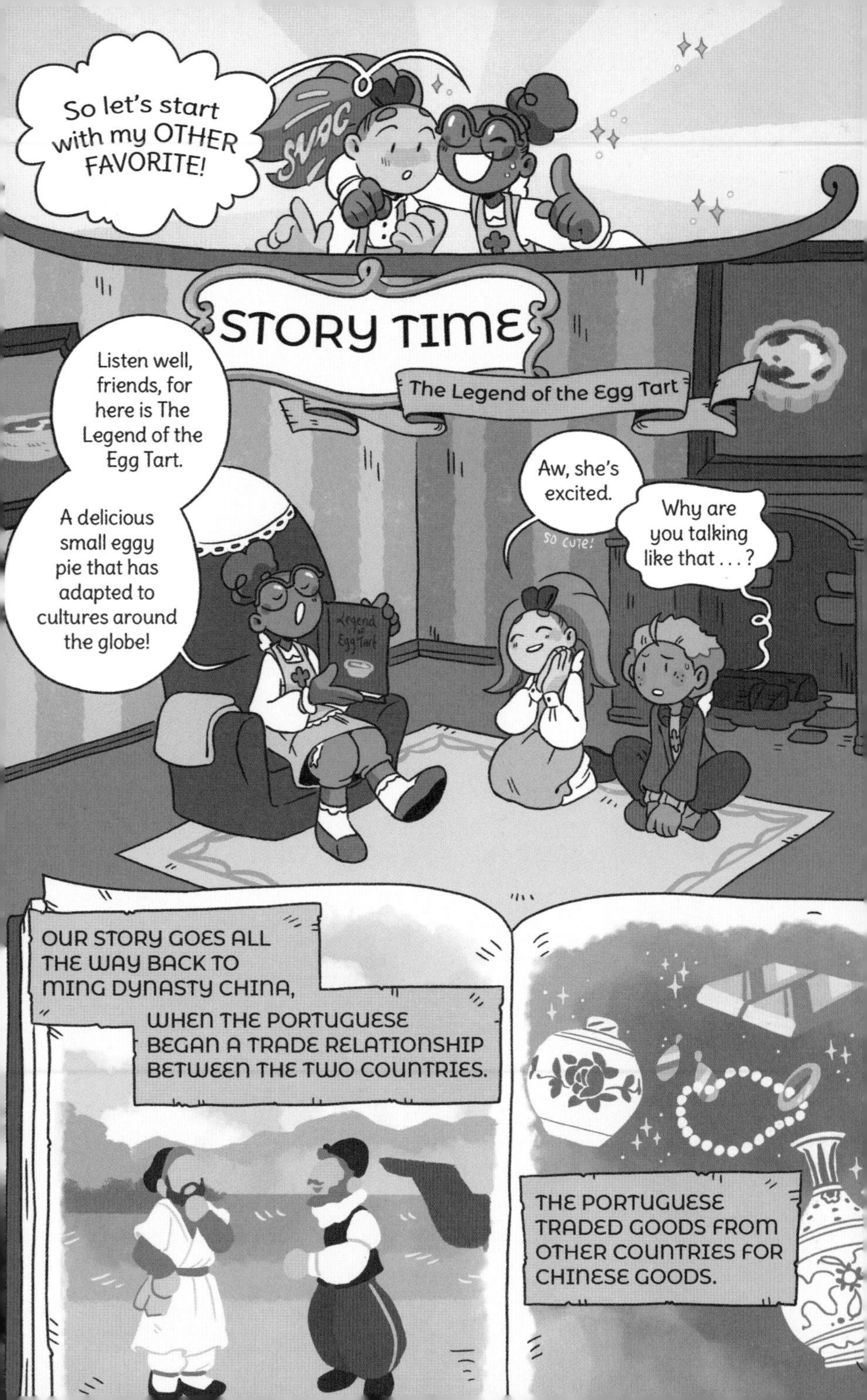

So let's start with my OTHER FAVORITE!
SNAG
STORY TIME
The Legend of the Egg Tart
Listen well, friends, for here is The Legend of the Egg Tart.
A delicious small eggy pie that has adapted to cultures around the globe!
Legend of Egg Tart
Aw, she's excited.
SO CUTE!
Why are you talking like that . . . ?
OUR STORY GOES ALL THE WAY BACK TO MING DYNASTY CHINA,
WHEN THE PORTUGUESE BEGAN A TRADE RELATIONSHIP BETWEEN THE TWO COUNTRIES.
THE PORTUGUESE TRADED GOODS FROM OTHER COUNTRIES FOR CHINESE GOODS.

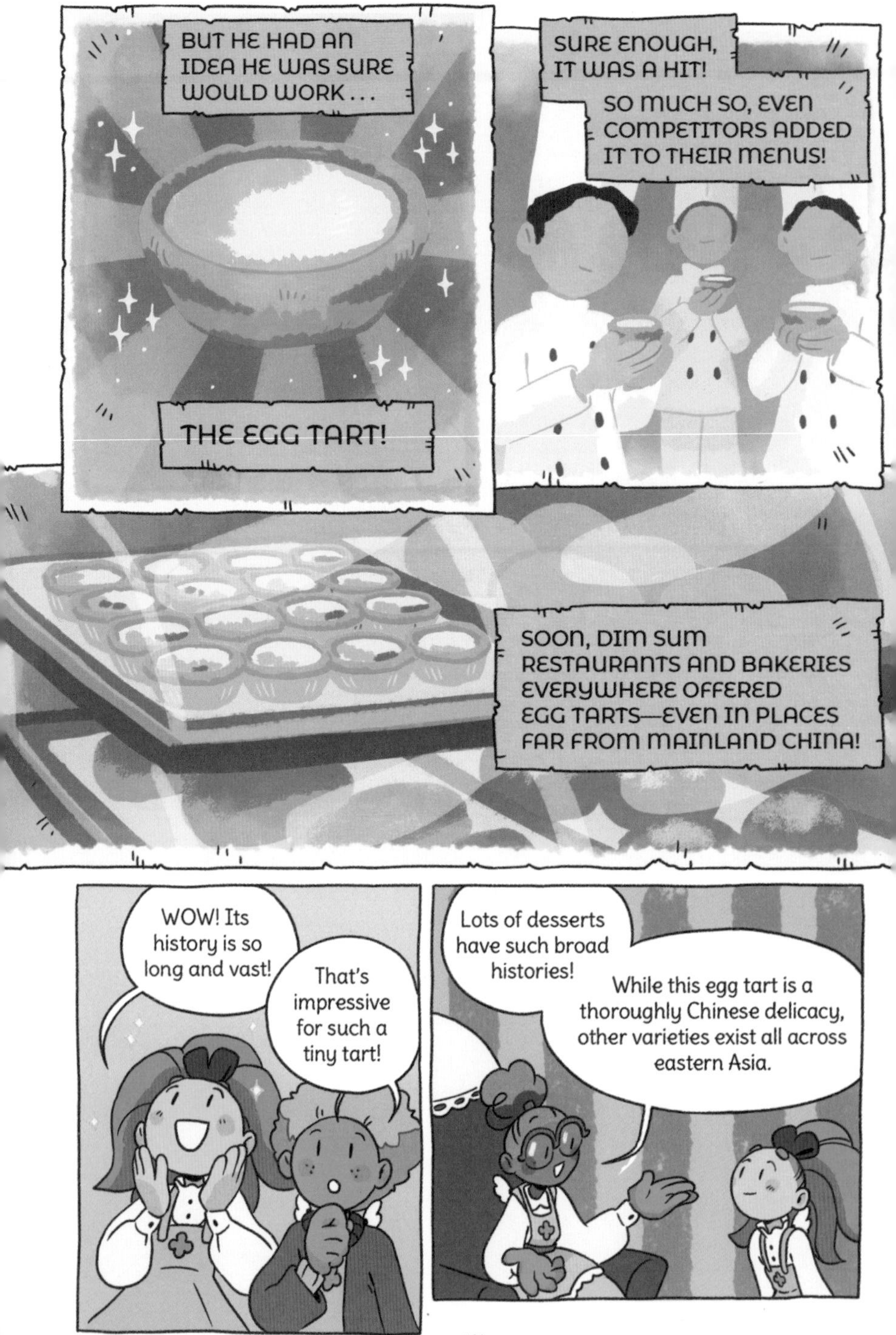
BUT HE HAD AN IDEA HE WAS SURE WOULD WORK . . .
THE EGG TART!
SURE ENOUGH, IT WAS A HIT!
SO MUCH SO, EVEN COMPETITORS ADDED IT TO THEIR MENUS!
SOON, DIM SUM RESTAURANTS AND BAKERIES EVERYWHERE OFFERED EGG TARTS—EVEN IN PLACES FAR FROM MAINLAND CHINA!
WOW! Its history is so long and vast!
That's impressive for such a tiny tart!
Lots of desserts have such broad histories!
While this egg tart is a thoroughly Chinese delicacy, other varieties exist all across eastern Asia.

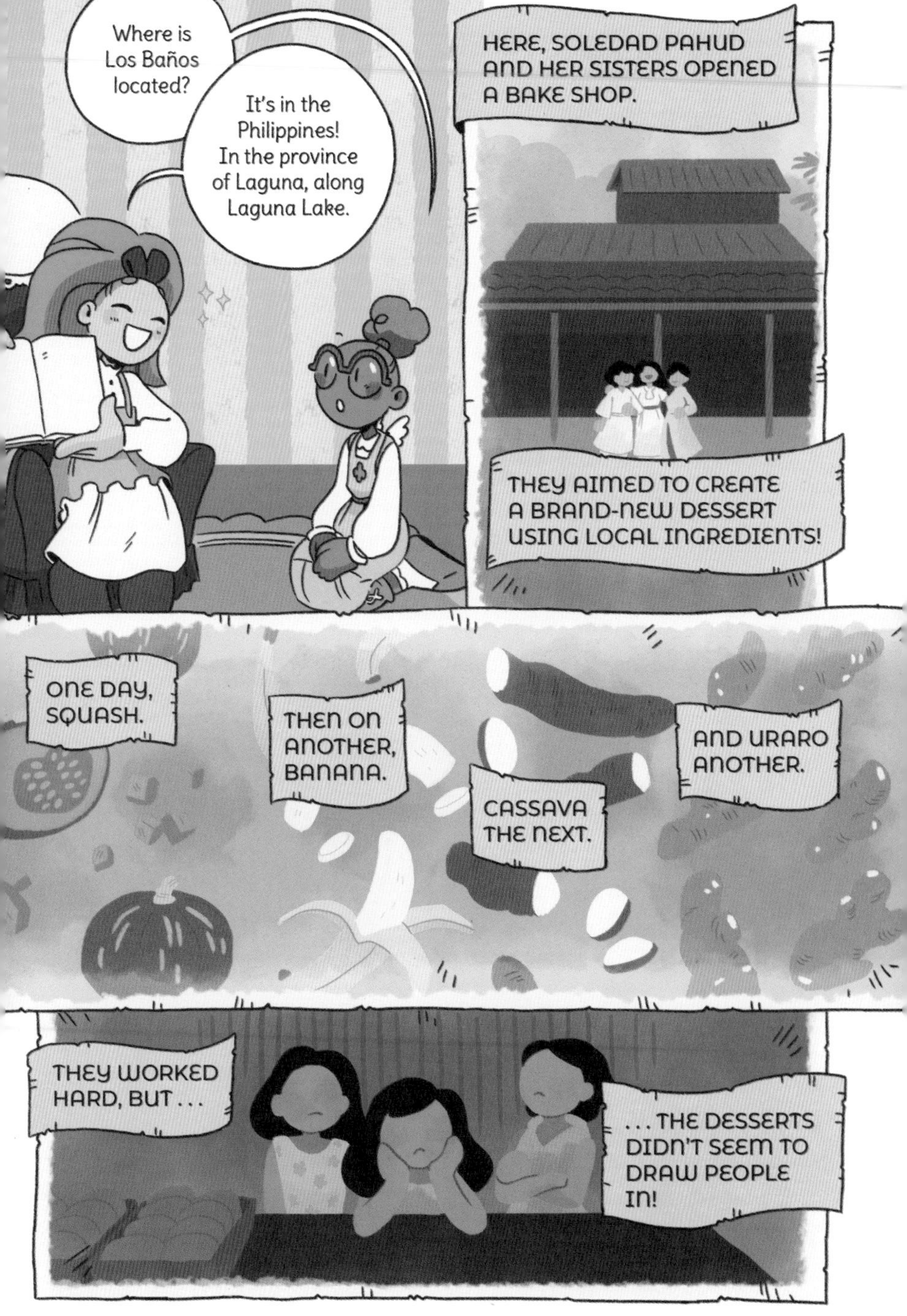
Where is Los Baños located?
It's in the Philippines! In the province of Laguna, along Laguna Lake.
HERE, SOLEDAD PAHUD AND HER SISTERS OPENED A BAKE SHOP.
THEY AIMED TO CREATE A BRAND-NEW DESSERT USING LOCAL INGREDIENTS!
ONE DAY, SQUASH.
THEN ON ANOTHER, BANANA.
CASSAVA THE NEXT.
AND URARO ANOTHER.
THEY WORKED HARD, BUT . . .
. . . THE DESSERTS DIDN'T SEEM TO DRAW PEOPLE IN!

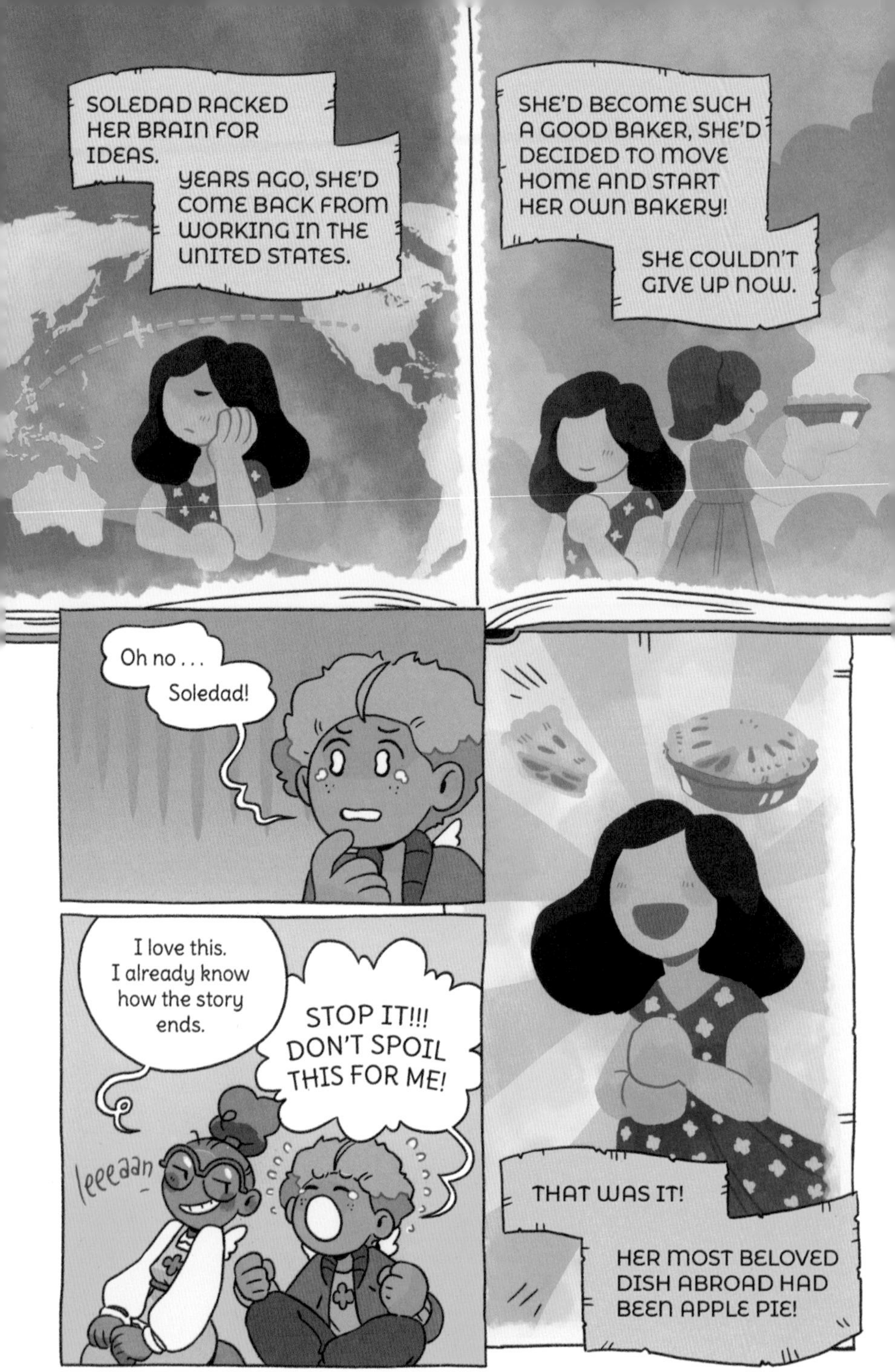
SOLEDAD RACKED HER BRAIN FOR IDEAS.
YEARS AGO, SHE'D COME BACK FROM WORKING IN THE UNITED STATES.
SHE'D BECOME SUCH A GOOD BAKER, SHE'D DECIDED TO MOVE HOME AND START HER OWN BAKERY!
SHE COULDN'T GIVE UP NOW.
Oh no . . .
Soledad!
I love this. I already know how the story ends.
STOP IT!!! DON'T SPOIL THIS FOR ME!
leeeaan
THAT WAS IT!
HER MOST BELOVED DISH ABROAD HAD BEEN APPLE PIE!

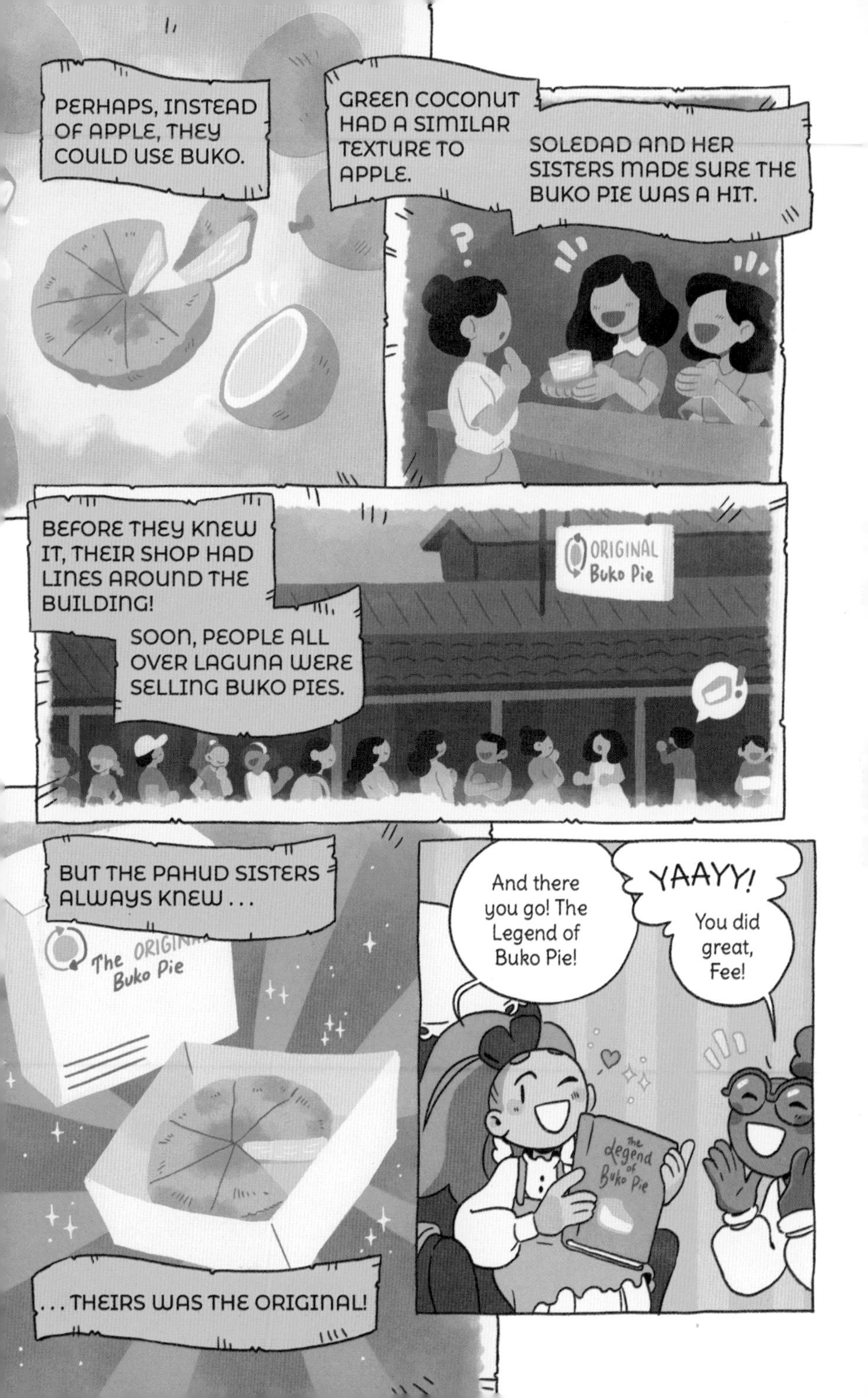
PERHAPS, INSTEAD OF APPLE, THEY COULD USE BUKO.
GREEN COCONUT HAD A SIMILAR TEXTURE TO APPLE.
SOLEDAD AND HER SISTERS MADE SURE THE BUKO PIE WAS A HIT.
?
BEFORE THEY KNEW IT, THEIR SHOP HAD LINES AROUND THE BUILDING!
ORIGINAL Buko Pie
SOON, PEOPLE ALL OVER LAGUNA WERE SELLING BUKO PIES.
BUT THE PAHUD SISTERS ALWAYS KNEW . . .
The ORIGINAL Buko Pie
. . . THEIRS WAS THE ORIGINAL!
And there you go! The Legend of Buko Pie!
YAAYY!
You did great, Fee!
The Legend of Buko Pie

BLUEBERRY PIE

YOU WILL NEED:

5 cups fresh blueberries

juice from ½ lemon

2 tablespoons milk or cream

4 tablespoons flour

½ cup brown sugar

¼ teaspoon ground cinnamon

9-inch pie dish

mixing bowl, spatula, and whisk

FOR THE CRUST:

2 ½ cups flour

1 teaspoon salt

¾ cup cold water

1 cup butter, chilled and cubed

1 egg for egg wash

1 teaspoon sugar

mixing bowl

pastry brush

OPTIONAL: cookie cutters

pastry cutter, knives, or forks

plastic wrap

rolling pin and spatula

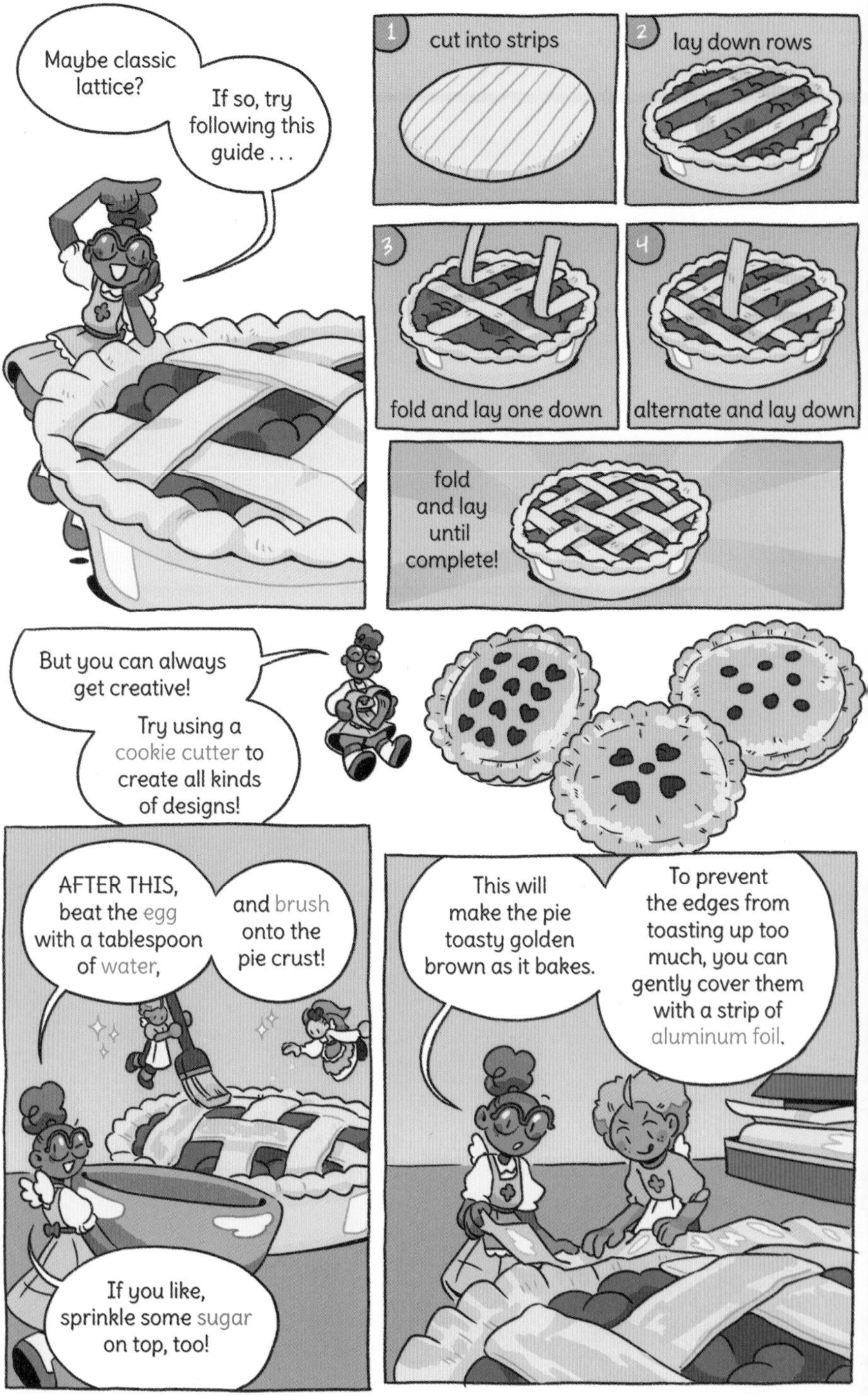
Maybe classic lattice?
If so, try following this guide . . .
1 cut into strips
2 lay down rows
3 fold and lay one down
4 alternate and lay down
fold and lay until complete!
But you can always get creative!
Try using a cookie cutter to create all kinds of designs!
AFTER THIS, beat the egg with a tablespoon of water,
and brush onto the pie crust!
If you like, sprinkle some sugar on top, too!
This will make the pie toasty golden brown as it bakes.
To prevent the edges from toasting up too much, you can gently cover them with a strip of aluminum foil.

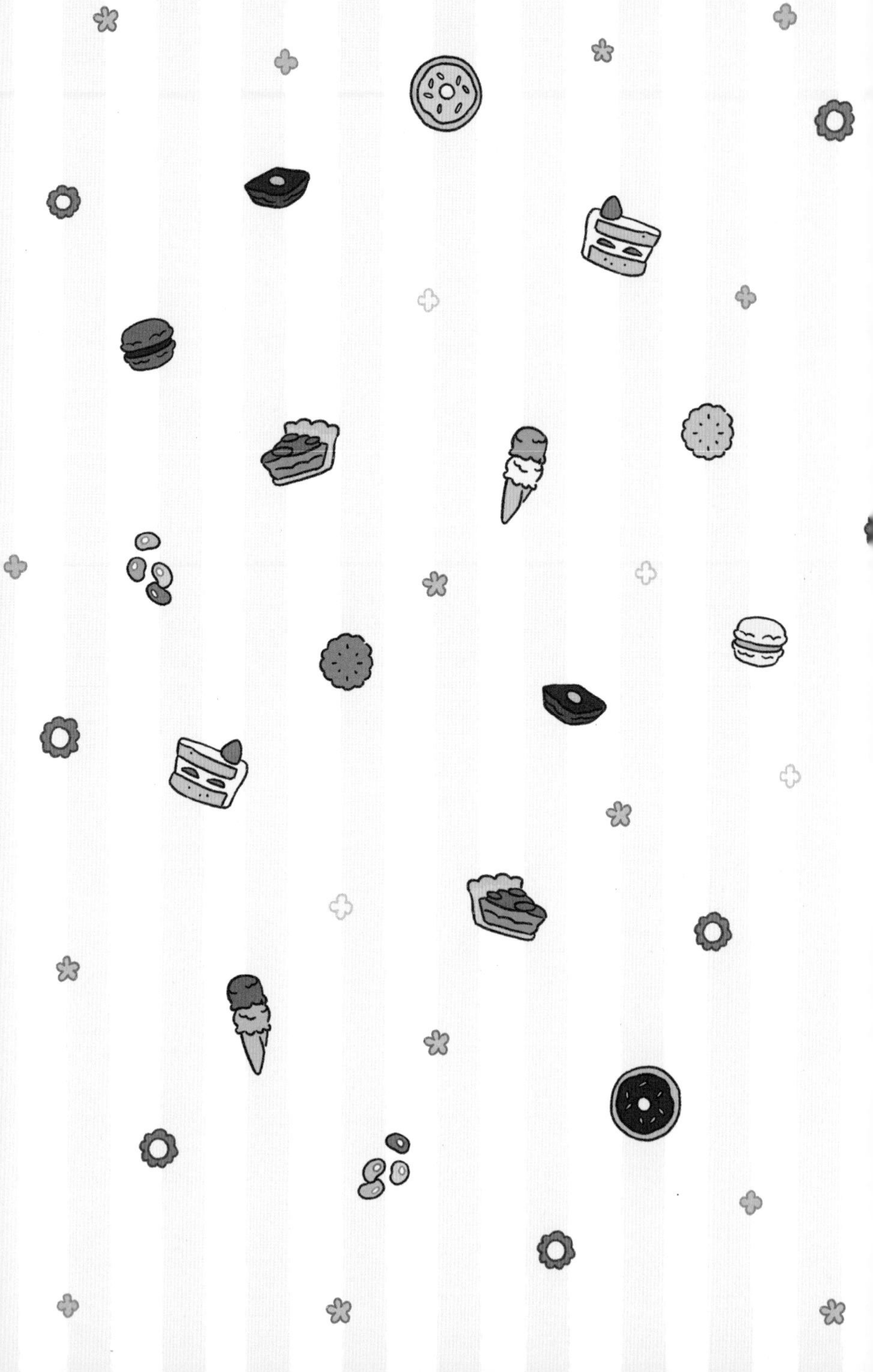

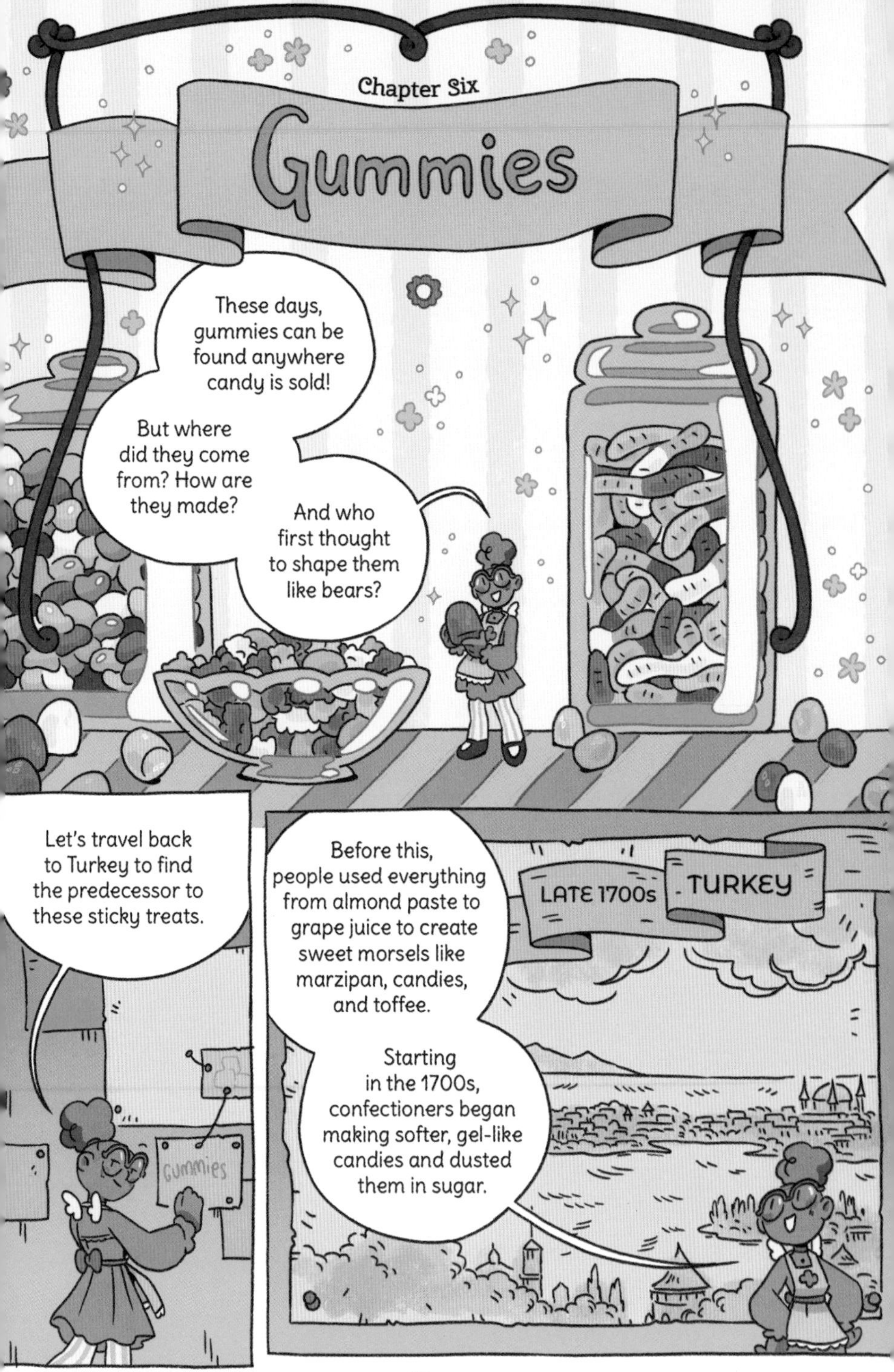

Chapter Six
Gummies
These days, gummies can be found anywhere candy is sold!
But where did they come from? How are they made?
And who first thought to shape them like bears?
Let's travel back to Turkey to find the predecessor to these sticky treats.
GUMMIES
Before this, people used everything from almond paste to grape juice to create sweet morsels like marzipan, candies, and toffee.
LATE 1700s
TURKEY
Starting in the 1700s, confectioners began making softer, gel-like candies and dusted them in sugar.

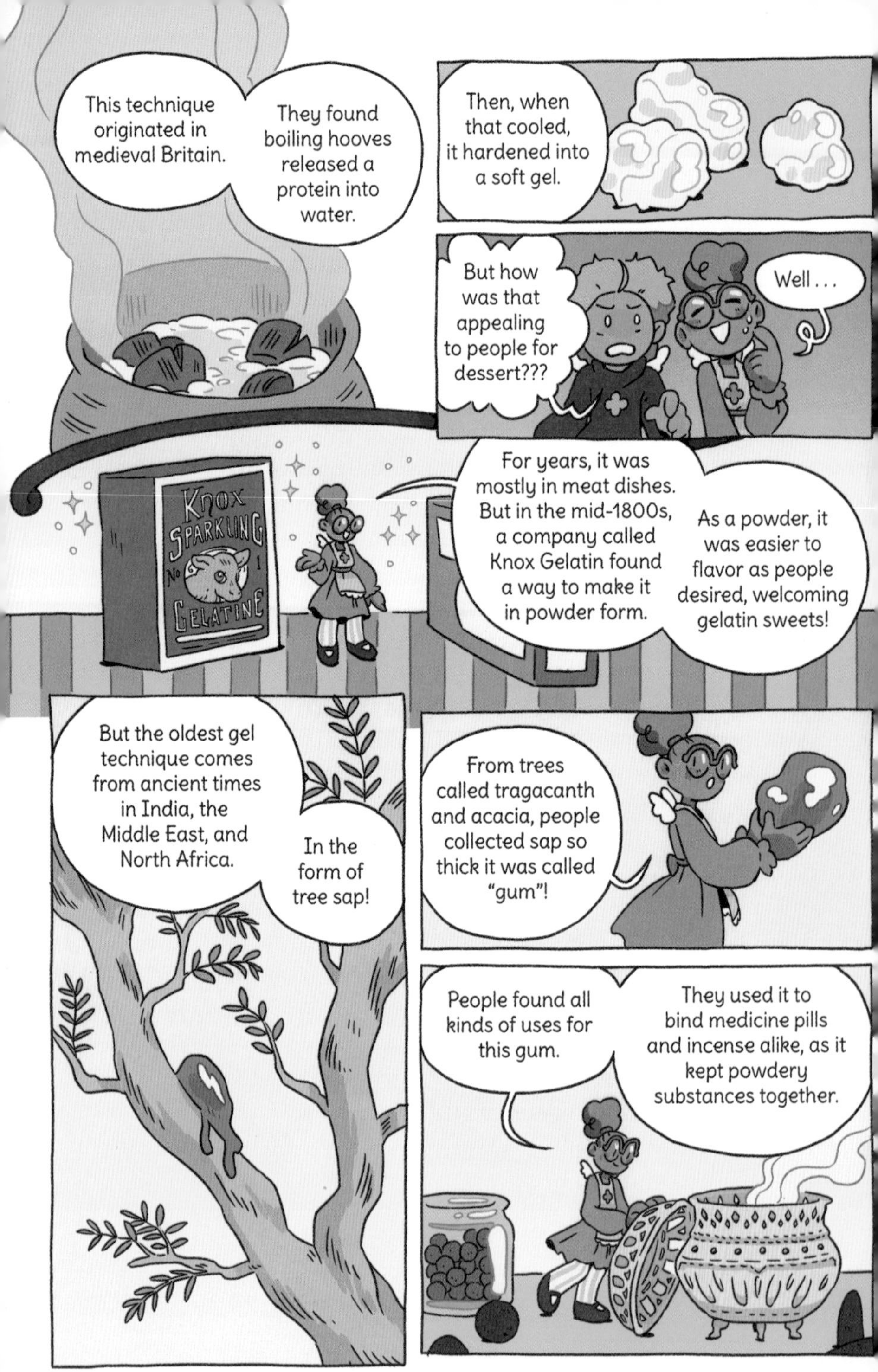
This technique originated in medieval Britain.
They found boiling hooves released a protein into water.
Then, when that cooled, it hardened into a soft gel.
But how was that appealing to people for dessert???
Well . . .
Knox SPARKLING No 1 GELATINE
For years, it was mostly in meat dishes. But in the mid-1800s, a company called Knox Gelatin found a way to make it in powder form.
As a powder, it was easier to flavor as people desired, welcoming gelatin sweets!
But the oldest gel technique comes from ancient times in India, the Middle East, and North Africa.
In the form of tree sap!
From trees called tragacanth and acacia, people collected sap so thick it was called "gum"!
People found all kinds of uses for this gum.
They used it to bind medicine pills and incense alike, as it kept powdery substances together.

The Abridged
Atlas of Cookie History

1. Ancient Roman Biscotus
2. Spread of Almond Flour Use from Islamic Cultures to Sicily
3. Persian and Arabic Qurabiya
4. Italian Biscotti
5. Egyptian Kahk
6. Levantine Ma'amoul
7. European Gingerbread
8. Indian and Pakistani Nankhatai
9. European Molded Spice Cookies
10. French Madeleines
11. Scottish Shortbread
12. Maria Sanders van Rensselaer's Handwritten Cook Book
13. British and Dutch Industrial Cookie Culture
14. Regions of Maria Cookie Traditions
15. American Drop Cookies
16. Ruth Graves Wakefield's *Toll House Tried and True Recipes*
17. Southeast Asian Kuih Cookie Traditions

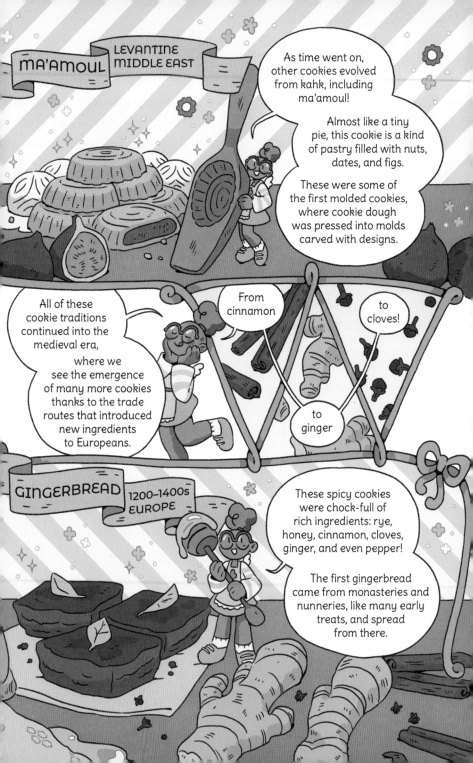

Ohh! Like gingerbread houses?
Not quite yet.
It'd be a hundred or so years before we see more molded and cut cookies.
But in that time we have so many other cookies to discover!
STORY TIME
The Legend of Nankhatai
Let's enjoy a Story Time! This time we have The Legend of Nankhatai!
What roads led to the creation of this tasty biscuit?
Well, if it's for a Story Time, I can wait.
MANY ROADS MEET IN THE INDIAN CITY OF SURAT,
AND MANY PEOPLE MADE IT THEIR HOME.
SOME DUTCH,
SOME PAKISTANI,
SOME IRANIAN.
SO IT WAS HERE A DUTCH COUPLE OPENED A DUTCH BAKERY.

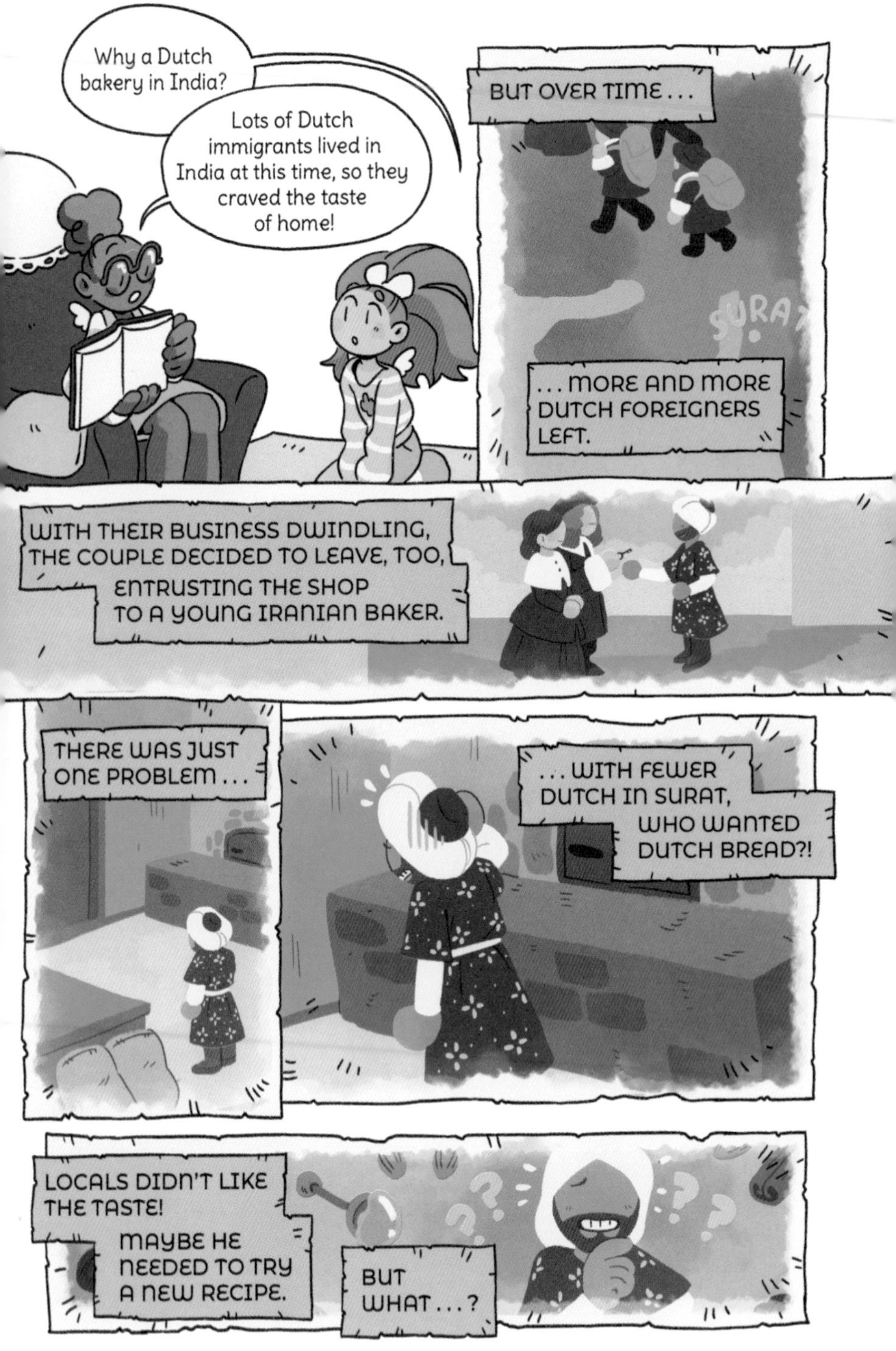
Why a Dutch bakery in India?
Lots of Dutch immigrants lived in India at this time, so they craved the taste of home!
BUT OVER TIME . . .
SURAT
. . . MORE AND MORE DUTCH FOREIGNERS LEFT.
WITH THEIR BUSINESS DWINDLING, THE COUPLE DECIDED TO LEAVE, TOO, ENTRUSTING THE SHOP TO A YOUNG IRANIAN BAKER.
THERE WAS JUST ONE PROBLEM . . .
. . . WITH FEWER DUTCH IN SURAT, WHO WANTED DUTCH BREAD?!
LOCALS DIDN'T LIKE THE TASTE!
MAYBE HE NEEDED TO TRY A NEW RECIPE.
BUT WHAT . . . ?

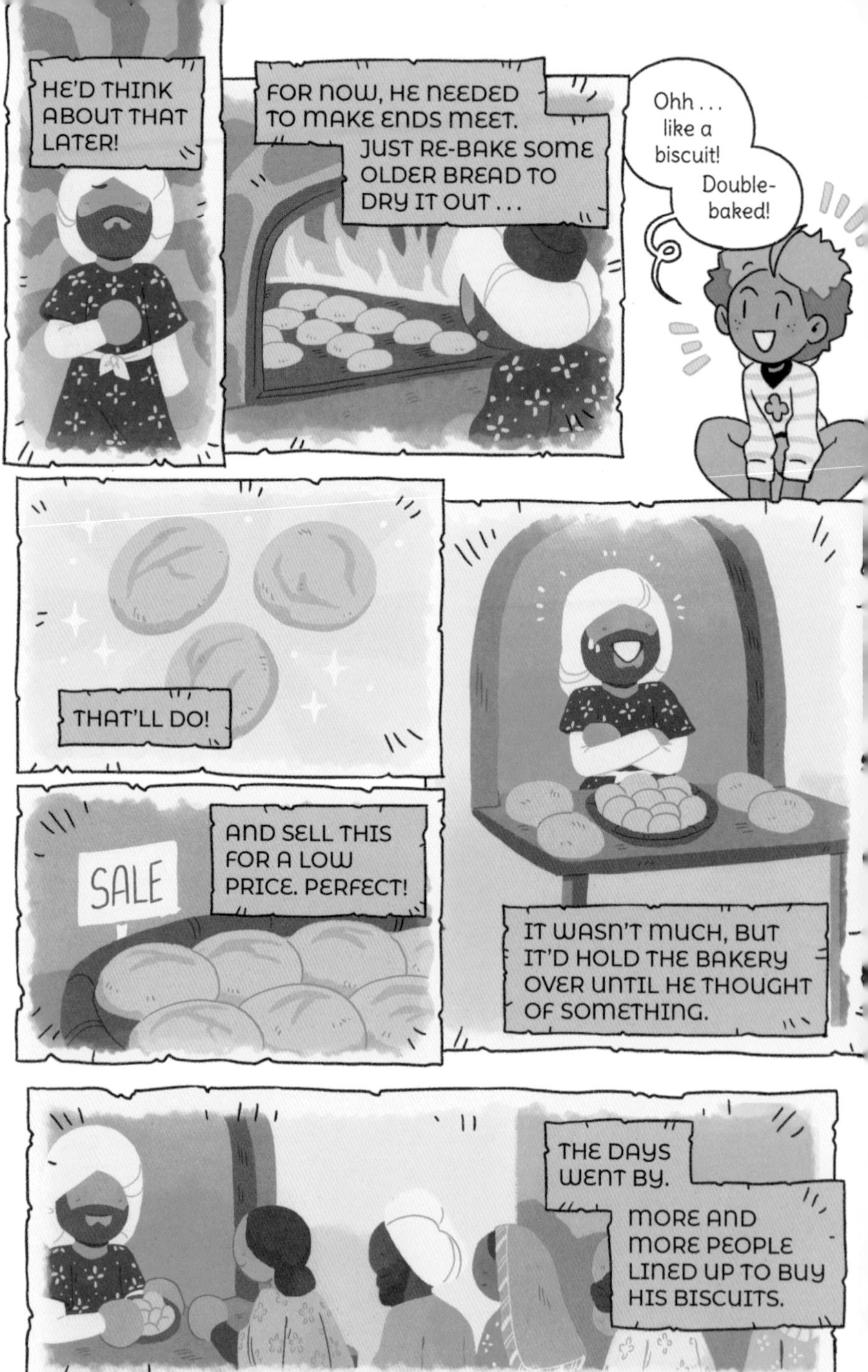
HE'D THINK ABOUT THAT LATER!
FOR NOW, HE NEEDED TO MAKE ENDS MEET.
JUST RE-BAKE SOME OLDER BREAD TO DRY IT OUT . . .
Ohh . . . like a biscuit!
Double-baked!
THAT'LL DO!
IT WASN'T MUCH, BUT IT'D HOLD THE BAKERY OVER UNTIL HE THOUGHT OF SOMETHING.
SALE
AND SELL THIS FOR A LOW PRICE. PERFECT!
THE DAYS WENT BY.
MORE AND MORE PEOPLE LINED UP TO BUY HIS BISCUITS.

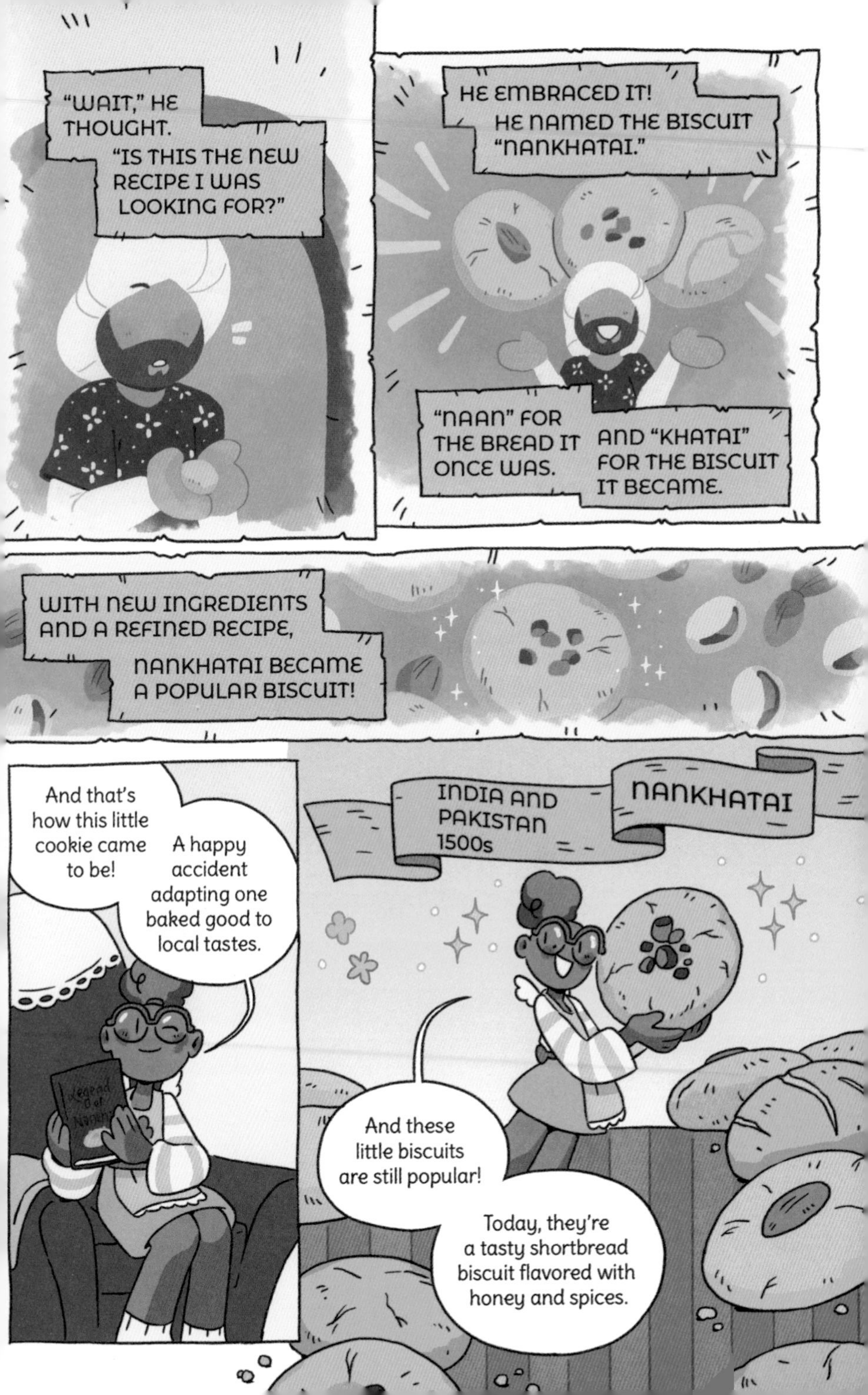
"WAIT," HE THOUGHT.
"IS THIS THE NEW RECIPE I WAS LOOKING FOR?"
HE EMBRACED IT!
HE NAMED THE BISCUIT "NANKHATAI."
"NAAN" FOR THE BREAD IT ONCE WAS.
AND "KHATAI" FOR THE BISCUIT IT BECAME.
WITH NEW INGREDIENTS AND A REFINED RECIPE,
NANKHATAI BECAME A POPULAR BISCUIT!
And that's how this little cookie came to be!
A happy accident adapting one baked good to local tastes.
INDIA AND PAKISTAN 1500s
NANKHATAI
And these little biscuits are still popular!
Today, they're a tasty shortbread biscuit flavored with honey and spices.

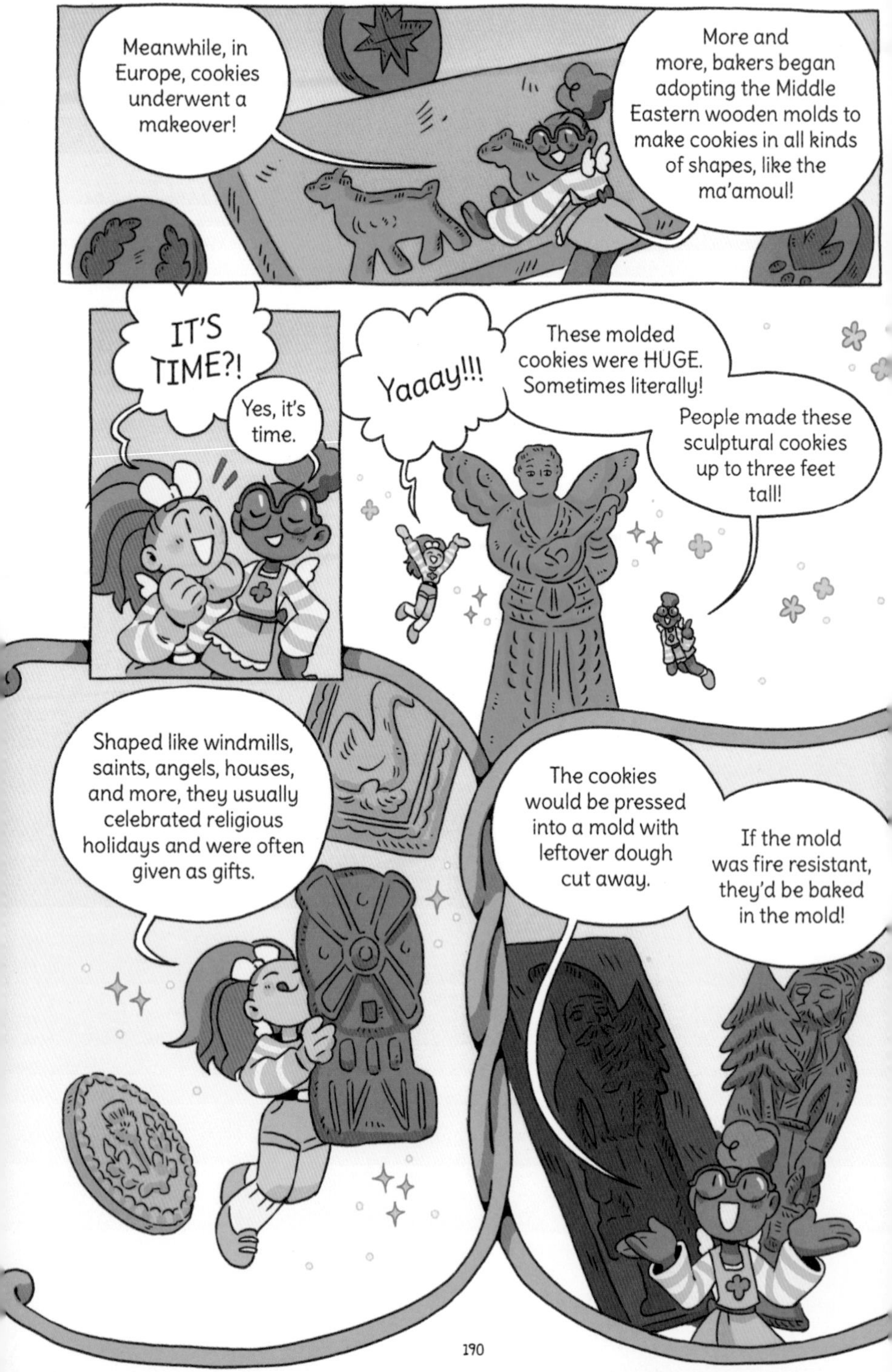

Meanwhile, in Europe, cookies underwent a makeover!
More and more, bakers began adopting the Middle Eastern wooden molds to make cookies in all kinds of shapes, like the ma'amoul!
IT'S TIME?!
Yes, it's time.
Yaaay!!!
These molded cookies were HUGE. Sometimes literally!
People made these sculptural cookies up to three feet tall!
Shaped like windmills, saints, angels, houses, and more, they usually celebrated religious holidays and were often given as gifts.
The cookies would be pressed into a mold with leftover dough cut away.
If the mold was fire resistant, they'd be baked in the mold!

SHORTBREAD — SCOTLAND 1500s–1700s

We see recipes for popular "short-cakes" starting in the late 1500s. "Short" meaning flaky, a texture which came from all the butter packed in there!

By the 1700s, Scottish shortbread is its own art form. Often pressed and baked in ceramic molds, these butter cookies melt in the mouth.

Up to this point, these treats were called lots of things:

biscuits, small cakes, even bread!

So... where'd "cookie" come from?

Well!

As far as we know, it first appeared in 1703 in Scotland.

1703: "cookie"

"cookie"

COOKIE

Oh! That's simple enough.

But, uh...

Pat Pat

It didn't... actually refer to cookies.

You see what I have to deal with here?

That's because sugar thrives in tropical regions, which Europe was not!

Indians and Southeast Asians were the first to cultivate and use sugar.

It wasn't until Europeans began colonizing these places that they started using more and more sugar.

SUGAR

The British and the Dutch in particular latched onto it, giving both countries access to cheaper sugar.

Cheaper sugar meant more desserts, including cookies.

So, during this era, both the British and Dutch developed tea-and-biscuit traditions.

INDUSTRIAL AGE EUROPE 1760s–1840s

With the rise of colonialism and trade, the British and Dutch names for cookies— "biscuits" and "cookjes"— spread.

By the 1800s, science had advanced so much that factories began to make cookies.

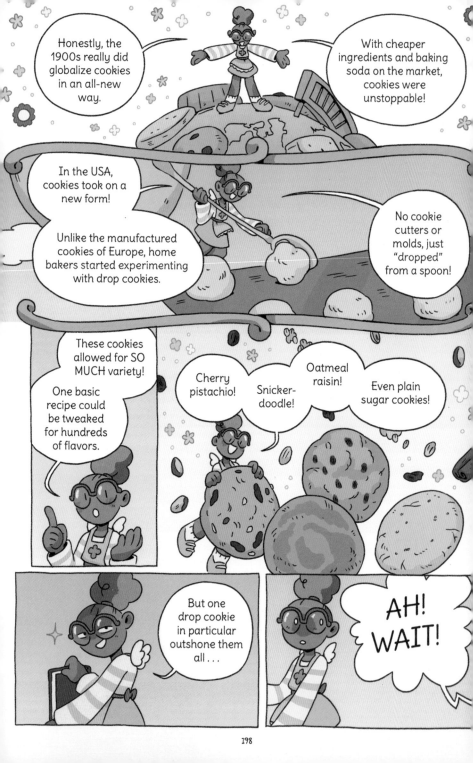

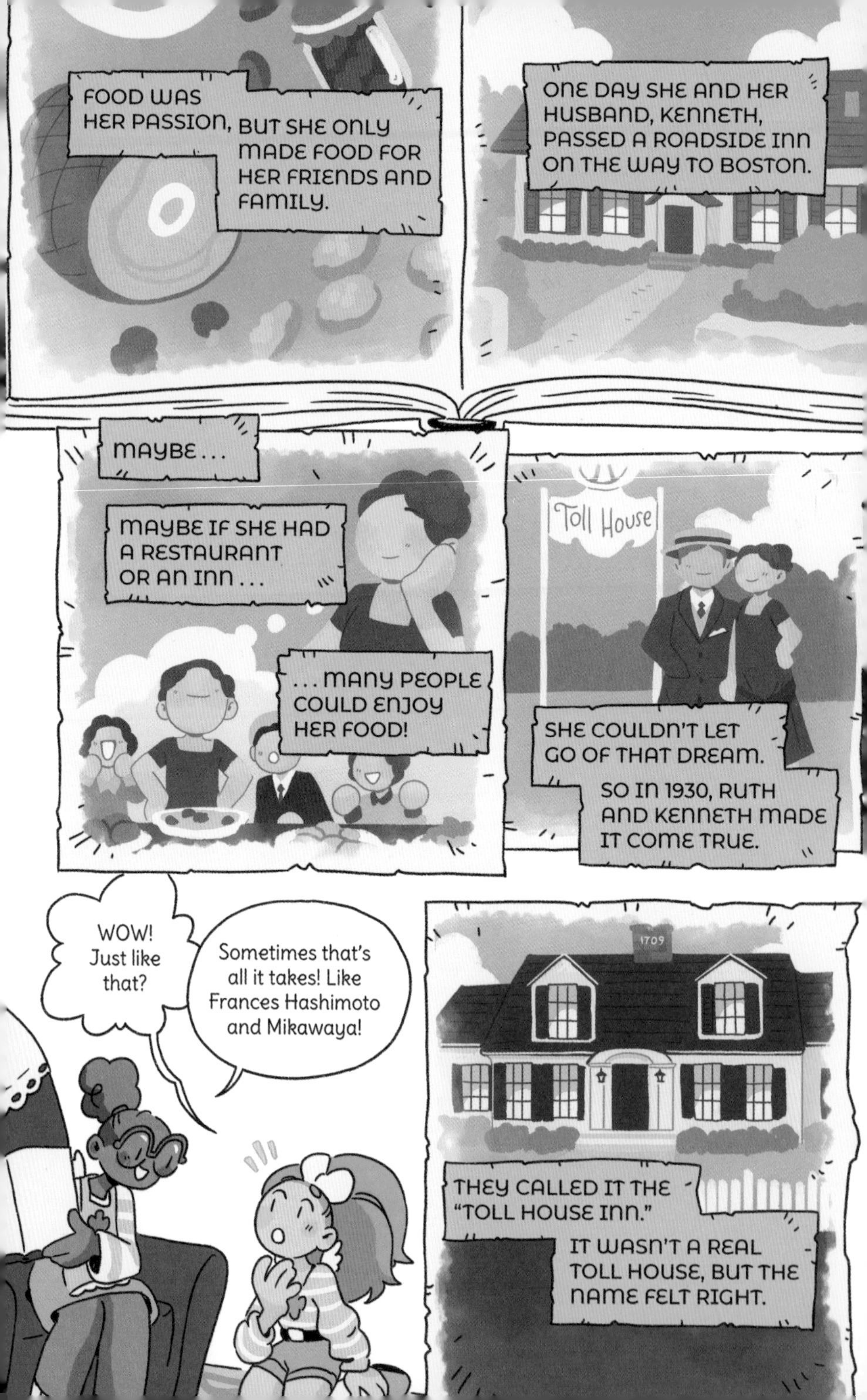
FOOD WAS HER PASSION, BUT SHE ONLY MADE FOOD FOR HER FRIENDS AND FAMILY.
ONE DAY SHE AND HER HUSBAND, KENNETH, PASSED A ROADSIDE INN ON THE WAY TO BOSTON.
MAYBE...
MAYBE IF SHE HAD A RESTAURANT OR AN INN...
...MANY PEOPLE COULD ENJOY HER FOOD!
Toll House
SHE COULDN'T LET GO OF THAT DREAM.
SO IN 1930, RUTH AND KENNETH MADE IT COME TRUE.
WOW! Just like that?
Sometimes that's all it takes! Like Frances Hashimoto and Mikawaya!
1709
THEY CALLED IT THE "TOLL HOUSE INN."
IT WASN'T A REAL TOLL HOUSE, BUT THE NAME FELT RIGHT.

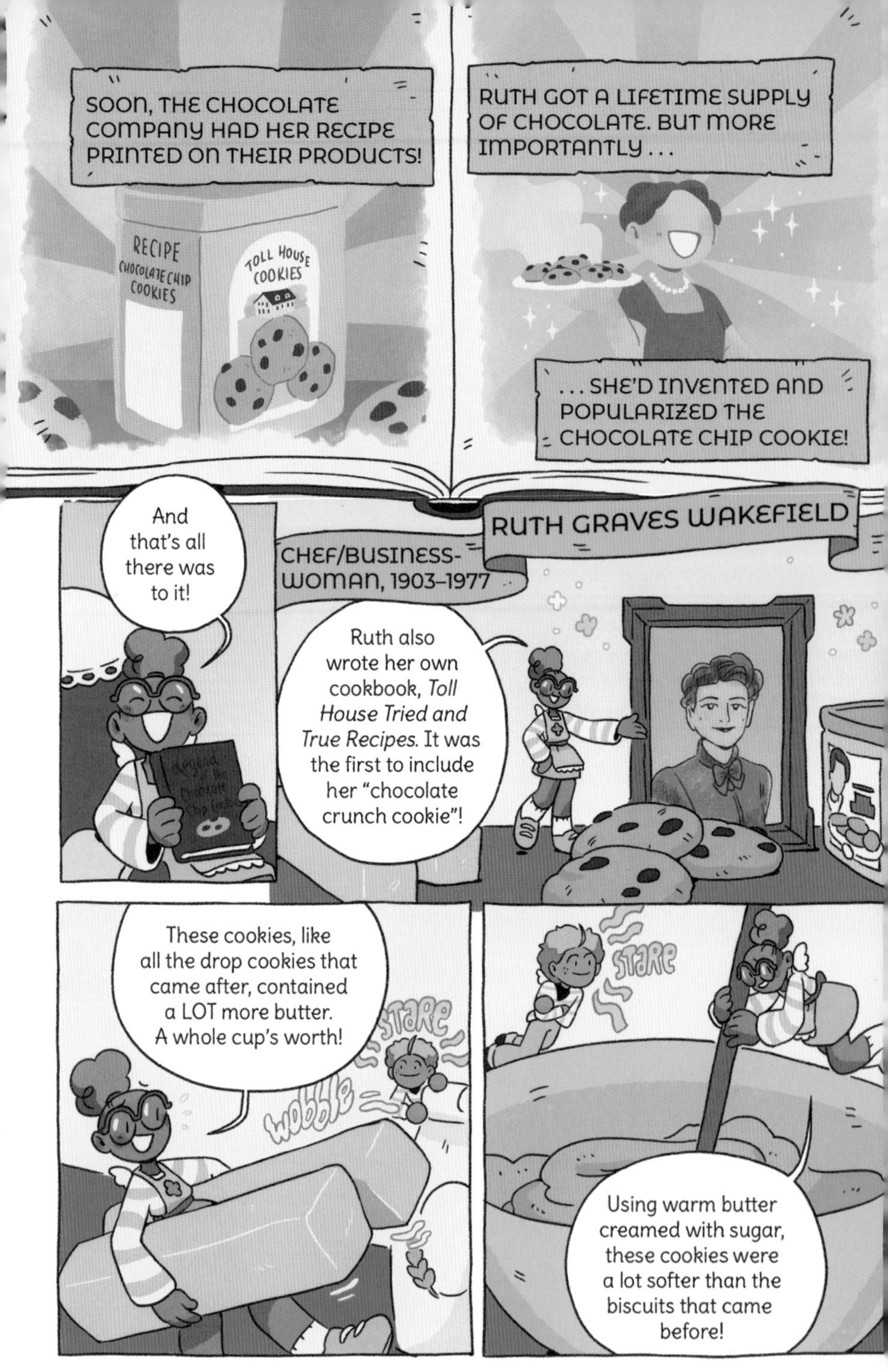
SOON, THE CHOCOLATE COMPANY HAD HER RECIPE PRINTED ON THEIR PRODUCTS!
RECIPE
CHOCOLATE CHIP COOKIES
TOLL HOUSE COOKIES
RUTH GOT A LIFETIME SUPPLY OF CHOCOLATE. BUT MORE IMPORTANTLY . . .
. . . SHE'D INVENTED AND POPULARIZED THE CHOCOLATE CHIP COOKIE!
And that's all there was to it!
RUTH GRAVES WAKEFIELD
CHEF/BUSINESS-WOMAN, 1903–1977
Ruth also wrote her own cookbook, *Toll House Tried and True Recipes*. It was the first to include her "chocolate crunch cookie"!
These cookies, like all the drop cookies that came after, contained a LOT more butter. A whole cup's worth!
STARE
wobble
STARE
Using warm butter creamed with sugar, these cookies were a lot softer than the biscuits that came before!

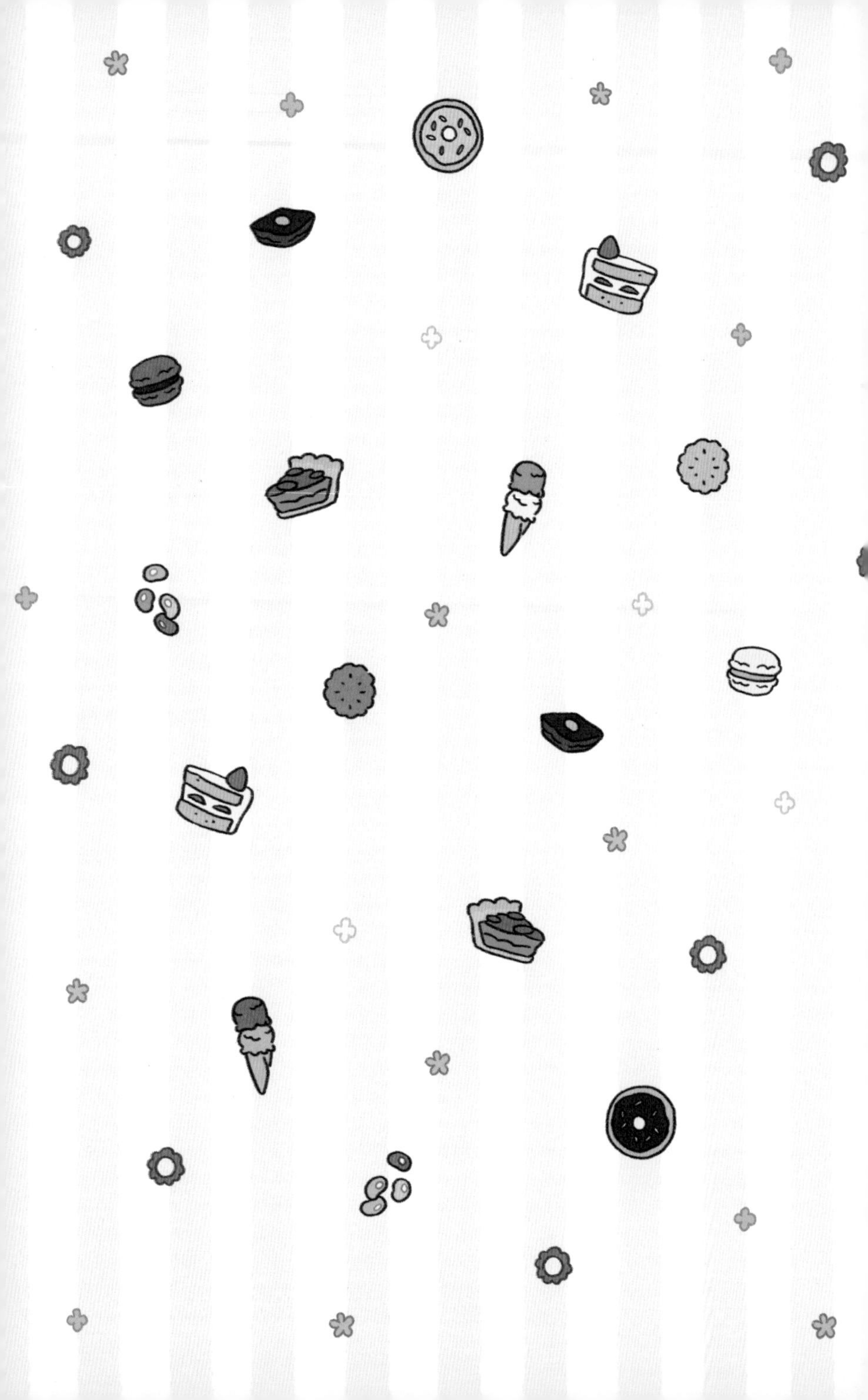

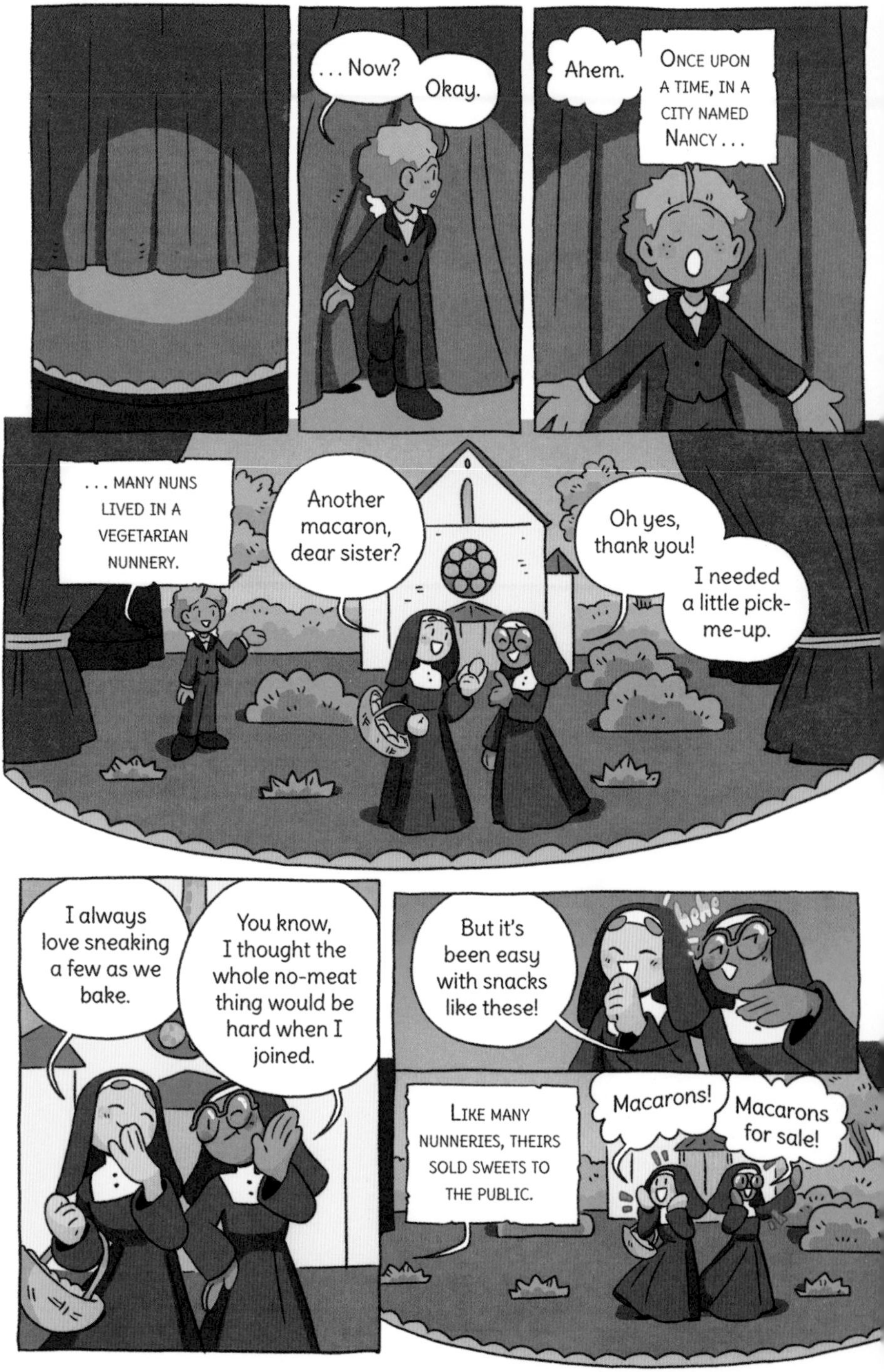
. . . Now?
Okay.
Ahem.
ONCE UPON A TIME, IN A CITY NAMED NANCY . . .
. . . MANY NUNS LIVED IN A VEGETARIAN NUNNERY.
Another macaron, dear sister?
Oh yes, thank you!
I needed a little pick-me-up.
I always love sneaking a few as we bake.
You know, I thought the whole no-meat thing would be hard when I joined.
But it's been easy with snacks like these!
hehe
LIKE MANY NUNNERIES, THEIRS SOLD SWEETS TO THE PUBLIC.
Macarons!
Macarons for sale!

But one day... Hear ye, hear ye!

According to the revolutionary government of France, all religious convents and monasteries are henceforth...

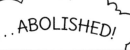

...ABOLISHED!

GASP!

Sister, what do we do??

Without the convent... we have no place to live!

How can we continue living like this?

WHY'D THEY CAST ME IN MULTIPLE ROLES?!

Should we run away to another country?

Can you speak any other languages?

That's not—

Pardon me, sisters.

It's a shame about what's happened.

Perhaps, if need be, I could offer you my home?

I mean... Latin.

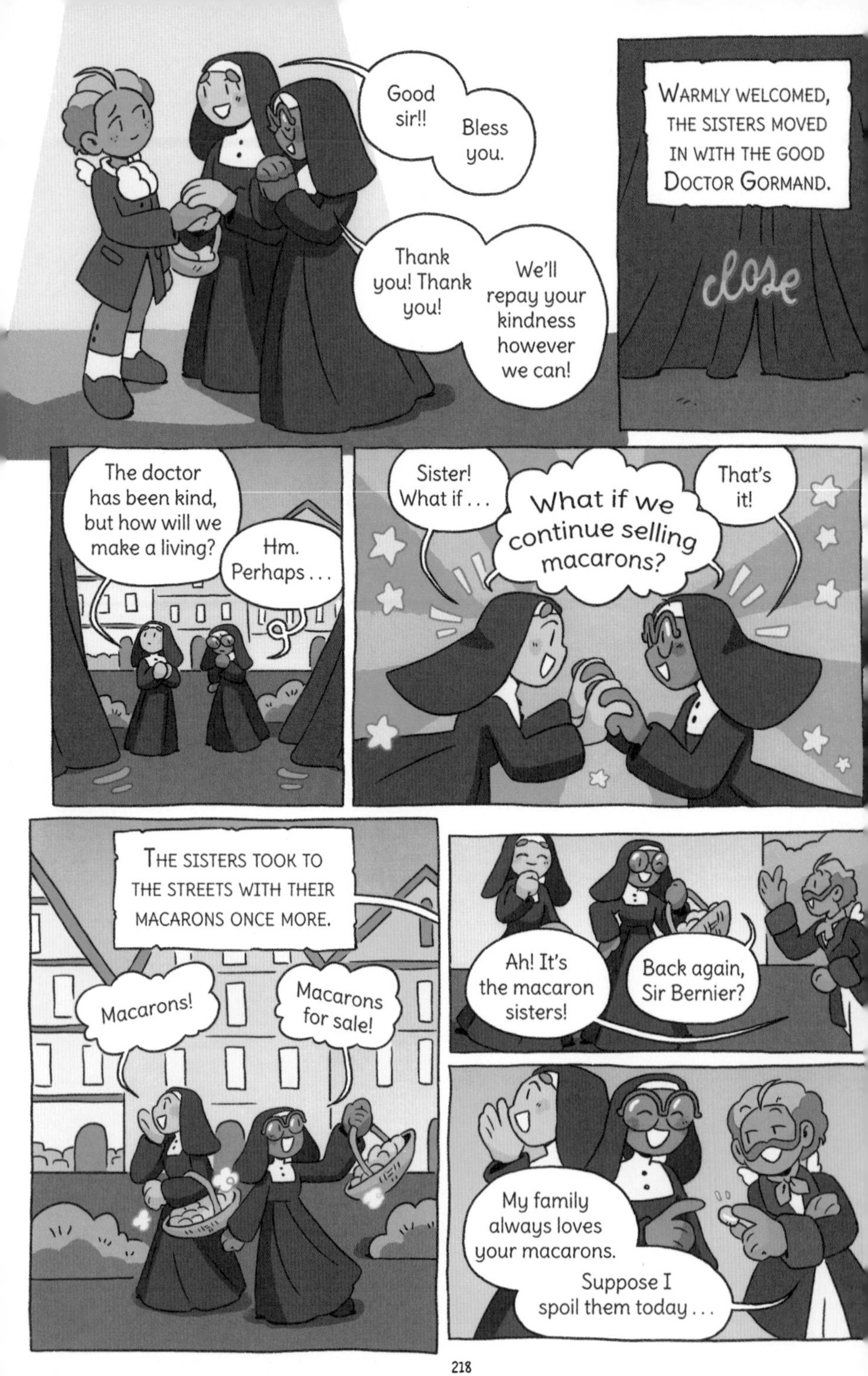
Good sir!!
Bless you.
Thank you! Thank you!
We'll repay your kindness however we can!
WARMLY WELCOMED, THE SISTERS MOVED IN WITH THE GOOD DOCTOR GORMAND.
close
The doctor has been kind, but how will we make a living?
Hm. Perhaps . . .
Sister! What if . . .
What if we continue selling macarons?
That's it!
THE SISTERS TOOK TO THE STREETS WITH THEIR MACARONS ONCE MORE.
Macarons!
Macarons for sale!
Ah! It's the macaron sisters!
Back again, Sir Bernier?
My family always loves your macarons.
Suppose I spoil them today . . .

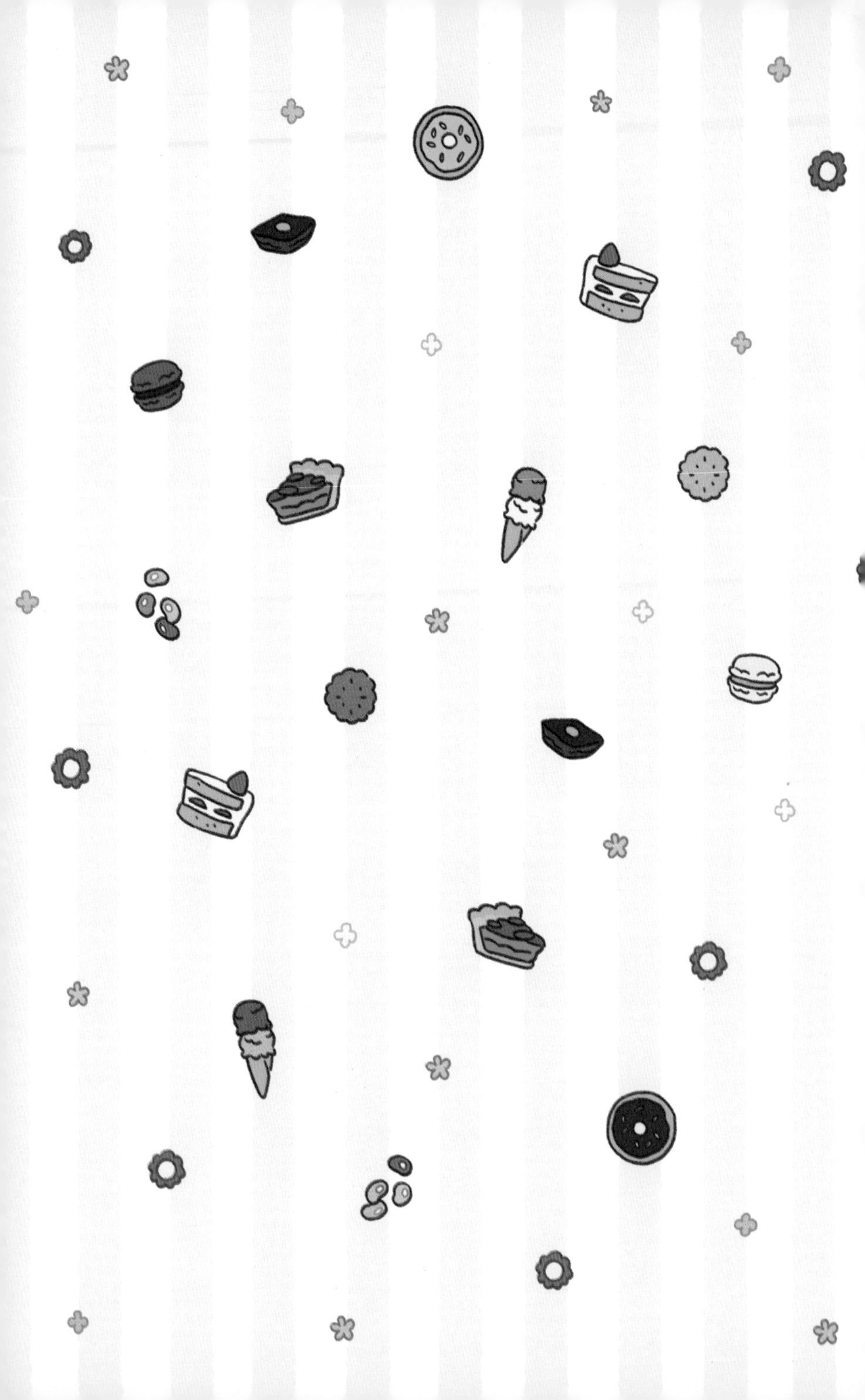

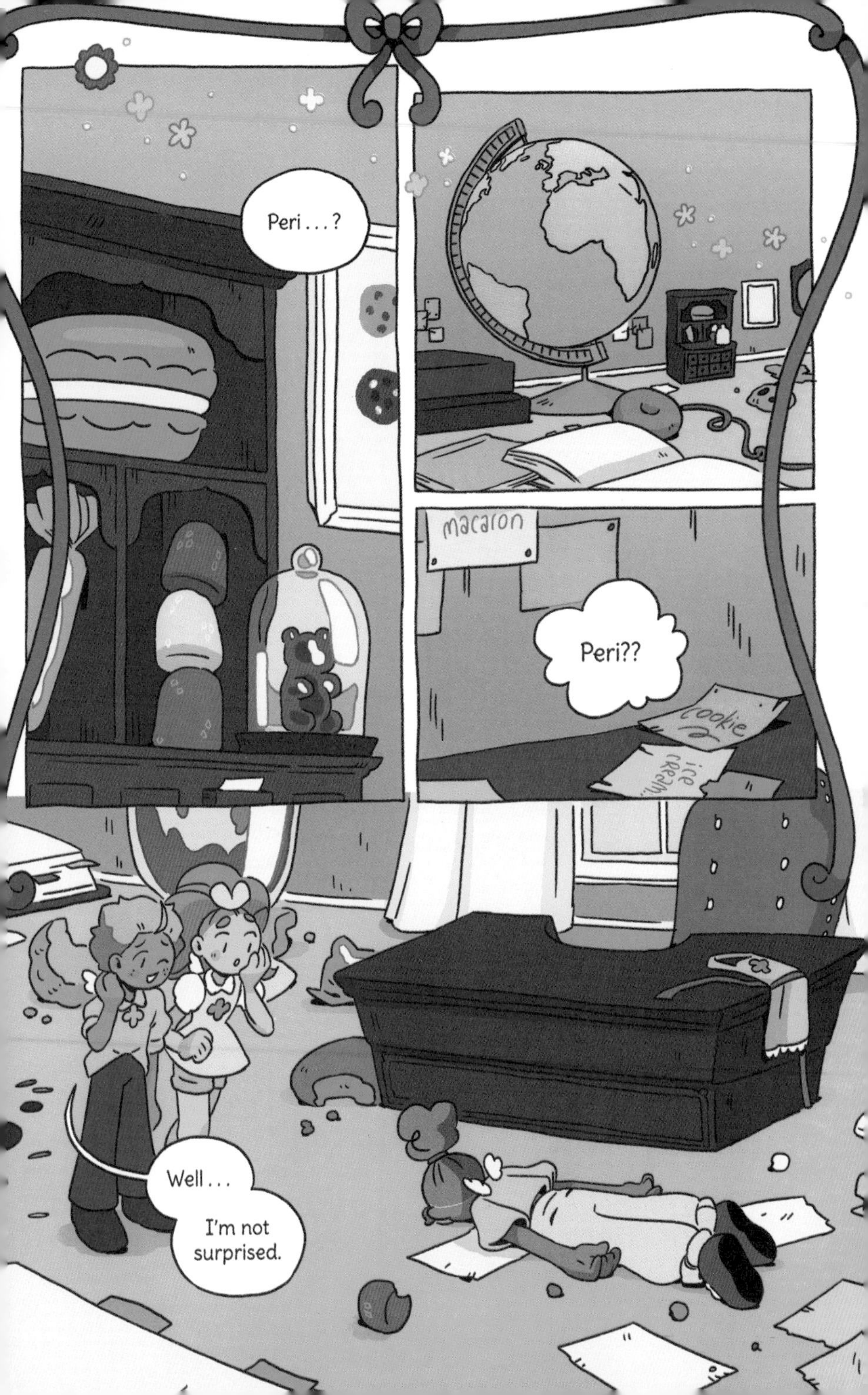
Peri . . . ?
macaron
Peri??
cookie
ice cream...
Well . . .
I'm not surprised.

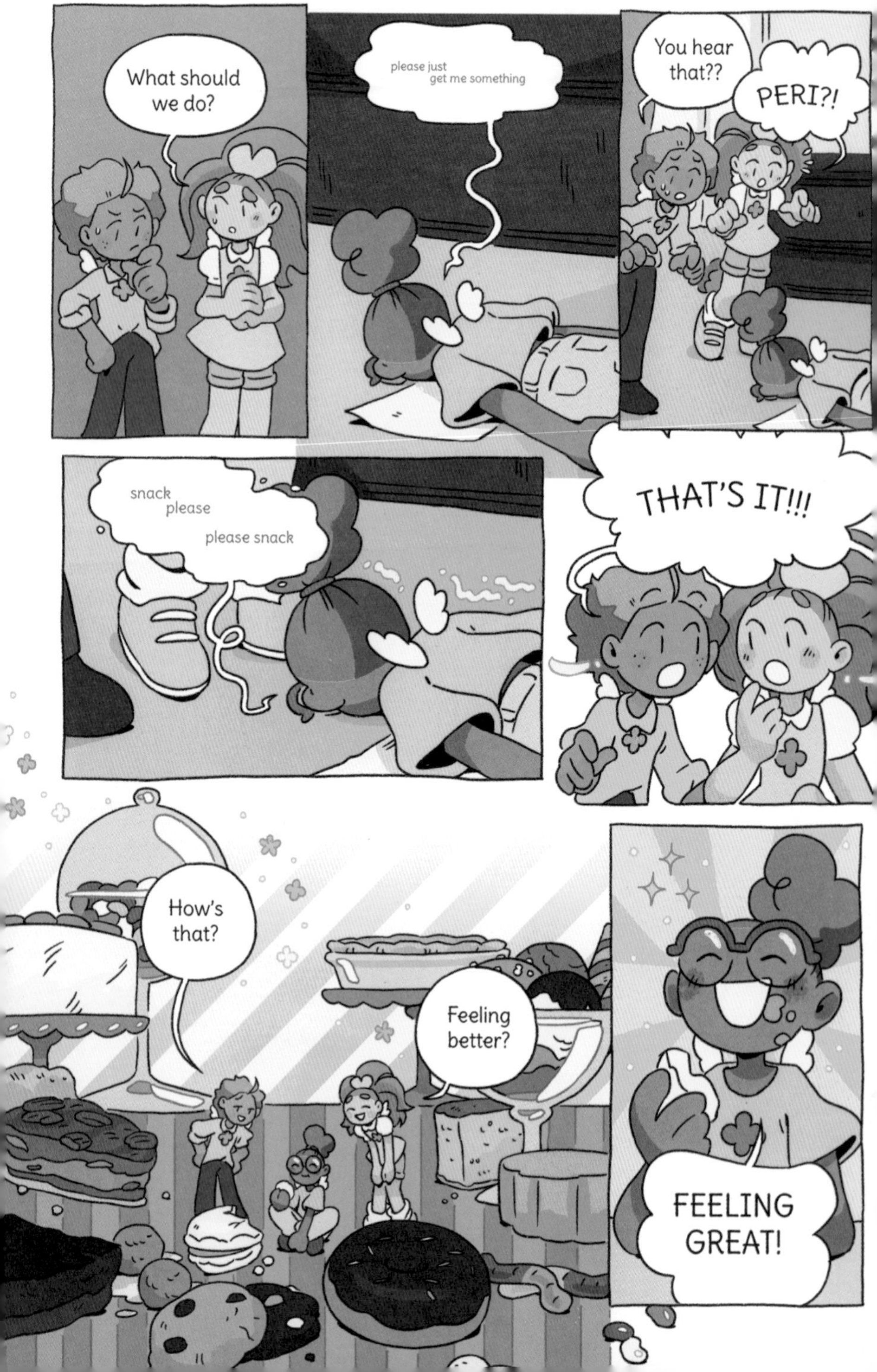

What should we do?
please just get me something
You hear that??
PERI?!
snack please please snack
THAT'S IT!!!
How's that?
Feeling better?
FEELING GREAT!

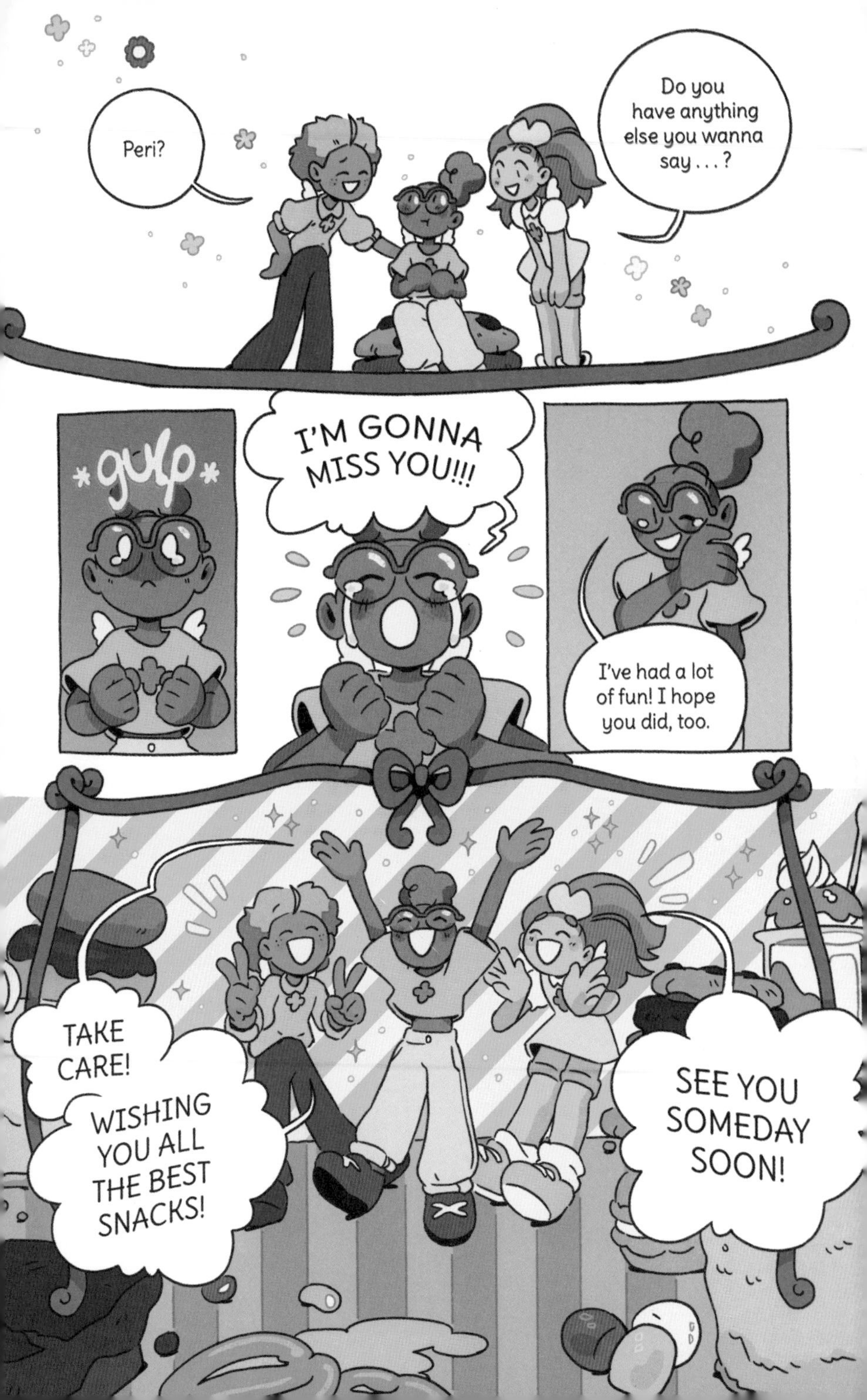
Peri?
Do you have anything else you wanna say . . . ?
gulp
I'M GONNA MISS YOU!!!
I've had a lot of fun! I hope you did, too.
TAKE CARE!
WISHING YOU ALL THE BEST SNACKS!
SEE YOU SOMEDAY SOON!

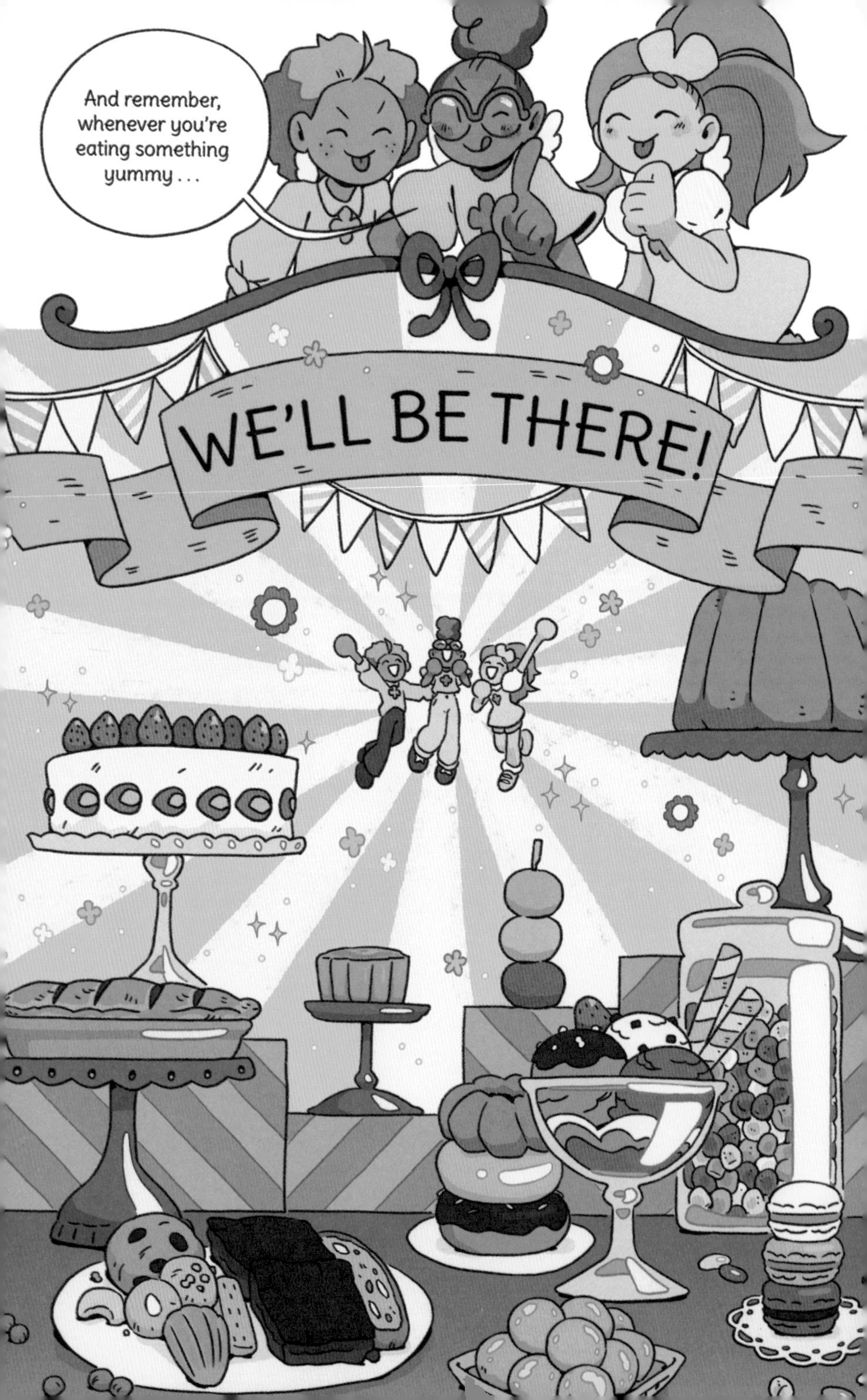
And remember, whenever you're eating something yummy . . .
WE'LL BE THERE!

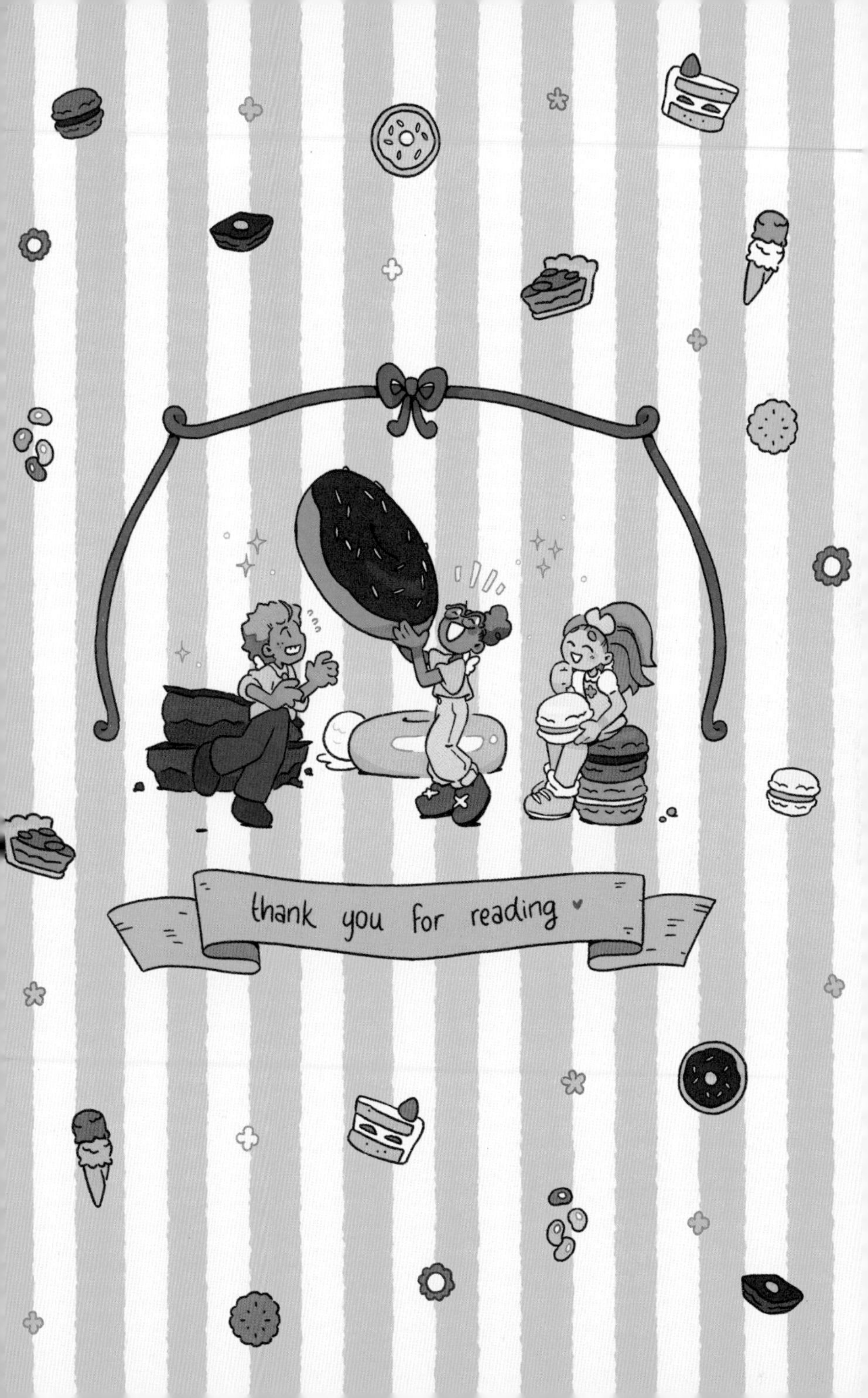
thank you for reading ♥

Bibliography

Adriano, Joel D. "By Popular Demand: This Native Delicacy Shop Has Established Itself as a Dominant Buko Pie Maker." *Entrepreneur Philippines.* web.archive.org/web/20170515032701/http://www.entrepreneur.com.ph/startup-tips/by-popular-demand

Balachandran, Mohit. "Nankhatai–The Dying Indian 'Biskoot.'" NDTV Food. food.ndtv.com/opinions/nankhatai-the-dying-indian-biskoot-696071

Byrn, Anne. *American Cookie: The Snaps, Drops, Jumbles, Tea Cakes, Bars & Brownies That We Have Loved for Generations.* New York: Rodale, 2018.

Clarkson, Janet. *Pie: A Global History.* London: Reaktion Books Ltd., 2009.

Corning Museum of Glass. cmog.org

David, Elizabeth. *Harvest of the Cold Months: The Social History of Ice and Ices.* New York: Viking, 1994.

Davidson, Alan. *The Oxford Companion to Food.* New York: Oxford University Press, 2014.

Donati, Silvia. "Taste the History of Gelato." *Italy Magazine.* italymagazine.com/featured-story/taste-history-gelato

Gage, Mary. "History of Brownies (Chocolate)." New England Recipes. newenglandrecipes.org/History_of_Brownies.pdf

Goldstein, Darra. *The Oxford Companion to Sugar and Sweets.* New York: Oxford University Press, 2015.

"The History of Macaron Sisters." Macaron de Nancy. macaron-de-nancy.com/en/history

Hochman, Karen. "The History of Brownies." The Nibble. thenibble.com/reviews/main/cookies/cookies2/history-of-the-brownie.asp

Humble, Nicola. *Cake: A Global History.* London: Reaktion Books Ltd., 2010.

Kiriyama, Iku. "Haru Hashimoto: Matriarch of Mikawaya." Discover Nikkei: Nanka Nikkei Voices. discovernikkei.org/en/journal/2015/2/2/haru-hashimoto-mikawaya/

Krondl, Michael. *Sweet Invention: A History of Dessert.* Chicago: Chicago Review Press, 2011.

Krondl, Michael. *The Donut: History, Recipes, and Lore from Boston to Berlin.* Chicago: Chicago Review Press, 2014.

Levene, Alysa. *Cake: A Slice of History.* New York: Pegasus Books, 2016.

Marlowe, Jack. "Zalabia and the First Ice-Cream Cone." *Aramco World.* archive.aramcoworld.com/issue/200304/zalabia.and.the.first.ice-cream.cone.htm

The Met. metmuseum.org

Padden, Kathy. "This Day in History: June 22nd–Captain Gregory and the Invention of the Doughnut." Today I Found Out: Feed Your Brain. todayifoundout.com/index.php/2015/06/this-day-in-history-june-22nd-captain-gregory-and-the-invention-of-the-doughnut

Quinzio, Geraldine M. *Of Sugar and Snow: A History of Ice Cream Making.* Berkeley, CA: University of California Press, 2009.

Robertson, Amy E. "Maamoul: An Ancient Cookie That Ushers in Easter and Eid in the Middle East." NPR: *The Salt.* npr.org/sections/thesalt/2017/04/11/522771745/maamoul-an-ancient-cookie-that-ushers-in-easter-and-eid-in-the-middle-east

Shapiro, Laura. *Something from the Oven: Reinventing Dinner in 1950s America.* London: Penguin Books, 2005.

Starr, Ben. "REAL Red Velvet Cake." *Have YOU Ben Starr Struck?* benstarr.com/blog/real-red-velvet-cake-with-no-food-coloring-or-beet-juice

Watanabe, Teresa. "Frances Hashimoto Dies at 69; Little Tokyo Leader, Mochi Ice Cream Creator." *LA Times.* latimes.com/local/obituaries/la-xpm-2012-nov-07-la-me-frances-hashimoto-20121107-story.html

Zheng, Limin. "Zhu Yuanzhang and Moon Cake Uprising." China Central Television. english.cctv.com/2016/09/14/ARTILP1KMo4BtfYKI6gOB2Q2160914.shtml

DESSERT HISTORY?!
MICHAEL KRONDL
DAVID
Thanks for all your help!

WHAT ARE FOOD SPRITES?

Food sprites are everywhere you find tasty food! They all gravitate toward different flavors and ingredients . . . After all, they have favorites, too! Their true names are usually very complicated. For example, Peri's real name is the first sweet snack given to you by a friend. But since most people have trouble remembering what that was, she uses her nickname Peri instead!

PERI

FAVE ICE CREAM:
bastani nooni

FAVE CAKE:
carrot cake

FAVE PIE:
PECAN!

FAVE COOKIE:
macarons

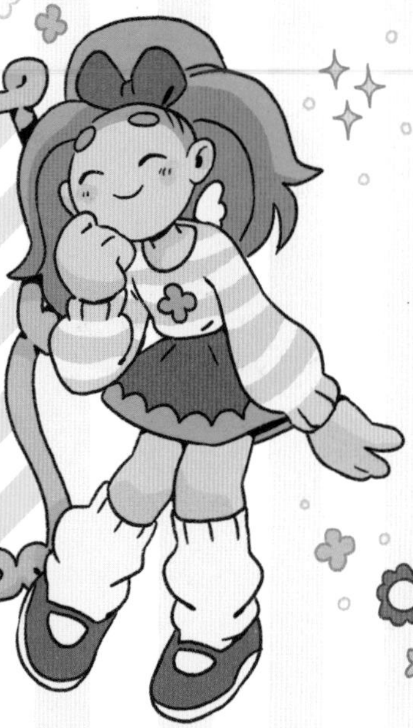

FEE

FAVE ICE CREAM:
mochi ice cream

FAVE CAKE:
strawberry shortcake

FAVE PIE:
apple with ice cream

FAVE COOKIE:
GINGERBREAD!

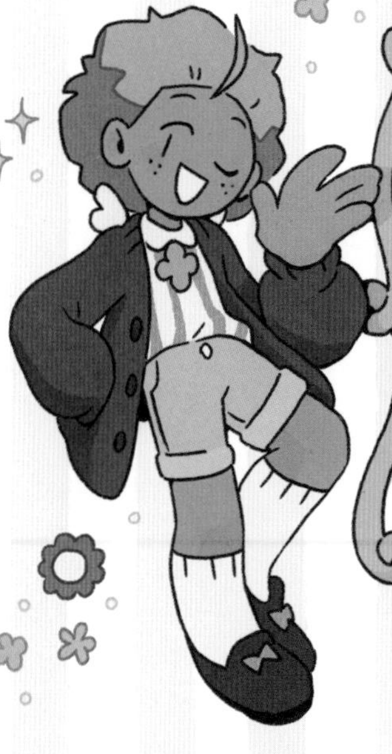

FADA

FAVE ICE CREAM:
chocolate chip cookie dough!

FAVE CAKE:
chocolate!

FAVE PIE:
chocolate peanut butter!

FAVE COOKIE:
CHOCOLATE CHIP!

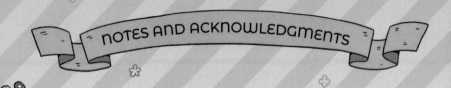

NOTES AND ACKNOWLEDGMENTS

In researching for this book, I recognize the political nature of food, both in its origin and spread. Many times, more often than not with European heritage foods, colonization and slavery are at the center of their histories. As such, I'd like to acknowledge that this book was written and drawn in Austin, Texas, on the traditional land of the Jumanos, Tonkawa, Numunuu, and Sana people, the rightful stewards of this beautiful land, where I am grateful to live.

I'd like to thank the team at RHG—particularly Whitney, Patrick, and Gina—and my wonderful agent, Steven Salpeter, for helping me make this book a reality. Thank you to my friend Gaby for all your suggestions, feedback, and encouragement.

Thank you to my lovely partner, Sergio, for always believing in my dreams, being my partner in life, and listening to me endlessly ramble on about whatever it is I'm into . . . in this case, dessert history.

I could pour out endless thanks and love to all my friends and family, those who worked with me, those who shared meals and holidays and boba with me, those who said they'd buy dozens of copies of this book (I'm holding you to it), and those who sent love and support from afar. Without you, I'd truly be eating desserts alone in my house. Thank you so, so much.

And, of course, thank you, dear reader. You're the reason I'm here!

This is my first book and first time publishing research. While *Yummy* is as thorough as I could make it with the resources available to me, it is by no means a definitive or flawless global history. Rather, it's more like dipping your toes into dessert history. Are you curious about the history of your favorite food? I hope this book encourages you to keep an open mind and think of history as a constantly growing, changing thing. Like the food sprites said, stay curious!

ABOUT THE AUTHOR

I'm Victoria Grace Elliott, a comic artist living in Austin, Texas. I love desserts (eating them, looking at them, making them, learning more about them), watching soap operas, and singing karaoke.

@fridayafternoon

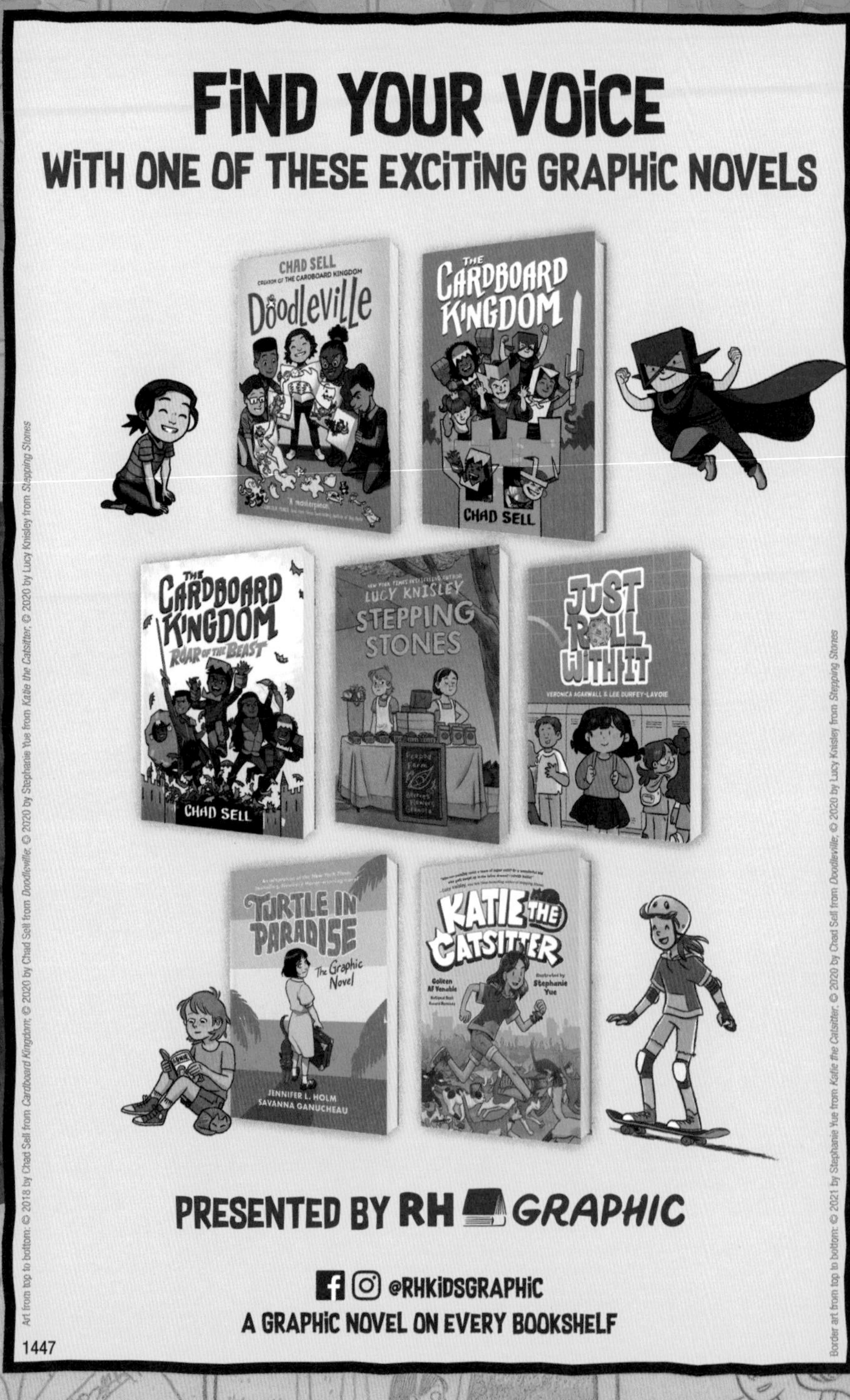

FIND YOUR VOICE
WITH ONE OF THESE EXCITING GRAPHIC NOVELS
CHAD SELL
CREATOR OF THE CARDBOARD KINGDOM
Doodleville
THE CARDBOARD KINGDOM
CHAD SELL
THE CARDBOARD KINGDOM
ROAR OF THE BEAST
CHAD SELL
LUCY KNISLEY
STEPPING STONES
JUST ROLL WITH IT
VERONICA AGARWALL & LEE DURFEY-LAVOIE
TURTLE IN PARADISE
The Graphic Novel
JENNIFER L. HOLM
SAVANNA GANUCHEAU
KATIE THE CATSITTER
Colleen AF Venable
Illustrated by Stephanie Yue
PRESENTED BY RH GRAPHIC
@RHKIDSGRAPHIC
A GRAPHIC NOVEL ON EVERY BOOKSHELF